The "Disguised" Political Film in Contemporary Hollywood

The "Disguised" Political Film in Contemporary Hollywood

A Genre's Construction

Betty Kaklamanidou

Bloomsbury Academic
An imprint of Bloomsbury Publishing Inc

B L O O M S B U R Y
NEW YORK · LONDON · OXFORD · NEW DELHI · SYDNEY

Bloomsbury Academic

An imprint of Bloomsbury Publishing Inc

1385 Broadway   50 Bedford Square
New York   London
NY 10018   WC1B 3DP
USA   UK

www.bloomsbury.com

BLOOMSBURY and the Diana logo are trademarks of Bloomsbury Publishing Plc

First published 2016

© Betty Kaklamanidou, 2016

Library of Congress Cataloging-in-Publication Data
A catalogue record for this book is available from the Library of Congress.

ISBN: HB: 978-1-5013-2230-3
          ePub: 978-1-5013-2232-7
          ePDF: 978-1-5013-2231-0

Cover image: FAIR GAME (2010) © ZUCKER PRODUCTIONS/THE KOBAL COLLECTION

Typeset by Fakenham Prepress Solutions, Fakenham, Norfolk NR21 8NN

To Alexandros Phaidon Lagopoulos
"Between you and me ... I think I'm getting there."

Contents

Acknowledgments   viii

1   Introduction: The "Disguised" Political Film   1
2   Political Comedies   35
3   Political Thrillers and US Foreign Policy   65
4   Political History Dramas and US Domestic Policy   105
5   Political Films From Antiquity to the Twentieth Century   121
6   Behind the Scenes of the Disguised Political Film Genre   143
7   Epilogue: Beyond the Corpus   157

Notes   171
Bibliography   175
Index   193

Acknowledgments

The summer of 2015 will soon be acknowledged as one of the most difficult—politically—periods in the history of modern Greece. Despite the uncertainty and indignation I felt alongside my compatriots, however, I will also personally remember the summer of 2015 as a period of intense and focused writing on this monograph. In fact, I believe that the book you are holding in your hands, or reading on the screen of your choice, is the main reason I escaped many heated discussions, even grave disputes, with friends and colleagues, and remained calm and concentrated during a storm of inane and simultaneously dangerous political decisions that even Hollywood's ingenious writers haven't come up with (perhaps they should look into that). So, in the midst of actual political chaos, I decided to concentrate on fictional politics and finally put into words the research I have been conducting in recent years, perhaps in an unconscious effort to find patterns and structures that would explain the oftentimes preposterous reality.

First, I should mention that the research for the monograph was facilitated by a grant awarded to young lecturers by Aristotle University of Thessaloniki in 2014, and I would like to thank the review committee for deeming my proposal worthy of the stipend.

My solitary writing was, of course, assisted by several individuals, without whom you would be reading a somewhat different version of the book. First and foremost, I'd like to thank my family: my loving husband Petros, who knows the meaning of the phrase "Baby, I'm at 845 words," my mom, Lia, Dimitris and the new love of my life, Eleni, and my brother-in-law Nikos, who didn't mind listening to my analysis on Gibson's *The Passion of the Christ* on the phone. Last but not least, Ella, my cat: your purring was all I needed after a good day's work.

Special thanks to Peggy Tally, a wonderful colleague, friend, and academic partner in crime, who read everything from first draft to final version offering valuable insight and encouragement. I feel blessed knowing her and fortunate to be able to work with her. Many thanks to Elizabeth Haas who took the time to read my first two chapters and whose comments and positive assessment empowered me in the early stages. Finally, I would like to thank Yannis Tzioumakis for that discussion at Aristotelous Square in May 2015, Sotiris

Petridis for crosschecking my corpus, and Ria Thanouli for all the phone conversations that may have seemed like my time off but were actually writing "triggers."

I had my first official talk about the book, when it was just a proposal in May 2015, with Bloomsbury's Senior Commissioning Editor Katie Gallof via Skype. I was immediately impressed by her knowledge and helpful advice, and little did I know—and despite the summer Katie and I both experienced (that's between Katie and me)—I would be fortunate enough to work with her after my proposal reviews finally arrived; I want to thank Katie for her professionalism and assistance all these months. Finally, I'd also like to thank Bloomsbury's Senior Editorial Assistant Michelle Chen and all the people who worked for my monograph during its production.

I keep writing "my" monograph, but now that the book is out, I feel it doesn't actually belong to me anymore; each reader will find things to agree or disagree with, passages he/she can stop and think about, perhaps even quote. Hopefully, there's even the chance that someone will find inspiration to go beyond something already written and produce a new chapter, article, book. To all the readers, then, I am honored you took some time to explore my thoughts on the "disguised" political film genre in contemporary Hollywood. Thank you.

Introduction: The "Disguised" Political Film

After the first US presidential debate took place on the evening of October 3, 2012, a single word dominated the next day's news reports on television, print and electronic media: the "narrative." For instance, most commentators and analysts insisted that candidate Mitt Romney's performance "changed the narrative" of the 2012 presidential campaign, while incumbent president Barack Obama appeared somewhat less authoritative.[1] A review of media articles on the Clinton campaigns (in 1992 and 1996), the W. Bush campaigns (in 2000 and 2004), and even Obama's 2008 campaign, does not yield any mention of "narrative," opting instead for other words, such as "strategy of the campaign."[2] The word "narrative" means an account of two or more events and does not discriminate between real and fictional ones. However, I should stress that I take the view that narrative—the arrangement of events into a specific order— always involves a degree of fabrication and has connotations of fictionalization. Therefore, I found the media's persistence in using the word "narrative" in 2012 a striking turn towards a media fictionalization of politics. This news narrativization was also a challenging way of moving away from the real political and social issues to viewing the campaign as a story with twists and turns, a story that is worth pursuing in an effort to attract the majority of viewers and/ or readers, and a story worth watching with the same pathos and/or interest that one watches a film in a theater. At the same time, the word "narrative" used time after time as a descriptive noun to clarify a real and quite significant event further blurs the "boundaries between 'factual' knowledge and 'fictive' representation" and "challenges the truth status of all disciplinary knowledge" (Shepherd 2013: 10).

The year of the presidential election not only witnessed a great number of real campaign narratives but also the release of three dramatic political narratives based on real events and one political comedy. The satirical *The Campaign* was released in August, *Argo* in October, less than a month before the November 6 election, *Lincoln* on November 16, and *Zero Dark Thirty* in January 2013. *Argo*, *Lincoln*, and *Zero Dark Thirty* were nominated for a total of twenty-four Academy Awards (seven, twelve, and five respectively) and won six (three, two, and one respectively), with *Argo* claiming the Oscar for Best Picture of 2012. Of course, political films have always been produced by Hollywood and every single annual box office contains relevant titles despite the fact that their number is quite small and their packaging and labeling usually "denies any political intention" (Giglio 2014: 1). However, I claim that there is a link between the release of these political films and their time of production and consumption, and I would suggest that it was not simply a coincidence that 2012 saw the release of some of the most powerful political narratives in at least a decade while simultaneously witnessing a compelling presidential race. The first Obama victory in 2008 also coincided with several acclaimed politically-centered films, such as *Vantage Point*, *Frost/Nixon*, *W.*, and *Milk*. An initial exploration of film titles reveals that since the election of Ronald Reagan in 1980, no other election year was accompanied by such prominent cinematic political narratives as 2012. Nevertheless, this observation leads to the obvious conclusion about an increase of political films during the Obama presidency. In fact, my research shows that it is not the number of films in production that has risen, but the number of acclaimed, lauded, and/or controversial political films that has risen gradually since 9/11, reaching an apogee in 2012.[3]

Cinema's growing interest in politics is accompanied by an even more impressive number of political shows on American television for at least the last two decades. It could be argued that the phenomenal success of *The West Wing* (NBC, 1999–2006) allowed the television industry to invest in both political dramas and comedies towards the end of the 2000s, and especially in the 2010s, most of which are both critically acclaimed and popular among viewers. Today, both the networks as well as the cable channels and the internet streaming service Netflix produce television shows that take place in Washington DC, and/ or focus on US policy. Shows such as *24* (Fox, 2001–10), *Homeland* (Showtime, 2011–present), *Boss* (Starz, 2011–12), *Madam Secretary* (CBS, 2014–present), *House of Cards* (Netflix, 2013–present), *The Americans* (FX, 2013–present), *Veep* (HBO, 2012–present), and *The Brink* (HBO, 2015) among others, offer a great variety of representations about the US government, issues of both domestic and foreign policy, as well as a host of subjects relevant to contemporary societal conflicts. They share, however, a dim view of politics and politicians, one that is fraught with corruption and intrigue while they also choose to center their narratives on mostly villainous characters, unlike their cinematic counterparts, which may underline the flaws of the political system but whose narrative protagonists are more often than not just, moral, and struggle to do the right thing. In the same vein, the rise of the political documentary in the new millennium (*Bowling for Columbine* [2002], *The Fog of War* [2003], *Fahrenheit 9/11* [2004], *The Corporation* [2004], *Sicko* [2007], *2016: Obama's America* [2012]),[4] and especially the controversy revolving around Michael Moore's films, on the one hand strengthened the documentary as a genre and, on the other, helped new filmmakers to secure capital more easily from relevant companies, as the financial success of contemporary political documentaries proved that this thematic preoccupation was also viable economically. The popularity of millennial political TV narratives and documentaries notwithstanding, I choose to focus exclusively on cinema in this monograph in order to define and construct a genre with specific conventions, modes of production and exhibition that differ from television and documentary practices, to have the opportunity to examine my corpus more meticulously, and to avoid minimizing the importance of the aforementioned groups of texts, that I believe should be autonomously explored. That being said, I include observations regarding the influence of television and/or documentary on contemporary political texts in some of the following chapters, as a consequence of cross-fertilization between contemporary narratives, but I do not divert my attention from film.

The Hollywood narratives that focus on political issues in the new millennium, and the media and artistic attention most of these films garnered, is indicative of film's continuing dual function as (a) a reflection, commentary, and/or critique of social events, and (b) a medium capable of foreseeing and/or assisting societal evolution. One could argue that politics has nothing to do with the fabricated nature of Hollywood film production whether or not its films are based on real events. However, as Sheldon S. Wolin (2004: 19) remarks, "imagination is also part of the political theorist's efforts." The author adds that since it can be impossible to directly observe societies, the theorist is compelled "to epitomize a society by abstracting certain phenomena and providing interconnections where none can be seen." Thus, imagination becomes "the theorist's means for understanding a world he can never 'know' in an intimate way," and also "to transcend history" (Wolin 2004: 19) the same way; I would argue that film imagines worlds and goes beyond historical representations.

The subject of this monograph is the "disguised" political films produced by Hollywood, the dominant cinematic paradigm in the world in the new millennium. The epithet "disguised" that also appears in the title of the book is not accidental as the overwhelming majority of the film titles that I have already mentioned, as well as the rest that form the corpus of this study, have been marketed and distributed to theaters worldwide with no mention of the word "politics" or its derivatives. The corpus discussed in the next pages comprises mainly "action thrillers," "historical dramas," "action/adventures," "biopics," "comedies," "spy comedies," and "crime dramas." I argue that these industry labels hide the fact that all the narratives belong to a political genre, a category that Hollywood is notorious for avoiding and is not interested in. That is why, I argue, this generic category can only exist as an abstraction, a theoretical construction, and not a widely acknowledged and/or used label. The aims of this study are, therefore, to define a political film genre based on a corpus of films produced and distributed between 2002 and 2012, group the films into subgenres, and analyze them. I believe that the data garnered from a ten-year period can assist in the compilation of a comprehensive corpus with a substantial number of films and can lead to valid conclusions. However, I would like to add that the last chapter also discusses some of the political narratives that were released in the 2013–15 period, to prove, on the one hand, the continuity of the genre and also verify the theoretical construction I am proposing in the next few pages.

The first step of every scientific endeavor is the demarcation of the object of study. However, the object of this book, namely political films, is not a clearly delineated object but rather an elusive one and resistant to clear boundaries. As Ian Scott puts it: "political films have never really had a working definition to speak of in any form" (Scott 2011: 14). Thus, the first part of the study endeavors to answer the following questions: What is a political film? Can *The Hunger Games*, 2012, belong to the same category as *Lincoln*, 2012? Is *Jarhead*, 2005, a political movie simply because it is set during the Gulf War but with no reference to the motives of the conflict and/or American and Arab relations, and thus in the same group of war films such as *Three Kings*, 1999, another narrative that focuses on the same military conflict but includes direct commentary on governmental and military strategies? Are historical films by definition political since their majority deals with significant events and/or people in a specific sociocultural landscape?

These are the questions that I set out to answer during my research in contemporary political cinematic narratives. It seems to me that the problems inherent in the effort to define and delineate a political film genre involve: (a) the term "politics", and (b) the theory of genre or absence thereof in the literature which leads to an empirical and not theoretical effort to define appropriately a political film genre. I therefore first try to unpack the problematic terms and concepts discussing the relevant literature and I provide a theoretical framework deriving from sociosemiotics on which I base my definition of the political film genre.

Politics: Choosing a definition and a theory

The first observation made during the study of the relevant literature is that the term "politics"—which is crucial for a study that includes the derivative term "political"—is not clearly defined. "Politics" is invariably used to designate both the more inclusive and exclusive definitions of the term. It can designate exclusively the governmental activities of a specific geographical area (country/ nation), the power relations between those individuals who hold positions of influence and the institutions that comprise the structure of the same area. The Aristotelian definition of politics as "the things concerning the polis," Max Weber's (1958) 1948 definition which sees politics as the allocation of a state's (the evolution of the Ancient Greek polis) power between various groups of people, and Bernard Crick's 1964 definition which designates politics as "the activity by which differing interests within a given unit of rule are conciliated by giving them a share in power in proportion to their importance to the welfare and the survival of the whole community" (Grant 2003), support the exclusive aspect of politics and limit its boundaries within a governmental and institutional structure.

On the other hand, during the late 1960s, "the personal is political" slogan of the second feminist wave blurred the lines between the public and the private spheres and drew "attention to the fact that power and advantage also characterize areas of life that are not usually thought of as political" (Chambers 2015, 267). Thus, "politics" became an inclusive term that could be used in every aspect of society (i.e., family politics, school politics). Harold Lasswell's (1936) definition of politics as "who gets what, when, and how," and David Easton's (1965) definition that designates politics as "the authoritative allocation of values for a society," as well as the more recent contribution by Jacques Rancière (2011, 3), who views politics as "the construction of a specific sphere of experience in which certain objects are posited as shared and certain subjects regarded as capable of designating these objects and of arguing about them," can support the more inclusive reading of the term. The number of definitions may hinder my goal but, at the same time, points to the fact that "the field of politics is and has been [...] a created one" (Wolin 2004: 5). Wolin observes that:

> The designation of certain activities and arrangements as political, the charac-
> teristic way that we think about them, and the concepts we employ to
> communicate our observations and reactions—none of these are written into
> the nature of things but are the legacy accruing from the historical activity of
> political philosophers. (2004: 5)

Following this continuity, Wolin (2004: 7) defines politics as the "institutionalized processes and settled procedures regularly used for handling public matters."

It is clear that the definition of the "political" in a political film genre is an important task because a broad definition, meaning one that includes social movements and not simply governmental and/or institutional practices, could lead to an inclusive corpus of political films while a narrower definition leads to a more exclusive categorization. Although I have argued and still maintain that "all films are political" (Kaklamanidou 2013: 3)[5] in the sense that "they offer competing ideological significations of the way the world is or should be" (Storey 2015: 4), all films do not belong to the same generic category. I choose, therefore, the more exclusive definition of politics, which can lead to a clearer definition of a political film genre.

My study focuses on fictional narratives, which by definition follow a clear path towards the resolution of an interior or exterior conflict. In other words, changes occur in political films, while stability rarely lasts for very long. Yet, I should note that conflict is *the* defining characteristic of the mainstream Hollywood film, irrespective of genre, and, as such, cannot constitute a criterion based on which one can demarcate any given genre; in this case, the political film. Interestingly, stability and change, along with peace, are among the basic concepts of political thought since Aristotle wrote his *Politics* and acknowledged that the stability of the polity is the index of its value, while change consti-tutes the index of its imperfection (Tzioka-Evangelou 2005: 41–2). After all, Aristotle's concept of the perfect polity and its goal, the attainment of bliss by an organized symbiotic group of people, can only be achieved in a politically stable environment. Of course, Aristotle wrote his thesis on politics during the era of the city-state (poli-kratos), but his observations, as well as those of Plato, ushered in the era of political theory and philosophy and became the basis of the future Western political tradition.

Almost invariably, narrative film includes change as a central structural device. Will the boy get the girl and form a union or will they remain two separate individuals? Will the hero vanquish the monster so that the community order is restored? Will the detective find the perpetrator of the crime so that they are justly punished? Will the sheriff arrest or kill the outlaw that threatens life in the town he tries to keep safe? Romantic comedies, horror films, crime films, and Westerns are just a few examples of popular Hollywood genres whose plot follows a pattern that moves from stability to change to a new stability. The electoral political comedies I examine in Chapter 2, for instance, also center on change as their protagonists—with the exception of *Swing Vote*, 2008—are first-time candidates who enter the political race to change what they believe is wrong in America, thus effecting change of a political nature.

Daniel P. Franklin (2006: 20–1) notes that classical liberalism, "the philosophy of the commercial middle class," is the political philosophy that is predominantly spread through the American motion picture. Indeed the majority of the films in my corpus ultimately promote democratic values, equality, liberty, and human rights. Nevertheless, the War on Terror that followed 9/11 also produced film narratives that go beyond liberal principles and embrace tactics that would have seemed unfathomable some decades ago. *Zero Dark Thirty* (2012) and *Rendition* (2007) are two films that show the CIA torturing foreigners to obtain information. Both films, and especially the first one, caused a media frenzy because of its depiction of "enhanced interrogation techniques", which violate "international law" despite being "universally practiced" (Giglio 2014: 240). Effecting change in a political structure is a difficult task since a structure is usually built, complemented, and solidified in a number of years, decades, even centuries. Nevertheless, change is possible through agency since it is agents to begin with that help the emergence of a structure. In this study, I am applying Colin Hay's (2002) strategic-relational theory to the examination of the narratives as I want to explore how agency affects structure, and vice versa, and how this relationship is, ultimately, a conveyor of political messages.

Hay's theory is based on the discussion between structure and agency, for which different approaches have been proposed. The one that Hay builds upon is Anthony Giddens's structuration theory that posits that "structure/agency is a duality [...]; they are interdependent and internally related. Structures constrain and enable agents, agents interpret structures and in doing so change them" (Marsh 2010: 216). Conversely, Marsh criticizes Giddens's approach because "methodologically, at any given time one can only study either structure or agency" (2010: 216), whereas it would be more productive to analyze the interaction between the two. Hay's (2002: 127) model solves Giddens's unilateral method as the author postulates that "neither agents nor structures are real, since neither has an existence in isolation from the other—their existence is relational (structure and agency are mutually constituted)." The center of Hay's approach is "the interaction between strategic actors and the strategic context within which they find themselves" (2002: 128). According to Marsh's argumentation, the "agent's strategic action both changes the structured context and contributes to the agent's strategic learning" (Marsh 2010: 218). Marsh finds that Hay's theory privileges agents because, in the strategic-relational approach, "it is agents' choices which are important and structures (which don't exist independently anyway) only affect agents to the extent that they recognize them and purposefully choose to be influenced by them" (2010: 218–19). Marsh emphasizes the dialectical relationship between structure and agency, not explicitly stated in Hay's approach, as consisting of six separate phases:

1. Structures provide the context within which agents act; these structures are both material and ideational.
2. Agents have preferences/objectives which they attempt to forward.
3. Agents interpret the context within which they act, a context which is both structural and strategic.
4. However, structures, both material and ideational, can have an effect on agents of which they are not necessarily conscious.
5. In acting, agents change the structures.
6. These structures then provide the context within which agents act in the next iteration. (Marsh 2010: 219)

Hay's theory and Marsh's additions provide the most appropriate methodology for this study as it not only complements the narratological approach I follow but also because it is based on clearly defined concepts and not only empirical observation.

Genre "fluidity"

Three Kings (1999) and *Jarhead* (2005) are both set during the Gulf War. The International Movie Database (IMDb) labels the first as an "action/adventure/comedy" and the second a "drama/war" film. Both films are discussed in scholarly volumes that examine war films and the relationship between film and history (see Barker [2011] and Rollins and O'Connor [2008] respectively) and are analyzed as "war" films. This example shows a discrepancy that exists between film genre categorization in academia and the industry/media. Genres are labels, generic categories, groupings that circulate among the Hollywood film industry, media outlets, and the audience, as well as academia. Genres are used by the industry as a marketing strategy to clearly define and appropriately market their product so that they reach the relevant audience. Genres are also used by academics to analyze their conventions, trace their historical evolution and/or demise, and reveal hidden commentary regarding sociopolitical circumstances.

The aims of industry and academia in genre categorization are not, therefore, necessarily similar. The media also uses and proposes new generic categories as evidenced by a search on the IMDb database and the approach proposed by the streaming service Netflix. IMDb categorizes the films of its database using a combination of only twenty-six categories (twenty-four relevant to film and two corresponding exclusively to TV programs), consisting entirely of nouns: Action, Adventure, Animation, Biography, Comedy, Crime, Documentary, Drama, Family, Fantasy, Film-Noir, Game-Show, History, Horror, Music, Musical, Mystery, News, Reality-TV, Romance, Sci-Fi, Sport, Talk-Show, Thriller, War, Western. Thus, *Selma* (2014) is a Biography/Drama/History film and *American Sniper*, 2014, an Action/Biography/Drama film. Interestingly, IMDb does not include political films in its classification system, while Netflix includes political dramas under the general label "drama," political comedies under "comedy," political thrillers under "thriller," and political documentaries under "documentary," thus treating films with political context only as subgenres of wide and established genres. In the second edition of *Projecting Politics*, Elizabeth Haas, Terry Christensen and Peter J. Haas (2015: 6) also note that there is not a single chapter from a total of thirty-six that "specifically addresses political films" in "the latest edition of the influential *Film Genre Reader*." The authors observe that this academic omission "contrasts with the decision of the Library of Congress's *Moving Image Genre Form Guide*," which includes the political genre—among a list of 125 genres—and a brief definition that limits the genre's boundaries to election films (2015: 6).

As noted, genre classification assists viewers in choosing a title based on personal preference. One can deduce that the more detailed the grouping the film belongs to, the more easily the viewer can be assisted in his cinematic selection. Netflix, which provides films on demand online to its more than fifty million global subscribers for a fee, went a step further in its film classification process and created 76,897 micro-genres. The company employed teams of people "to watch films and tag them with all kinds of metadata," based on "a 36-page training document that teaches them how to rate movies on their sexually suggestive content, goriness, romance levels, and even narrative elements like plot conclusiveness" (Madrigal 2013). Netflix may present all its genres in a quite traditional way on its official site, but its micro-genres are suggested to subscribers based on previous choices and create a personalized film universe. "Critically-acclaimed Fight-the-System Documentaries," "Dark Independent Dysfunctional-Family Movies," "Cynical Comedies Featuring a Strong Female Lead," and "Critically-acclaimed Emotional Father-Son Dramas" are a few of the micro-categories Netflix creates to maximize its profits.[6]

Media genre categorization is based on journalistic inspirations, ideas, and/or intentions as well as on the industry's promotional material. Hollywood does avoid the word political, even in films that could not be categorized otherwise. Why would obvious examples of political cinema, such as *Lincoln* be marketed as a biopic, *Argo* a thriller, and *The Ides of March* (2011) a drama? "If you want to send a message, use Western Union," is producer Samuel Goldwyn's alleged retort to someone who wanted to make a political film. Giglio (2014: 5), who cites Goldwyn's phrase, notes that Hollywood is not overtly sympathetic to political narratives, yet also "delivers political messages in a minority of its films." Nevertheless, this minority has yet to be clearly delineated.

The industry and media reluctance to use the word political is the first obstacle in the genre's definition. After all, genres are usually born through studio labeling and press categorization. Through a detailed account of archival material, Rick Altman (2006) concludes that generic film categories are initially described with the use of adjectives, which then take the status of a noun. "Before the Western became a separate genre and a household word, there were [...] Western chase films, Western scenic, Western melodramas, Western romances, Western adventure films, and even Western comedies, Western dramas and Western epics." Similarly, "the musical was preceded by musical comedy, musical drama, musical romance, musical farce, farce, and even the double redundant *all-talking, all-singing, all-dancing musical melodrama*" (Altman 2006 52–3). The process of "full genrification" had to include three changes. First, the studios had to standardize and automatize the transgeneric forms (i.e., musical + comedy); second, the films had to display a set of recognizable conventions;

and third, the audience had to develop "expectations that come with generic identification" (Altman 2006: 53). Thus, Altman concludes:

> Genre films are films produced after general identification and consecration of a genre through substantification, during the limited period when shared textual material and structures lead audiences to interpret films not as separate entities but according to generic expectations and against generic norms. (2006: 53)

It becomes clear that the political film is still in the first stage of the genrification process and it remains to be seen whether it will ever acquire the status of an acknowledged film genre. For this to happen, and if one follows Altman's theory, then the word political will acquire the status of a noun and thus the "political" will not have to be accompanied by a defining term, such as comedy, drama, or thriller.

The second obstacle in the definition process is the theoretical view that claims there are no "pure" genres. Janet Staiger (2003: 185) observes that "Hollywood films have never been pure. [...] All that has been pure has been sincere attempts to find order among variety." Staiger proves that the purity argument cannot be upheld as careful analysis confirms the existence of at least two plots (one of which is often a romance) in most Hollywood films. Yet, the author also notes that "grouping films can still be an important scholarly act because it may elucidate what producers and consumers of films do" (2003: 186), and uncover the contribution of film narratives to the sociocultural landscape of a specific time period.

I agree that films usually belong to more than one genre. Most romantic comedies, for instance, include dramatic scenes but that does not change their "status" as romantic comedies. Romance as a secondary plot is a ubiquitous presence in almost any genre—from the Western, horror, sci-fi to the action/adventure film, without confusing the viewers as to the conventions of the fictional world portrayed on their screen of preference. How does one determine the overarching generic category in a given film narrative? The formalist concept of the "dominant" is a useful tool, frequently used in film genre theory (Glitre 2006; Kaklamanidou 2013). According to Roman Jakobson (1981: 751), "[t]he dominant may be defined as the focusing component of a work of art: it rules, determines, and transforms the remaining components." It is "the element which specifies a given variety of language [or any narrative element] dominates the entire structure and thus acts as its mandatory and inalienable constituent dominating all the remaining elements and exerting direct influence upon them." Based on this theory, films that I initially and empirically included in the corpus as political narratives were excluded upon a second viewing. For instance, *Australia*, 2008, is first and foremost a romantic drama set during a turbulent pre-Second World War period while also examining the Stolen Generations. Romance also prevails in *Cold Mountain* (2003) which, despite being set during the American Civil War and examining political and gender issues, is dominated by the long and tumultuous journey of a deserter from the Confederate Army back to the woman he loves. Finally, although I remembered *The Last Samurai* (2003) as a film that centered on the Westernization of Japan in the nineteenth century and the intricate business of war—issues that belong to the political sphere—I concluded after the second viewing that its dominant feature is loyalty, overcoming adversity, and exploring the male bond between two men. These conclusions are based on the narrative time allotted for the subjects covered in the films, and are discussed in the relevant chapter.

Political film: Literature discussion

Film genre theory discussion is largely avoided in the literature concerning politics and films and/or the political film. This is perhaps mainly due to the different fields of study that the authors are experts at; the majority, such as Terry Christensen, Peter M. Haas, Ernest Giglio, Daniel P. Franklin, Brian Neve, and Phillip L. Gianos are political scientists, M. Keith Booker and Harry Keyishian are both English professors, while Philip John Davies and Ian Scott are professors of American Studies. Another reason can be the impasse the researcher can reach if genre theory enters the discussion of a political film genre. The relevant literature can be divided into two broad categories: the "inclusives," that is, authors who discuss a variety of genres as instances of political critique, and the "exclusives," the smaller percentage of authors who try to define the genre and delineate its boundaries.

The first group includes a number of insightful analyses of diverse films and examination of the relationship between Hollywood and politics in a broader sense. Phillip L. Gianos's *Politics and Politicians in American Film* (1998) examines films on the Cold War and Vietnam as well Ford's Westerns, and classics, such as *Citizen Kane* (1941). Similarly, Philip John Davies and Paul Wells's (2002) edited collection *American film and Politics from Reagan to Bush Jr.* discusses a variety of 1990s films, from the animated *Mermaid* (1990) to

Fight Club (1999) and *Magnolia* (1999) while Daniel P. Franklin's *Politics and Film* (2006), also studies a cluster of heterogeneous films from different eras, from *Mr. Smith Goes to Washington* (1939) to the sci-fi action *X2* (2003) and *The Coneheads* (1993). Brian Neve's (1992) *Film and Politics in America: A Social Tradition* examines "questions concerning politics and American film" covering the 1930s to the 1960s (1992: ix). No genre definition is provided and, again, diverse genre films are covered while there is analysis of the production side of certain films and special emphasis on specific directors (such as Elia Kazan, Robert Rossen and Abraham Polonsky). Lastly, Douglas Kellner's *Cinema Wars* includes films that speak to all aspects of American politics, as the author wants "to show that the turbulence of the era is reproduced in the Hollywood films of the 2000s" (Kellner 2010: 1). Kellner claims that "Films are an especially illuminating social indicator of the realities of a historical era" (2010: 4) and adds films, such as the sci-fi *Transformers* (2007) and the *Star Wars* trilogy (1999–2005) to his discussion of explicitly political narratives.

As mentioned, only a few authors attempt to delve into questions of genre boundaries. In *From Office to Ballot Box. The American Political Film*, Booker (2007) focuses on political films produced after the Second World War and defines the genre as "a species of film which is directly concerned with the workings of politics and the role of politics in our lives" (2007: 3). The author insists on films that center on "the political process," "the process of government," "films about specific politically charged topics or phenomena," "films that deal with the role of the media in American political life," and "films that deal with the Vietnam War and its immediate impact on American society" (2007: 4–5). Booker succeeds in providing a definition that can unite different subgenres, such as the war film, the terrorist film, and the courtroom film, under the common heading of the genre of political film, but does not offer a systematic analysis of the genre's conventions and/or narrative characteristics.

The focus of Michael Coyne's (2008) *Hollywood Goes to Washington* is "films set centrally and specifically in the milieu of American politics—foregrounding political figures (whether historical or fictional), and depicting expressly political melodramas and crises on screen, ranging from bio-pics to movies about election campaigns and, of course, conspiracy thrillers." Coyne excludes films with "a pronounced political dimension and often impact upon the arena of US politics," such as films on "feminism, gay rights, environmentalism" (2008: 8). Coyne's contributions are the observations that "the American political film is a genre by virtue of content rather than form," that it "is essentially fluid," and that "it crosses the borders of various Hollywood genres" (2008: 9). Indeed, whereas a horror film can be acknowledged with ease through both narrative strategies (a monster of whatever form threatens a community, claiming innocent lives only to be vanquished by a hero/heroine to restore normalcy) and cinematic form (i.e., ominous music, specific *mise-en-scène* techniques, such as point-of-view shots), a political film is a rather ambiguous category. For instance, I doubt that one would place *Man of the Year* (2006) *Valkyrie* (2008) and *Salt* (2010)—at first glance, a comedy, a historical war film, and an action/thriller—in the political film genre. It is obvious that "political film content may occur in narratives that are dramatic, comic, or even exciting" (Giglio 2014: 26).

The expanded second edition of Scott's *American Politics in Hollywood Film* (2011) is an informed monograph that examines the political ideas Hollywood disseminates through relevant films and studies relevant films from the 1930s to the 2000s. Scott rightly concludes that in the 2000s and especially thanks to the critical appraisal and popular appeal of the TV series *The West Wing*, which helped introduce political practices—even those that would be considered dull and indifferent to a wide audience—politics and politicians enter the cultural zeitgeist. The phenomenal success of *The West Wing* with both the critics and the viewers, and the special sociohistorical circumstances of the early 2000s, contributed to the re-emergence of political narratives on the silver screen. Scott does not provide a clear definition of the genre, yet his four analytical chapters on specific groups of political films (from classical paradigms and campaign films to paranoia thrillers and political biographies) offer insightful explanations and valuable sociopolitical contextualization of the films examined, explaining the continuity and endurance of these subgenres in the 1990s and 2000s.

One of the most important works on the subject is Haas, Christensen, and Haas's (2015) *Projecting Politics: Political Messages in American Films*, an expanded second edition of their 2005 monograph, based on the 1987 *Reel Politics*. Haas, Christensen, and Haas also underline the ambiguity surrounding the delineation of political films. They suggest that the lack of a definition is due to the variety of forms that political films can take (they can be comedies, dramas, thrillers, etc.), the fact that they "do not share as many conventions of plot and character as do other genres," the fact that "overtly political films often allow for variation within the genre by combining descriptions, as in 'political comedy' or 'political thriller,' thus vitiating their status," and the unwillingness of Hollywood to use the label "political" resulting in filmmakers avoiding "making political films or attempt to depoliticize the ones they do" (2015: 7).

Haas, Christensen, and Haas create a typology of four categories of political films based on two criteria they consider the "two predominant dimensions of political films," namely content and intent, which they find "parallel the two major strands of political theory—empirical and normative" (2015: 9). For the authors, political content "entails more or less accurately depicting some aspect of political reality [...], political institutions, processes, and actors," while they find political intent in films "that are loaded with intentional political messages," which "explicitly challenge the values of the audience and may even incite it to political action" (2015: 9–10).

Haas, Christensen, and Haas's (2015: 10–14) subsequent categories of political film are:

1. Political reflexive films (with high political content and low political intent, such as *Independence Day* [1996], as well as several Westerns and gangster films).
2. Pure political films (with high political content and high political intent, such as *The Candidate* [1972], and propaganda films).
3. Socially reflective films (with low political content and low political intent, such as *Pretty Woman* [1990] and *Gone With the Wind* [1939]).
4. Auteur political films (with high political intent and low political content, such as *Natural Born Killers* [1994]).

Haas, Christensen, and Haas's categorization is most useful as it actually shows that the overwhelming majority of films produced by Hollywood contain political messages, despite the industry's reluctance and/or denial of purposely mixing politics with filmmaking practices. However, I would argue that the criterion of intent is problematic in that it is quite difficult to prove. As I understand it, it would require systematic research and wide industry knowledge to conclude that a given film was purposely made to include a political message. Interviews with screenwriters, directors, producers, composers, and actors (not to mention other members of the crew and industry executives who could influence filming, such as marketing and media strategists) should be available if one is to begin discussing the intent of a film narrative.

In addition, Haas, Christensen, and Haas insist on content rather than the form of a political film, like several other authors, such as Coyne (2008) and Giglio (2014), which is the first, natural step in trying to analyze a genre. However, no systematic corpus of political films has been created to date, with the exception of a helpful political filmography from the 1930s to the 2010s, included in Haas, Christensen, and Haas's monograph. In addition, if one is to examine content and/or form, one would unavoidably step into the field of narratology. Revealing the surface structure could not only lead to a more concrete definition but also elucidate patterns not easily observed without systematic analysis. Although structural analysis is not considered the theory *du jour*, I maintain it provides us with the only tangible tools to unlock a text. After all, the overwhelming majority of authors who examine film narratives apply textual analysis or close readings to prove their arguments, thus using tools from semiotics.

The narrative discussion of the films is based on a semiotic analysis of the audiovisual text. The reason semiotics is used in this study is perfectly summed up by Alexandros Ph. Lagopoulos and Karin Boklund-Lagopoulou (1992: 35) below:

> Semiotics is a powerful tool—the most powerful tool we possess—for the in-depth analysis of ideology, culture, and the systems of meaning. It studies the universe of signs and its structure in all their aspects and complexity. It can study the articulation and classification of signifiers; penetrate into the phenomenon of perception; analyse in detail the structure of conception; describe the direct, denotative meaning of semiotic messages; discover the ideological presuppositions of scientific modes of discourse; explore the hidden, connotative meaning of cultural texts and together with this their fundamental value systems or world views; formulate the surface and deep structures of these texts; [...] Semiotics offers not only a theory of meaning, but has also elaborated methods for operating on meaning and qualitative techniques for detailed analysis.

One would argue that although semiotics is useful in analyzing all kinds of texts—including cinematic narratives—the end result is a series of patterns, models of deep and surface structures, which are ahistorical in nature and do not take into account production or sociocultural parameters. Lagopoulos and Boklund-Lagopoulou acknowledge that "[c]ultural systems [such as cinema] do not exist without a material vehicle" (1992: 39) and that no semiotic analysis can be complete without taking into consideration this materiality, thus canceling every argument that may imply semiotics cannot be used to examine cultural texts. Lagopoulos and Boklund-Lagopoulou further propose to complement the examination of the narratives' meaning with the "exo-semiotic" (the material production). More recently, Lagopoulos and Boklund-Lagopoulou (2014) have become proponents of "social semiotics," arguing that "the viewpoint of social semiotics, the articulation and integration of culture within material society reflecting the foundational process creating culture, leads to the articulation of semiotic analysis with its sociological determinants, thus allowing, beyond *description* and *understanding*, the sociohistorical *interpretation* and *explanation* of the semiotic."

Many are the monographs on film studies that opt for textual analysis as their methodological tool. However, the majority take the definition of the text as well as the semiotic context of textual analysis for granted. I would like to briefly clarify some widely used terms, such as text, actor, transformation, and isotopy, that I am using. I would also like to underscore at this point that I do not aim to present a new theory or enter in a theoretical discusssion of the rich literature. My aim is to explain from the outset the theoretical context I am working in and, hopefully, to propose a more concrete model of analysis of audiovisual texts.

There are a number of definitions of the text in semiotic theory, that mainly originate from French semiotics and the study of literature. Nevertheless, these definitions can be directly applied—and have already been widely used—to the study of film texts. Gérard Genette (1972: 71) defines the text—*récit* in French— as "the narrative enunciation, the oral or written discourse that undertakes the relation of an event or a series of events." Joseph Courtés (1991: 70) first notes that, quite simply, the main characteristic of the text is "that something happens," and defines it as the "transformation between two successive/reversible and different states" (1991: 72). As an example, Courtés (1991: 73) uses a random TV commercial that advertises a floor cleaning product. The commercial shows the dirty floor (state 1) and then a woman cleaning it with the advertised product (T = transformation). The next state of the floor, cleanliness (state 2), can be shown or not as Courtés argues the viewer has already predicted what will happen. Consequently, the text narrates the transformation of a dirty floor into a clean one through the use of a detergent. Thus, Courtés arrives at a basic diagram, following his definition of the text.

Table 1 The text according to Courtés

State 1 (dirt)	T= transformation of floor	State 2 (cleanliness)

Based on the above, the film text consists of the moving images, the sounds, the music, and the characters' speech, that begin after the production company's logos—or after the credits when the latter are not shown during the film's beginning—and end with a title card reading "The End" or the final credits.

Narratology is based on an analogy: a narrative is like a sentence (phrase) and, as such, it can be analyzed with the assistance of a narrative grammar. Every narrative includes a subject that acts, and an action, while there can also be objects that the action can be driven towards. According to Algirdas J. Greimas (1986: 176–178), there are six "grammar" roles present in a narrative: the subject and object of action, the sender and receiver, the helper and the enemy. Every character in a narrative can assume more than one role, and thus, a number of narrative combinations can be created. However, an important observation made by Jacques Fontanille (2003: 150) should be made here. Fontanille notes that "the notion of actant is an abstract notion that, first of all, must be distinguished from the traditional or intutive notions of character, hero, actor or role." Fontanille argues that we need to conceive the notion of actant in a context that presupposes that "nothing in the text is given by default," and "that everything is to be constructed" (2003: 150). He stresses the importance of first establishing the development of the plot and defining its functions. Fontanille concludes that "[t]he actant is therefore this abstract functional entity that is necessary for the narrative predication." In his application of semiotic and narrative theories to film, André Gardies (1993: 33) agrees with Fontanille and points out that actants can take the form of "characters, animals, objects, even sentiments." For instance, in several political thrillers it is anger or revenge, that is, emotions, that act as "senders" and prompt the subject/character towards action.

Finally, I am also examining the major isotopies of the films. An isotopy is a semantic repetition that may appear in the text. In film, this can take the form of repetitive settings (the vast frontier vs. the small town in the Western), characters (the good guy vs. the bad, in Westerns, horror films etc.), and even narrative structures (the romantic comedy's boy meets girl, boy loses girl, boy gets girl in the end formula). Distinguishing isotopies is useful in constructing the overall structure of a genre—that is, a group of films that share semantic as well as syntactic traits—as well as observing their association with their exo-semiotic environment.

My first step in defining a political genre is the compilation of a corpus of films and the analysis of their narrative grammar. The hypothesis is that if we could examine the narrative grammar of a cluster of similar films, we would see the same patterns emerging and thus arrive at a more appropriate genre definition.

Corpus construction

As the political film remains a rather elusive category, I believe systematic research with specific criteria can clarify its borders. That is why I chose to begin with the construction of a corpus. The initial compiled corpus comprised two hundred films taken from the annual top-100 US box office data, found on boxofficemojo.com (http://www.boxofficemojo.com). The criteria followed for the inclusion of a given title in the initial corpus were: the films had to have a relevant political subject, have been produced and/or coproduced in the United States, and have been shot and/or released between 2002 and 2012. Finally, their gross proceeds had to be at least $15 million worldwide and/or match their budget. This number matches approximately the returns of *The Conspirator*, which was the 200th film in the initial corpus. I decided to limit the search to two hundred films as I wanted to ensure that the films in the corpus had an average to positive appeal, and their journey was not limited to the festival circuit or a couple of theaters. This meant that I had to exclude films such as *Grassroots* (which was shot on a low budget but returned only $12,000 in 2012, and was not released worldwide), *War, Inc.* (which cost $10 million but earned a little over $1 million in 2008), *The Lucky Ones* (budgeted at $14 million, it did not even reach $300,000 in admissions), the 2006 remake of the classic *All The King's Men* (which cost $55 million but earned only $9.5 million), and *Spartan* (which cost $20 million but returned $8.1 million).

The selection of the films followed three of the four methods proposed by Andrew Tudor in 1973 regarding genre classification and labeled by Janet Staiger in 1997. Before deciding on the inclusion of the titles, I began with a relatively preconceived idea of what a political film is and had decided that politics should be used in an exclusive context (the "a priori" method according to Staiger [2003: 187]). Secondly, I used empirical evidence in order to include films in the corpus (the "empiricist" method, [Staiger 2003: 197]). I had already watched the majority of the films, approximately 90 percent, during their initial release in the theaters, which facilitated the compilation. For the rest of the included films in the initial corpus, I also relied on plot summaries, reviews, and relevant information, such as interviews with filmmakers, actors, etc. (the "social consensus" method, [Staiger 2003: 187]),[7] as "industrial and journalistic labels and terms constitute crucial evidence for an understanding of both the industry's and the audience's generic conceptions" (Neale 2003: [1990] 167–8).

After the initial selection of films, all the titles were crosschecked using the American Film Institute (AFI) Catalog of Feature Films, which includes data on almost 60,000 films. As mentioned, IMDb does not include a political genre in its film categorization. Boxofficemojo.com, on the other hand, includes 211 different generic categories under its link "Genres" on the lower left-hand menu of its web page. Among them, there are four categories that include the word political: political documentaries, political campaign/election films, political satires, and political thrillers. Each genre is followed by the number of relevant films that exist in the database, which leads to a new page with the specific genre films listed according to their financial success. However, when one searches for the profits of a given film using the search button on the top left-hand corner or simply googles the film title followed by keywords, such as financial return, success, or box office, the film page that opens includes a different genre classification and the word political disappears. So, *The Ides of March* is only a thriller if one searches using the title of the film, but turns into a political thriller if you look it up in the Genre section. In other words, no film in the final corpus was categorized as a political narrative on either imdb.com (http://www.imdb.com) or boxofficemojo.com, two of the largest and most informed movie databases in the world. That is why I also used the AFI Catalog to check the films a third and final time. The AFI Catalog does not provide a list with its genre categories. However, a simple search to find political films yielded 265 titles from approximately 60,000 entries, which only accounts for 0.44 percent of all the films in the Catalog. In a database that comprises 4723 Westerns (7.87 percent), 2244 crime films (3.74 percent), 1382 horror films (2.3 percent), 1086 romantic comedies (1.81 percent) or even 781 science fiction films (1.3 percent), it becomes evident that the political film is a category not promoted, encouraged, or even acknowledged, by Hollywood. I should also note that the AFI Catalog also includes documentaries, so the 265 titles do not refer exclusively to fiction films. To conclude, only seven of the final seventy-eight films of the corpus were characterized as political narratives in the AFI Catalog: *Man of the Year* (2006), *Lions for Lambs* (2007), *Swing Vote* (2008), *The Ides of March* (2011), *Syriana* (2005), *W.* (2008) and *Frost/Nixon* (2008). The data above prove, with tangible evidence, the disinclination of the industry (the AFI comprises film leaders, business people, and academics), and the media (imdb.com and boxofficemojo.com are both subsidiaries of amazon.com, owned by billionaire Jeff Bezos, who in 2013 expanded to media with the purchase of *The Washington Post*) to acknowledge the existence of films that can be labeled as political. Yet, the genre obstinately continues its secret life and it is up to the researcher to define its borders and describe its specific parameters.

Proposing a definition of the disguised political film genre

Once the list of all the films was compiled, I watched them again and proceeded to a surface narrative analysis. The analysis I followed focused on the protagonist's personal narrative program. In other words, I examined and noted the main subject's object, without taking into account the other subjects/characters. Once the films were viewed, the narrative programs of the protagonists were written down. The main observation made once I examined the basic structure of the initial films in the corpus is that the basic narrative program of the protagonist is that he/she acts for the greater good of the state and not exclusively for their own benefit, whether he/she understands it or not. Before I go any further, though, I have to stress that I acknowledge the limitation of this criterion in solely defining the genre. The fact is that many genres have their protagonist act for the greater good; in horror, for instance, the hero/heroine has to vanquish the monster not only to save his/her life, but to exterminate the threat for the good of the community/world. The same applies to the superhero films. Thus, I needed to complement the criterion of this narrative program with a specific context. The object of the protagonist is to affect the political structure (the three branches of the government: executive, legislative, judiciary), electoral procedures, and/or established institutions (police, CIA, FBI). In films, this object can take many forms: the assassination of an oppressive leader (*Valkyrie* [2008]; *Inglorious Basterds* [2009]), the overcoming of a speech impediment to uphold the monarchy (*The King's Speech* [2010]), a personal sacrifice (*The Passion of the Christ* [2004]), the passing of new legislation (*Lincoln* [2012]; *Legally Blonde 2: Red, White & Blonde* [2003]), or the exposure of governmental corruption (*Shooter*, 2007). In this way, I arrived at the following definition of the "disguised" political film:

> The political film is a narrative whose story can take place in the past or the present, follow the dramatic or comedic mode, originate from real or fictional events—or a combination of both—with a subject/protagonist whose narrative object is situated in the political structure of a state and its attainment will affect society as a whole in a positive or negative way.

The process was quite intriguing as films I had initially considered as explicitly political were excluded from the corpus based on a second viewing and my definition of a political film genre. Based on the definition and the patterns that emerged after viewing the 200 films of the initial corpus, only seventy-eight made it to the final corpus of political films, while more than 120 had to be excluded. A closer examination of some of these titles follows:

Excluded films

Other genres

Sci-fi/action/adventure films (such as *The Hunger Games* franchise [2012, 2013, 2014, 2015], *Stealth* [2005], *Déjà vu* [2006], *Adjustment Bureau* [2011], *V for Vendetta* [2006], and *Battleship* [2012]), Westerns (such as *Open Range* [2003], *The Missing* [2003], and *3:10 to Yuma* [2007]), gangster films (such as *The Departed* [2006], *American Gangster* [2007], and *Public Enemies* [2009]), horror films (such as *Abraham Lincoln: Vampire Hunter* [2012], and *Chernobyl Diaries* [2012]), are not considered political films despite their partial focus on governmental and/or established institutional practices. Of course, I believe that the above genres function as political allegories. They have offered and still produce narratives that convey astute critique and commentary, and this particular function has been meticulously documented in academia.[8] However, I maintain that the spectacular aspects promoted by both science fiction and horror, whether they come in the form of stunningly choreographed and filmed action sequences or gore and splatter, are the dominant narrative elements to the detriment of political content.

Films mistaken as political

Michael Shapiro (2009: 41) and Gianos (1998) observe that usually politically-centered films revolve around an individual story and not a collective one. Gianos argues that this trend is due, on the one hand to "the interests of story-telling," and the powerful Hollywood classical narration (the three-act structure and the emphasis on the hero/heroine's desires and actions), and, on the other, to the establishment of the star system and the "U.S. cultural emphasis on individualism" (1998: 170). The emphasis on a single protagonist is a widely established narrative trope and, as the definition above shows, political films do usually center on a single protagonist/subject. However, the difference lies in the object of the protagonist and its effect. Thus, even films that can be thought of as political narratives are instantly excluded from the genre if the protagonist's goal is (a) not situated in a political context, and (b) will affect his/her own interests. During the viewing of the films, I came across a number of films I have always thought of as political narratives, mainly because their stories centered on politically important subjects, such as the 9/11 attacks, or because the narratives were steered by or starred individuals with a well-known affinity with political filmmaking, such as Oliver Stone and George Clooney. However, after the analysis of the films' narrative grammar, I realized that these films do not belong to the genre.

For instance, Stone's *World Trade Center*, 2006, was an empirically easy inclusion in the first corpus. The director's body of work, his reputation as a political filmmaker and the 9/11 theme of the film were the three reasons why I included the film in the initial corpus. *World Trade Center* focuses on two Port Authority police officers, about to assist the rescue efforts after the attack in New York on 9/11, only to find themselves trapped when the South Tower collapses over them. By focusing on the story of these officers, the film celebrates the people who died on duty and those who tried to rescue them, which we only see during the finale. The film is an intense drama but not a political narrative as all the political implications of 9/11 are absent and no cause or responsibility is examined. The object of the protagonists' efforts is to save people but the political context is missing. As Kellner (2010: 104) observes, *World Trade Center* "is the ultimate un-Oliver Stone film: restrained, understated, often slow and somber, and conservative [...] It is conservative in following traditional Hollywood generic forms and storytelling, in failing to deal with the political context." I do not believe Stone "failed" to deal with the politics surrounding the 9/11 attacks as Kellner notes above, but instead chose another path. By following the conventions of the disaster or the survival film, genres which usually celebrate human will and power in the face of extreme adversity and/ or danger, Stone opted to approach a traumatic event in a humanistic way, and perhaps assist in his nation's mourning process. The same argument could be made about the first narrative film which dealt with the 9/11 attacks, *United 93*, released three and a half months earlier than *World Trade Center*. Again, the reputation of the director, Paul Greengrass, "whose pedigree was in political documentaries for British television," and the theme, "which told the story of the passengers whose intervention caused one of the planes hijacked on September 11 to crash in Pennsylvania" (Holloway 2008: 86) could easily lead to the inclusion of the film into a political film genre. Nevertheless, as with Stone's contribution, *United 93* is not asking questions about the political reasons and/ or consequences of the attacks but is more interested in the human factor.[9] I would argue that *World Trade Center* and *United 93* are in the same category as *Reign Over Me* (2007) and *Extremely Loud and Incredibly Close* (2011) two films that also center on the implications 9/11 had on the lives of individuals that lost loved ones in the attacks but leave any political questions aside, functioning as traumatic appeasement rather than polemical statements.

Motorcycle Diaries (2004) was also added to the first corpus as the film centers on Ernesto "Che" Guevara, a significant political figure. However, after the second viewing, it became clear that the narrative was more interested in exploring specific personality characteristics of its protagonist that were tied to his private life, and was not concerned with Che's political decisions and or legacy. In particular, the film follows Ernesto and his friend Alberto Granado in their motorcycle journey across South America. Both men are in their early twenties, and their adventure away from their comfortable lives in Buenos Aires will transform their lives forever. The film focuses on how the journey and the encounter with everyday people along the way inform Ernesto and Alberto about the social injustice and deep-seated class division in South America. Basically, the film conveys what shaped Guevara's political beliefs but stops just before he becomes a political leader. Therefore, and despite the obvious political subtext and social commentary embedded in the plot, *Motorcycle Diaries* is not a political film.

War films

One of the definitions of war is that it "is the application of state violence in the name of policy," involving "killing and wounding people and destroying property until the survivors abandon their military resistance or the belligerents come to a negotiated agreement" (Otterbein 2004: 9). As such, the initial corpus contained, as one might expect, a significant number of war films since politics and war have a close relationship. War films have been around ever since the birth of Hollywood and have been, for the most part, "expected to play the patriotic game" (Alford 2010: 9). In his examination of the Hollywood war film tradition, Alford underlines the creation of the Office of War Information

(OWI) in 1940 as the key to understanding how the war film was shaped in the subsequent decades, as one of its purposes "was the development of strategies for using film [...] to propagate its messages" (2010: 9). The OWI still functions today and there have been cases where "branches of the Pentagon successfully steered film scripts in some very precise directions, or effectively prevented others from being made" (2010: 11). As a detailed account on the OWI role in the films on the corpus falls beyond the scope of this, it can be safely hypothesized that war films with no political commentary or, by contrast, with conservative and propagandistic undertones, can be the result of pressure and/or influence by factors outside the film industry.

In *Tears of the Sun* (2003), a US Navy SEAL team, headed by Lieutenant A. K. Waters (Bruce Willis) is on a mission to extract Dr. Lena Fiore Kendricks (Monica Bellucci), an American citizen by marriage, two nuns, and a priest, during a Nigerian civil unrest between the Fulanis and the Igbos at an unidentified moment in time. The object of the protagonist may be set during a political context (civil war) but it will not have any effect for the whole community. The film cannot be categorized as political, yet the narrative offers several instances for political commentary. The film begins with a news report presenting the clash between two ethnic groups, while a female reporter, in voice off, explains the situation, and sets the scene for what will follow:

> TV REPORTER: Tension that had been brewing for months in Nigeria exploded yesterday as exiled General Mustafa Yakunu orchestrated a swift and violent coup against the democratically elected government of President Samula Azuka. In the land of 120 million people and over 250 ethnic groups, there'd been a long history of ethnic enmity, particularly between northern Fulani Moslems in the North and southern Christian Igbo in the South. The victorious Fulani rebels have taken to the streets as periodic outbursts of violence continue all over the country [...] There's no word yet on the United Nations' reaction to the coup, but United States forces have already begun to evacuate its embassy.

While Waters's mission does not contain any elements of American interventionism in the region initially, everything changes when the soldiers witness a massacre at an Igbo village and decide to engage by killing the Fulani attackers. From that moment, the US soldiers become ethically involved. In addition, and unbeknownst to Waters, among the Igbo refugees that Dr. Kendricks has demanded also be saved along with her, is the only son of the murdered President Azuka and Nigeria's hope for democracy. For the first time in his military career, Waters disobeys orders and decides, along with his soldiers, to save everyone and not just Dr. Kendricks. However, throughout the narrative, no commentary is made by the characters regarding the civil war, and/or the US role in the region. The sole exception is Captain Rhodes (Tom Skerritt), who, while briefing the team at the beginning of the film about the Fulani's whereabouts and military equipment, states: "unfortunately, we have been supplying them for far too many years." *Tears of the Sun* misses every opportunity for political insight despite the setting (the Nigerian Civil War), and the themes (ethnicity, genocide, religion, the US involvement). In the end, American interventionism is reduced to a "morally justified" act as the soldiers led by Waters are shown to be "informed by deeply entrenched values of democracy and multiculturalism" (Alford 2010: 52), thus empowering the patriotic sentiment.

Jarhead, 2005, "the first major film about the first Gulf War," was, initially, destined to become "the definitive film about the 1991 Gulf War." However, as Rollins and O'Connor (2008: 29) observe, *Jarhead* is "Not political in any way," but mostly "preoccupied with the issue of character." The film, based on US Marine Anthony Swofford's same-titled 2003 memoir, is, indeed, "a compelling account of life in the Marine Corps [...] just before and during the war" (Booker 2007: 205). Nevertheless, it "carefully avoids any real engagement with the numerous political issues surrounding the war, opting instead to comment on those issues only peripherally or in passing" (2007: 205). Contrary to *Tears of the Sun*, which sets a clear objective for the main character from the beginning, *Jarhead*'s narrative is more ambiguous. Anthony's (Jake Gyllenhaal) objective is never made clear. The plot is focused on a single individual and the practical and psychological ordeal he is facing to the detriment of examining the political implications of its context.

Clint Eastwood's *Flags of Our Fathers*, and *Letters of Iwo Jima* (both released in 2006), are two films that focus on the same event, the 1945 Battle of Iwo Jima during the Second World War, and constitute "a unique contribution to film history," as this is the "first time a director made two films at the same time" on the same subject (Schubart and Gjelsvik 2013: 1). The first film concentrates on the American soldiers, and especially those who were photographed by Joe Rosenthal—who immortalized the event—raising the second flag on the island of Iwo Jima, situated in the Pacific Ocean, after its successful capture, and follows their life after their return home. The latter takes the point of view of the Japanese, and similarly focuses on a few Japanese soldiers just before and during the battle. Both films castigate the US and Japanese governments in their meddling in military operations during the course of the narrative. In particular, in *Flags of Our Fathers*, upon their return, the young soldiers are used by the government to promote war bonds and help the war effort by making speeches and appearances all over the country. However, despite the critique the filmmaker incorporates in two narratives, he is clearly more interested in investigating the traumas of war and how they affected the young soldiers in both countries. After all, the protagonists' goal in the first film is to find peace and quiet and lead a normal life, while in the second they aim at fighting for their lives. Thus, neither of Eastwood's films can be characterized as political, although the filmmaker is clearly aware and mindful of the era's political strategies. Finally, other war films excluded from the corpus are *Windtalkers* (2002), which centers mostly on male bonding and race, *Flyboys* (2006), which takes a biographical approach following a small group of Americans who become fighter pilots during the First World War, and *War Horse* (2011), which examines the human/animal relationship in times of conflict.

Dramas on socially charged issues

In the initial corpus, several films that dealt with socially charged issues, such as gender relations, immigration, race, etc., were included. However, their overwhelming majority focused on the struggles of individuals to overcome adversity while the outcome of the protagonists did not have a wide social effect. Interestingly, almost all films that focus on race relations opt for an approach that does not involve political institutions. *The Human Stain* (2003), *Crash* (2004), *The Great Debaters* (2007), *The Freedom Writers* (2007), *The Help* (2011), and *Django Unchained* (2012), concentrate on racial tensions from contemporary and historical perspectives. Nevertheless, the core subject of racial acceptance and racism is limited within the boundaries of each protagonist's narrative program and never enters the political arena. The exception in this cluster of films is *Lincoln*, which revolves around the President's efforts to abolish slavery in 1865 by passing the Thirteenth Amendment by the House of Representatives.[10]

Other excluded films include *The House of Sand and Fog* (2003), *The Visitor* (2007), and *The Namesake* (2006), three films that examine Middle-Eastern and Asian racial identities in a post-9/11 world, *Changeling* (2008), and *North Country* (2005), which focus on female disempowerment and gender inequality, and *Babel* (2006), whose episodic structure may contain political commentary (such as the treatment of Mexican immigrants by Americans), but again chooses to limit its critique within the parameters of its characters' microcosm.

Anglophone films produced outside Hollywood

Lastly, Anglophone films not produced or coproduced by US companies were excluded from the corpus in accordance with the criteria outlined above. I am therefore not discussing such films as *The Pianist* (2002), *The Iron Lady* (2011), *Hyde Park on Hudson* (2012), *Tinker, Tailor, Soldier, Spy* (2011), *In The Loop* (2009), or *Pan's Labyrinth* (2006), despite their obvious political character.

Final corpus: Initial observations and categorization

From the initial 200 films, the final corpus includes seventy-eight films that, according to the proposed definition, can be considered political films. I'd like to stress again that the political film can only exist as a theoretical construction and that all the films in the corpus can belong to other generic categories as well. The first observation has to do with the repetition of the same names in the director's chair and the screenplay department. Two directors have helmed three political films each: Ridley Scott (*Robin Hood, Kingdom of Heaven, Body of Lies*) and Paul Greengrass (*The Bourne Ultimatum, The Bourne Supremacy, Green Zone*), and six directors were behind the camera of two films each: Robert Redford (*Lions for Lambs, The Conspirator*), Oliver Stone (*W., Alexander*), Steven Spielberg (*Lincoln, Munich*), Doug Liman (*State of Play, The Bourne Identity*), Antoine Fuqua (*Shooter, King Arthur*), and George Clooney (*Good Night, and Good Luck,* and *The Ides of March*). Although not all of the titles above are explicitly political, sometimes it suffices to mention the name of the director to know that the film touches upon political subjects. As Haas, Christensen, and Haas (2015: 35) note, "next to John Sayles, Oliver Stone, Spike Lee, and Robert Redford," who "espouse a well-known political agenda," the growing bodies of work by "the Hughes Brothers [...], Ben Affleck, Lee Daniels, Kathryn Bigelow, and George Clooney [...] may belong in the coterie of political directors," along, I would add, with Liman, Greengrass and Scott.

Similarly, writers Brian Helgeland (*Green Zone, Robin Hood, Salt*—the last was cowritten with Kurt Wimmer), Matthew Michael Carnahan (*The Kingdom, Lions for Lambs, State of Play*—the last was cowritten with Tony Gilroy and Billy Ray), and Peter Morgan (*Frost/Nixon, The Other Boleyn Girl, The Queen*) are responsible for the scripts of nine films. George Clooney and Grant Heslov cowrote *Good Night, and Good Luck,* and *The Ides of March,* Tony Kushner is the writer of *Lincoln* and cowriter of *Munich*, William Monaham wrote the screenplay for *Kingdom of Heaven* and *Body of Lies*, and Tony Gilroy wrote *The Bourne Identity*, *The Bourne Supremacy* and cowrote *The Bourne Ultimatum*, *The Bourne Legacy*, and *State of Play*.

A number of actors also repeatedly appear in the cast of political films. Matt Damon has not only starred in the *Bourne* trilogy but also *Green Zone*, *The Good Shepherd* and *Syriana*; Clooney is the lead in *Syriana*, *Good Night, and Good Luck*, *The Men Who Stare at Goats*, and *The Ides in March*; David Strathairn appears in *Lincoln*, *The Bourne Legacy*, and *The Bourne Ultimatum*; Sean Penn is the lead male in *Milk*, *Fair Game*, and *The Interpreter*; Chris Cooper stars in *Breach*, and appears in *The Kingdom*, *Syriana*, *The Bourne Supremacy*, and *The Bourne Identity*. Since the making of a film requires significant capital, I think the examination of these individuals linked to the political film along with a discussion regarding the production, marketing, and distribution of the films can provide inside information regarding political narratives in contemporary Hollywood. That is why the penultimate chapter of this monograph is dedicated to these industry players in front of and behind the camera.

A second observation is that forty-three out of the seventy-eight films (55.1 percent) are based on novels, memoirs, television series, and historical research while thirty-six are based on original screenplays. This remark is not very significant in itself, as the political film follows a trend that is common in Hollywood regarding the based-on-a-previous-source/original screenplay ratio. However, if we combine the percentage with the fact that the top-twenty of the highest grossing political films and the most critically acclaimed and award-winning narratives in the corpus comprises fifteen cinematic adaptations—irrespective of their type of source—and only five films that derive from original stories, then we can reach some worthy conclusions. Adaptation scholars have repeatedly pointed out that cinematic adaptations, and especially literary adaptations, are among the most recognizable parameters of "quality" filmmaking (McFarlane 1996; Kaklamanidou 2006; Hutcheon 2006).[11]

The "quality" parameter does accompany most political films—irrespective of their box office performance—that are based on (a) memoirs, such as *Argo*, *Syriana* and *Fair Game*, (b) novels, such as the *Bourne* trilogy, and *Body of Lies*, and (c) historical research, such as *The Conspirator*, *The Queen*, and *The King's Speech*. It seems that the source, especially the memoir and the historical evidence, lends to the cinematic text an aura of gravitas and authenticity and transforms it into an audiovisual version of a "this is how it really happened" story. Although I am not delving into an in-depth discussion of whether the history film is a suitable conveyor of historical truth or not, it is useful to note that history films are more often than not regarded a priori as "serious" productions rather than entertainment vehicles.

The third observation regards Hollywood's industry gender disparity. From the seventy-eight films, only two were directed by female filmmakers: Kathryn Bigelow's *Zero Dark Thirty* and Betty Thomas's *I Spy*. The 2.56 percent of female directors is lower than the already small percentage of 4.6 percent, which designates the women who directed studio films in 2014 (Silverstein 2015), and corroborates my suspicion about the "disguised" political film being predominantly a male genre. The screenwriting section of the films included only three women (3.85 percent), two of whom participated in a writing group with two and three male writers respectively; Kate Condell wrote the screenplay for *Legally Blonde 2: Red, White & Blonde*, Marianne Wibberley cowrote *I Spy* with Cormac Wibberley, Jay Scherick, and David Ronn, and Laeta Kalogrids cowrote *Alexander* with Oliver Stone and Christopher Kyle.

The situation improves a little if one turns one's attention to the narrative itself. Of the seventy-eight films, ten (12.8 percent) had a female lead (*The Queen, Zero Dark Thirty, Fair Game, Legally Blonde 2: Red, White & Blonde, The Interpreter, Salt, Elizabeth: The Golden Age, The Young Victoria, The Other Boleyn Girl,* and *The Debt*). This percentage is actually a little higher than the average of 12 percent that describes the percentage of films of the top 100 highest grossing productions with female protagonists in 2014 (Silverstein 2015). I should note, however, that the male leads in *Fair Game* and *The Interpreter* share almost as much screen time as the female protagonist. In addition, *Salt* was initially conceived as a Tom Cruise vehicle. When he refused, due to scheduling conflicts, Sony's cochairwoman, Amy Pascal, contacted Angelina Jolie who, two years earlier, had been asked if she wanted to play a Bond girl. Jolie may have refused but she added that she would gladly play Bond instead. Pascal, therefore, knew that *Salt* would definitely interest her and eventually the role in *Salt* was rewritten for the female star (Cohen 2010). Narratively significant female roles, and not simply female characters as love interests, were part of a few political narratives, such as the *Bourne* tetralogy (with the exception of *The Bourne Identity*), *The Manchurian Candidate, Rendition, The Conspirator,* and *Get Smart*.

The data provided by the corpus can lead to a number of initial observations regarding the genre as whole, which are as follows:

1. The contemporary political film is a male-centric genre regarding both the narrative and the filmmaking team behind the camera, echoing the real political landscape, which sees few women in positions of power. According to Steven Hill's (2014) article in *The Nation*, "[t]he percentage of women holding statewide and state legislative offices is less than 25 percent, barely higher than in 1993." However, at a time where women lead a number of countries around the world (i.e., Germany, Liberia, Argentina, Norway, Poland), and where US television broadcasts shows with politically powerful women, such as *Madam Secretary* (CBS, 2014–present), *Veep* (HBO, 2012–present), and *Homeland* (HBO, 2011–present), the Hollywood film industry persists in following a less progressive and more traditional path regarding political narratives.
2. The contemporary political film performs best, in the box office and/or in reviews, when its plot is based on previously written material.
3. The contemporary political film is represented by a specific group of people in front of, and behind, the camera.

Sub-genres and book chapters

The categorization of the films was based on their narrative mode, prevailing theme, and the use of conventions from a variety of genres. Based on the first criterion, the films were divided between dramas and comedies. It is no surprise that among the seventy-eight films, only fifteen (19.2 percent) were comedies, while the rest followed the dramatic mode. These fifteen political comedies can be further sub-categorized among spy spoof films or spy parodies (*Get Smart, I Spy, Bad Company*, the two *Johnny English* films, and the two *Agent Cody Banks* productions), election comedies (*Head of State, Man of the Year, Swing Vote, The Campaign*), a satire (*The Dictator*), two history comedies (*Charlie Wilson's War, The Men Who Stare at Goats*), and a legal comedy (*Legally Blonde 2: Red, White & Blonde*).

Taking into consideration genre hybridization, and the political focus of the narrative, the rest of the films were divided into four categories which, along with the political comedies, constitute Chapters 2 to 6 of this monograph. Chapter 2 is dedicated to political comedies and focuses on the election cycle, mentioned above, which includes films that follow a tradition that goes back to the late 1930s and Frank Capra's classic *Mr. Smith Goes to Washington*, 1939.

Chapter 3 examines political thrillers, primarily represented via two established and well-recognized genres: the action genre and the thriller. I argue that the combination of conventions from both generic groups with a politically charged subject gives birth to the "political thriller," which shares both semantic and syntactic elements from action films and thrillers (such as spectacular chases, location shooting, frequent use of slow motion in editing, a central conflict between good and evil) to critique or support US foreign policies and/or their formation and execution. The majority of political thrillers involve CIA agents, military personnel, and the Secret Service and struggles to eradicate a foreign threat or a corrupt individual inside the domestic structure, which threatens stability. I should note, however, that based on the definition I propose, the majority of thrillers that set their action in the espionage world are by definition political, because their main protagonist acts in the line of duty and is obliged to protect the nation and its citizens. Exceptions do exist, however, and are presented in the same chapter. Furthermore, these spy/action thrillers convey interesting messages regarding US foreign policies, and that is why part of the chapter studies the relationship between the narrative and the sociopolitical climate. The films in this chapter are divided in two groups: films that are based on novels or original screenplays, such as the *Bourne* tetralogy, *Vantage Point*, *The Manchurian Candidate*, *The Interpreter*, and *The Sentinel*, and films that are based on real events and/or memoirs of real incidents, such as *Argo*, *Syriana*, *Traitor*, and *Breach*. I believe this division better assists both the narrative analysis, as well as the examination of the plot, *vis-à-vis* the potential political messages included in the film.[12]

Chapter 4 focuses on the examination of US domestic policies through political dramas, and/or biopics that refer to past historical events (*Good Night, and Good Luck, Milk, The Conspirator, Lincoln*), a fictional drama (*The Life of David Gale*), and two action/thrillers (*xXx: State of the Union, State of Play*). Historical dramas, or "dramatic feature films," as Robert A. Rosenstone (2012: 18) labels films that "reach a wide audience and sometimes become the focus of public debate about history," dominate this sub-category in my corpus. They also constitute films that were among the best films of their release years, garnering critical acclaim and a host of awards and accolades, while their majority also enjoyed substantial financial returns. This chapter discusses the representation of domestic policy in these films, and shows that despite differences in subject matter (from the passing of a revolutionary new law to the intricate relationship between the press and political power), style, context, and tone, the narratives focus on how the United States has dealt, and is dealing, with the continuation of its Republic.

Chapter 5 includes the examination of sixteen political films that fit the criteria of the proposed definition but are marketed and distributed under different labels by the industry, such as historical dramas, epics, action/adventure, or thrillers (i.e., *The Passion of the Christ* [2004]; *Troy* [2004]; *Kingdom of Heaven* [2005]; *300* [2006]). This discrepancy between industry categorization and theoretical assessment further reinforces my argument about how a political film genre can only exist in Hollywood as a theoretical construction and not an industry label. On the other hand, the existence of political narratives in a variety of genres also points to the filmmakers' continuing propensity to deal cinematically with political subjects and avoid Hollywood's aversion to political films by camouflaging their narratives into labels the industry usually relates to and accepts to market. I mainly concentrate on the monarchy film that prominently features in the late 2000s (i.e., *The Queen* [2006]; *Elizabeth: The Golden Age* [2007]; *The Other Boleyn Girl* [2008]) as it is the only subgenre in the corpus that concentrates on female protagonists.

Chapter 6 is an attempt to go behind the scenes of political narratives. In the relevant literature there are authors who use the criterion of "intent" in order to define political films. I find the inclusion of this criterion problematic, at least as far as it concerns fiction features, as it is not based on actual journalistic material (that is, interviews with filmmakers). Moreover, the criterion of intent is quite difficult to prove without systematic research and wide industry knowledge. However, as the internet today provides the theorist with a great amount of information, I endeavor to go beyond the political films discussed in the previous chapters and search for the "intent" of some of them, in interviews by directors, writers, and/or actors. Based on the statistical data drawn from the corpus, this chapter includes media interviews and articles on directors, writers, and actors mostly associated with the genre. Since the making of a film requires significant capital, I think the examination of these individuals linked to the political films of the corpus can yield helpful insights regarding the state of the genre in contemporary Hollywood. The book closes with Chapter 7, including a brief discussion of political films released between 2013 and 2015, and some concluding remarks on political films as a constructed category as well as some thoughts on the future of the genre.

2

Political Comedies

As noted in the introduction, the number of political comedies included in the corpus constitutes the smallest group in a general division of the narratives between comedy and drama. Only fifteen out of the seventy-eight films are comedies (19.2 percent) while five of them (33.3 percent) belong to the comedy/action genre, including the two *Johnny English* films, 2003 and 2011, that spoof the James Bond character, the two teen/action/comedy *Cody Banks* films (2003 and 2004), that focus on a teen CIA agent, and the Jackie Chan vehicle *The Spy Next Door* (2004). The rest of the films can be grouped in two broad categories: (a) comedies that deal with presidential campaigns, and presidents (*The Campaign, Man of the Year, Swing Vote,* and *Head of State*) and the Washington political scene (*Legally Blonde 2: Red, White & Blonde*) and mostly comment on domestic policies and procedures, and (b) films that satirize foreign policies and predominantly US-Arab relations (*The Dictator, The Men Who Stare at Goats*) or comment on political diplomacy (*Charlie Wilson's War*). As comedy is by definition based on hyperbole, I want to explore if the texts systematically acknowledge and/or castigate political mistakes that happen in the actual US political scene or if they tend to perpetuate the structural status quo of American politics. To do so, I analyze the cycle of the electoral process as this is the only group in the comedy category that produced narratives on the same subject from 2003 to 2012 and can lead to a semi-diachronic assessment of the subject.

The electoral process cycle

The films in this group share a focus on the electoral process, the defining praxis of the democratic system, and follow a long tradition of Hollywood narratives that extol the power of the popular vote and/or follow a candidate on the campaign trail.

From *All the King's Men* (1949), to *The Candidate* (1972), *The Distinguished Gentleman* (1992), and *Primary Colors* (1998)—to name but a few—the American film industry has always found a way to depict and simultaneously examine and/or criticize the way political power works, the rise and fall of politicians, and the intricacies involved to gain a seat of power and influence in Washington. However, as with the majority of the older films I just mentioned, their post-9/11 counterparts did not fare well at the box office, unlike the success encountered by the other political comedies discussed later in this chapter. Despite the modest budgets of the first three films—*Head of State* cost $35.2 million, *Man of the Year* $20 million, and *Swing Vote* $21 million—and the $95 million budget of *The Campaign*, the films' worldwide gross was $38.6 million, $41 million, $17.6 million, and $104 million respectively. To put this in perspective, suffice it to say that the gross of these four films combined amounts to $201 million and is less than *The Avengers'* opening weekend in 2012, which surpassed $207.5 million. As the general rule of thumb of measuring commercial success is that for a film "to break even, box office gross must be 2.5 times production costs" (Kuhn and Westwell 2012: 42), it is evident that these political comedies did not appeal to a wide audience. The star power and worldwide appeal of the film's main protagonists, consisting of experienced and usually bankable comedians such as Robin Williams, Will Ferrell, and even Academy Award recipient Kevin Costner, was not enough to attract viewers to the theaters. Marketing reasons and lack of sufficient and/or clever advertising may account for the disappointing financial outcome but this research is beyond the scope of my examination and should be reserved for a different study. After all, the film industry is notorious for targeting young and mostly Caucasian males, aged eighteen to twenty-four, and political comedies do not appeal to this demographic. Despite the revealing data of the 2014 Theatrical Market Statistics Report, published by the Motion Pictures Association of America (MPAA), that show that theatre attendance "increased for 40–49 year olds [...] and 50–59 year olds [...]," and that female moviegoers continue to comprise "the larger share [...] consistently since 2010," the film industry still caters to the tastes of the eighteen to twenty-four male populace, which may "represent 10% of the population, but 13% of moviegoers and 16% of tickets sold."

Although the goal of this chapter—and the whole monograph for that matter—is not to account for the films' commercial success or failure, I would like to hypothesize the following: political comedies can only be commercially successful if (a) they are first marketed as belonging to another specific genre (i.e., *Get Smart* is a suspense comedy that lampoons action thrillers, the two *Johnny English* films parody the James Bond franchise, *Legally Blonde 2: Red, White & Blonde* was a Reese Witherspoon vehicle and was viewed as the twenty-first-century *Clueless*), and/or (b) if their critique on the system is more radical and/or powerful than the boundaries set by such television political satirists as Jon Stewart and Stephen Colbert, as was the case with the irreverent Sacha Baron Cohen's commercially successful *The Dictator*.

Main actors' narrative program

As mentioned, all the films focus on the electoral process. Three (*Head of State, Man of the Year*, and *Swing Vote*) center on presidential elections and one (*The Campaign*) on congressional elections. The narratives unfold in a linear manner with the exception of *Man of the Year*, which is narrated by the protagonist's best friend and campaign manager. Yet, despite the occasional presence of the character in the fictitious present and some voice-overs, the story/*syuzhet* of the main characters also unfolds linearly.

Head of State, Man of the Year, and The Campaign follow the course of American men towards public office while Swing Vote follows an American worker as he single-handedly determines the outcome of the presidential elections. In *Head of State*, Mays Gilliam (Chris Rock) serves as an alderman of the impoverished 9th Ward in Washington DC, the unglamorous and poverty stricken part of the capital which is rarely featured in films that take place in Washington. Due to a conflict with a major developer, Mays loses his job and his fiancée at the beginning of the film. Despair lasts for a brief moment as the protagonist is chosen by the—unnamed in the narrative—Democratic Party to become their presidential candidate once their previous candidate and his nominated vice president are killed in an aviation freak accident. The Democrats are sure to lose the 2004 election and they are looking for an unknown candidate that could help them pave the way for the 2008 elections. Mays's brief media presence as the hero that saved an elderly woman from a vicious developer that demolished her house gives the Party the idea to use an African-American man as a candidate, and therefore become the first party to ever nominate a minority. Senator Bill Arnot (James Rebhorn), the mastermind of the plan, is certain that despite their upcoming defeat the electorate will remember their bold choice and will reciprocate in 2008. Mays accepts the nomination and the rest of the film concentrates on his adventurous campaign, concluding with his victory and the inaugural ball. In *Man of the Year*, Tom Dobbs (Robin Williams) is a popular television comedian and satirist of public affairs who decides to run for president as an independent nominee after an impromptu encouragement by his fans. Because of a technical problem in the electronic voting system that the manufacturing corporation does not fix, despite being notified by a competent employee, Dobbs wins the election. However, he soon learns the truth and has to confront the dilemma of stepping down and revealing a corporate intrigue or continue being a president who has not actually been chosen by the people. *The Campaign* follows two main characters as they vie for Congress at the 14th District of North Carolina. Marty Huggins (Zach Galifianakis), a very reserved, soft-spoken family man and tourism director in the small town of Hammond, becomes an unlikely political candidate after two businessmen convince him he can make a change for the better, while Cam Brady (Ferrell) is confident this election will mark his fifth term as congressman. Finally, although *Swing Vote* does not focus on a candidate, it does make elections its narrative center. The film plot revolves around Bud Johnson (Costner), a factory worker and single dad, who becomes the single voter who will determine the result of the presidential election because of a voting machine mishap.

As is evidenced by these condensed plot summaries, the films' narratives present great similarities regarding the actants/characters and their personal narrative programs. All the protagonists are heterosexual males in their thirties or forties and, in their majority, they present variations of singledom. Mays, in *Head of State*, is abandoned by his fiancée in the second sequence, *Man of The Year*'s Dobbs (Robin Williams) is single, and Bud in *Swing Vote* is divorced and raises his young daughter, while only the two congressional candidates in *The Campaign*, Cam and Marty, have wives and children. In addition, none of the protagonists—with the exception of *The Campaign*'s Cam, a film which boasts two equally important main characters and their electoral rivalry—enter the electoral race as a result of their individual decision. Instead, in *Head of State*, Mays is chosen by the Democrats to head the Party's ticket after their candidates die. In *Man of the Year*, Tom decides to run only after a woman in his audience asks him to do so during a show, and a few million enthusiastic emails follow that same night to support this impromptu idea. In *The Campaign*, Marty is convinced to run by two of his father's business acquaintances, while in *Swing Vote* it is Bud's daughter, Molly (Madeline Carroll), who believes in the sanctity of democracy's voting system, who tries to vote in place of her dad—who is drunk and has forgotten to meet her at the voting polls—only to find herself unable to actually register her choice because the machine is accidentally unplugged by a cleaning lady in the empty hall. The next morning, it is discovered that this unregistered vote is the one that will reveal the next president, and Bud becomes the person who holds the course the United States will take for the next four years in his hands.

Therefore, the basic linear and shared syntax of these films, based on the six grammar roles (sender, subject, object, receiver, enemy, friend) outlined by Greimas and discussed in the introduction, is as follows:

Sender of action (The Party, Fans, Businessmen, Daughter) ➜ Subject of action (Mays, Tom, Marty, Bud) ➜ Object of action (winning or determining a Public Seat) ➜ Receiver (the American people)

As previously mentioned, each character—which is not to be confused with the term "actant," or the role, or the real actor who incarnates the role—is part of the fictional world and has specific functions, following his/her own narrative program. Each character in the text can assume more than one role; consequently, a number of narrative programs evolve simultaneously, and characters can have different roles according to each subject of action. For instance, in *Head of State*, Mays is the main character/protagonist (subject) who wants to become president of the United States (object); yet, in the narrative program of Debra Lassiter (Lynn Whitfield), the campaign manager, he becomes an instrument (the helper) in her effort to win the election. Similarly, in *Man of The Year*, Tom Dobbs also wants to become president. However, the narrative program of Eleanor Green (Laura Linney), the tech employee who discovers her company helped elect the wrong person, evolves in tandem with that of Tom's, creating a secondary plot, and meets towards the climax of the film to include Tom as a helper to uncover a corporate fraud.

The sender of the action may or may not be a major character in the rest of the film. For instance, the woman in Dobbs's studio audience, who first asks him to run for president, appears for a couple of seconds in *Man of the Year*. However, senator Bill Arnot and campaign manager Debra remain part of the fictional universe in *Head of State*, even after they persuade Mays to accept the Party's candidacy, as do business moguls Glenn and Wade Motch (John Lithgow and Dan Aykroyd respectively) in *The Campaign*. Similarly, in *Swing Vote*, it is Bud's daughter's effort to vote, combined with his registration as a voter, that lead to his discovery and the subsequent pressure exercised on him by officials to choose the next president.

Iconography

One of the defining characteristics of a genre is its iconography, a cluster of similar settings, objects, and buildings that are repeated in the films and connote a direct relationship with the genre in question. Vast, open spaces, horses, cacti, a sheriff star, or a cowboy easily indicate the viewer's entrance to the world of the Western. Menacing music, an isolated house, and a group of young adults welcome us, more often than not, to the horror universe. The use of these semantic "building blocks" (Altman 2003: 31) helps not only the creation of the genre but also assists viewers in identifying each film's generic identity. *Head of State, Man of the Year, Swing Vote,* and *The Campaign* present a variety of shared semantic elements, which I group under the headings: (a) setting, (b) media spectacle, and (c) media presence.

Setting

The images in Figures 1–4 do not belong to the same film, although one could easily mistake them as stills from the same narrative, despite differences in their choice of color palette. The first figure (from *Head of State*) shows the Capitol in Washington DC, the seat of the US Congress, while the last figure (from *The Campaign*) also includes the Washington Monument, the tallest monumental obelisk in the world. Figures 2 and 3 (from *Man of the Year* and *Swing Vote* respectively) depict the Oval Office, the office of the President of the United States. The four films include more images that are politically charged, but I chose to show these two pairs, in order to emphasize the similarities of the narratives at a pictorial level. One could argue that it goes without saying that political films include images of Washington buildings and settings as their seats of government. Indeed, the majority of the films in my corpus, as is shown in the rest of the chapters, present similar images. Nevertheless, this helps only to consolidate the genre's semantic side that along with my proposed narrative syntax can lead to a more concrete theorization. On the other hand, an image of a government building cannot automatically label a film as political. For instance, Giglio (2014: 35-6) compares two films set in Washington DC, *Mr. Smith Goes to Washington* and *No Way Out* (1987), rightly concluding that while the former falls under the category of political film, the second does not. Giglio's observation is in tandem with Altman's semantic/syntactic approach that claims

Figures 1–4 (Left to right, top to bottom) Still frames[1] of buildings and settings from *Head of State, Man of the Year, Swing Vote*, and *The Campaign*.

that it is not enough to find the semantic ingredients or the syntactic ones to delineate a genre but to combine both approaches for a more accurate corpus compiling.

The political debate as media spectacle

The similarities of Figures 6 and 8 (*Man of the Year, The Campaign*) are impressive. Two long shots present a spacious hall while the stage accommodates two wooden rostrums from where each candidate will present his views. Behind them, we see the American flag and the President's flag. The lighting of the scene is also similar in that only the candidates are well lit while the rest of the room is darker. Figure 5, from *Head of State*, is also quite similar in its décor although the flags are missing; the shot is a medium one, allowing the viewers to recognize the characters. Finally, Figure 7, from *Swing Vote*, differs from the rest in that the debate seems to take place outdoors and not inside a building. However, other than that and the photography choices and filter that give the illusion of a grandiose event, the stage, the rostrums, the placing of the candidates at the center, that is, the *mise-en-scène*, remains the same.

Figures 5–8 (Left to right, top to bottom) Still frames from political debates in *Head of State, Man of the Year, Swing Vote,* and *The Campaign.*

These televised political debates belong to a group of representations of events, and/or reporting of events, that Kellner calls media spectacles. Drawing from Guy Debord's concept of the "society of the spectacle" (1967), Kellner defines media spectacles as "those phenomena of media culture that embody contemporary society's basic values, serve to initiate individuals into its way of life, and dramatize its controversies and struggles, as well as its modes of conflict resolution" (2003: 2). These spectacles "include media extravaganzas, sporting events, political happenings, and those attention-grabbing occurrences that we call news" (2003: 2). Thus, presidential debates become something more than an instrument to inform the American voters about key political issues and to try and convince them of their candidates convictions, the usefulness and viability of their proposed measures and actions regarding policies in different sectors, and ultimately even determine their vote; they become a media spectacle, a dramatic narrative staged, photographed, and executed like a game with winners and losers.

This spectacle is also in tandem with the television industry's profit-making incentive and capitalistic practices, proved by the impressive ratings. According to *The Hollywood Reporter*'s Michael O'Connell (2012), the first Mitt Romney–Barack Obama presidential debate, on October 4, 2012, drew more than sixty-seven million viewers to their screens. O'Connell notes (2012) that "No first round debate has hit that high of a number since President Jimmy Carter went up against Republican candidate Ronald Reagan in 1980 for 80.6 million viewers." Without using the word "spectacle," O'Connell clearly treats the debate as a special event, while his use of the phrase "first round debate" is indicative of how the Romney–Obama televised discussion has turned into a type of game, a boxing match where only one person will be left standing at the end. And although real political debates retain their austere format, more or less, their fictional ones go a step further. *Borgen* (DR1, 2010–13), a critically acclaimed televised Danish political drama, included a storyline in its last season where a news station decides to host political debates in the form of matches, with a referee/moderator, buzzers, and even cheerleaders; acknowledging that for the sake of ratings and subsequent cash flow, every issue, however serious, can be transformed into a sensational spectacle. The importance the news put on the Romney–Obama debate as well as the far-fetched—or isn't it?—Danish representation also confirms Kellner's (2003: 7) point about how "contemporary television exhibits more hi-tech glitter, faster and glitzier editing, computer simulations," even when dealing with political news.

Finally, I could not but point out that while watching the 2012 Romney–Obama debate, I observed a striking resemblance to the imagined debate in *Head of State* (see Figures 9 and 10), filmed nine years before. From the choice of a medium-long shot, the camera angle, the blue background, and the wooden rostrums, to the fact that an African-American is debating a Caucasian candidate, it's no wonder that *Head of State* is credited with paving the way for the first African-American president five years after its release, however modestly, as Manohla Dargis and A. O. Scott contend (2009). As the discussion on the influence of cinematic narratives on actual events is discussed in a later section of the book, I now turn my attention to the third shared type of

Figures 9–10 Find the differences.

iconography among the films, which is also related to the media, and especially the reporting, and/or dissemination, of news.

The media as "actant"

Figures 11 to 18 are a small sample of the presence of media in the four political comedies in question. The first four frames show how both everyday people, as well as political professionals (politicians, campaign managers, etc.) learn the news from the small screen. Figures 15 and 16 depict the presidential candidates of *Head of State* and *Man of the Year* in close-up shots, as covers of two US high-profile weekly magazines, *Newsweek* and *Time*. Figure 17 is a shot from *Swing Vote* that shows Bud's friends reading the popular lifestyle magazine *In Touch*, featuring their former colleague on the cover, and the last (Figure 18) depicts Cam preparing for an interview with British journalist Piers Morgan on the *Piers Morgan Live* show (CNN, 2011–14). Media presence in the form of journalists reporting outside government buildings, or waiting to question candidates; TV screens that are watched by the fictional characters or are on in a room while the viewer listens to a piece of news; shots of news magazines and newspapers, or shots of TV news reports or breaking news; media strategists that contact

Figures 11–14 (Left to right, top to bottom) Still frames from the presence of TV as a source of news in *Head of State, Man of the Year, Swing Vote,* and *The Campaign.*

Figures 15–18 (Left to right, top to bottom) Still frames from the presence of TV as a source of news in *Head of State, Man of the Year, Swing Vote,* and *The Campaign.*

journalists with specific information—whether positive or negative—they want disseminated widely; journalists working in networks, writing up a story or getting ready to report the news on location or present it from a studio; all abound in these political comedies—and many other subgenres of the political film genre for that matter. However, discussion on its function in political films in the relevant literature is rare, despite the fact that televised news can "shape [people's] perceptions, beliefs and opinions about current events and issues" (Gunter 2015: 16) and, in a fictional universe, dispense information to both the characters and the viewers and shape their point of view. Eleftheria Thanouli (2013: 30) is one of the few scholars that has noticed the presence of TV screens, in her book-length analysis of *Wag the Dog*, and maintains that, "the televised image is a narrative force of its own, working above and beyond the diegesis and establishing a level of mediated reality that runs parallel to the diegetic reality of the characters." Thanouli (2013: 30–1) analyzes specific relevant scenes, and concludes that the film narrative offers "the possibility of objects to carry the weight of story transmission."

Going a step further, I maintain that the representation of media in political films, irrespective of the form it may take, has a specific narrative function that helps to advance the plot. As such, it should be analyzed and discussed to theorize its place in the narrative. The representation of media (mainly television, the press, and online news outlets and blogs) in the four political comedies of this section can take a variety of forms. First, it can be represented by a secondary character with his/her own narrative program—i.e., the female reporter, Kate Madison (Paula Patton), who discovers the name of the last voter in *Swing Vote* and tries to secure an exclusive interview so that she is promoted to a national network, and also serves as the romantic interest of the main protagonist. Second, media is portrayed via cameos of professional news people that appear briefly in a scene or two, assuming their real, professional role in the fictional cosmos (i.e., Faith Daniels appears as a debate moderator in *Man of the Year*, while a host of well-known television news people, such as Wolf Blitzer, Mika Brzezinski, and Chris Matthews, and political commentators Bill Maher, Dennis Miller, and Ed Schultz, appear on TV screens in *The Campaign*, reporting on the fictional campaign course of Cam and Marty). Finally, media is present in the form of TV screens in houses, campaign buses, offices, and the groups of unnamed journalists that gather around a political candidate and/or voters outside buildings. This media omnipresence plays an important part in the narrative as it informs both characters and viewers, reveals news previously unknown, and therefore leads to specific actions on the part of the protagonists.

I therefore argue that the media constitutes an "actant," and takes one of the six grammar roles in Greimas's actantial layout (sender, subject, helper, object, receiver, enemy) as discussed in the introduction. In the four films, media news usually assumes the role of the "sender," as the disseminated reports encourage or oblige the characters to act. For instance, in *Head of State*, it is a news report that sets the plot in motion. Mays's appearance on the news when he saves his neighbor, and the journalists' subsequent labeling him as a hero, is what leads to his being chosen by the Democratic Party as their presidential candidate. The news "sends" the information to the Democrats (subjects) who invite previously unknown to them Mays (object) to their offices. The same function of the news as sender is observed in *Swing Vote*, where a reporter uncovers the last voter's identity and triggers the exhaustive dissection of Bud that soon takes national proportions. In other words, even when journalists and/or news reporters remain unnamed, as part of a group of professionals trying to get a quote from a major character, or even when a TV report is being watched, a significant narrative function takes place: that of news transmission that inevitably advances the plot in one way or another.

Aside from its narrative function, the representation of media also comments on its state and role in the real world, and merits some attention. Televised news is a powerful instrument as it not only communicates information about events and people but it "can set an agenda of events or issues for the public," "can cause events, issues and featured people to be brought to mind rendering them more accessible in memory," and "[p]otentially [...] might determine what people think about" (Gunter 2015: 16). Gunter claims that this kind of influence "has been labeled as 'framing'" and derives from the earlier experimental psychological work of Daniel Kahneman and Amos Tversky (Gunter 2015: 16–17). Framing is defined by a special focus on certain elements of a news report rather than others. This exclusion/inclusion strategy creates the desired narrative on the part of the political agenda followed by a number of individuals, such as TV journalists, news editors, network executives, or the industry itself. After a public debate between Cam and Marty in *The Campaign*, the two candidates run toward a baby so that they can be photographed as wholesome, family men. As Marty approaches first, Cam tries to punch him in the face but after Marty avoids it, Cam accidentally hits the baby. The scene is shot in slow motion, satirizing that there is almost nothing political candidates will not do for some positive press coverage. The next sequence shows how TV "frames" the incident. They exclude the accidental nature of Cam's action completely, focusing on the unfortunate punching; thus, contributing to a grave decline in Cam's popularity in the polls.

Man of the Year also suggests another aspect of media and news power, in particular the influence of what has been labeled as "fake" news, or news satire, best exemplified in the United States of the late 1990s, 2000s, and 2010s by *The Daily Show with Jon Stewart* (Comedy Central, 1999–2015), and its spin-off, *The Colbert Report* (Comedy Central, 2005–14) with Stephen Colbert. As Tom Dobbs' first public debate as a presidential candidate, his campaign team— comprised of his fake news show colleagues—urge him to abandon his rather solemn approach and include a joke or two to maintain and/or increase his popularity. In particular, Dobbs's campaign manager, Jack Menken (Chistopher Walken), tells him that people get their news from Jon Stewart, a comedian, and do not really care about the issues at hand. Later in the film, a fictional journalist on a TV screen cites a study that confirms that Americans are informed by Jay Leno, David Letterman, Jon Stewart, and Tom Dobbs. The discussion on the status and impact of fake news may take place in the fictional environment of a political comedy but the question has been the locus of contemporary academic examination as well. Although the division between fake and real news could easily, at first, denote that fake news cannot be taken seriously and is usually tampered with, and/or manufactured, recent studies claim differently. Mark K. McBeth and Randy S. Clemons (2011: 79) contend that fake news shows "are not only at least as real as the mainstream news, but also that they contribute more to the type of deliberative discourse essential to genuine democracy and public policy." After all, these shows repeatedly broadcast real relevant videos and comment on political issues. McBeth and Clemons (2011: 79–80) also add that fake news shows have been acknowledged as important sites of political news dissemination by candidates as well, and cite a number of instances where politicians even thanked the hosts for their presence at the shows, which resulted in an increase in the polls. The same sentiment is echoed by Jonathan Gray and Jeffrey P. Jones (2009: 28) who note that "some of the most influential programs are now considered by the political establishment to be necessary stops to stoop for votes, remake public images, or build a nationwide persona." At the time of the writing (August 2015), news articles appeared, online and in print, revealing that Stewart had secretly visited President Obama at the White House. In *The New York Times* article, White House media liaison Dag Vega stressed that "Stewart was a key influencer for millennials," and that "[t]hey relied on him for an honest take on the news, and the president and senior staff know that" (Shear 2015).

To confirm the previous writers, suffice it to say that Barack Obama appeared on *The Colbert Report* three times (as a senator in 2008 and twice as the President in 2010 and 2014) and on *The Daily Show with Jon Stewart* six times (three times as a senator and presidential candidate—in 2007 and twice in 2008—and three more times as the sitting President in 2010, 2012, and 2015). Of course, these appearances were vehemently criticized by conservative media. Especially after Obama appeared on Zach Galifianakis's comedy show *Between Two Ferns* (Funny or Die, 2008–present) in March 2014, CNN's conservative political commentator David Gergen "fired off three tweets decrying Obama's appearance, the last of which read, "Unimaginable that Truman, Ike, JFK, Reagan would appear on Between Two Ferns. They carefully protected majesty of their office" (Beinart 2014). Of course, as some research would prove, and Rachel Maddow's show was quick to point out using archival footage, "Presidents Dwight Eisenhower, Richard Nixon, Ronald Reagan, and George W. Bush [...] appeared with popular comedians at some point in their presidency" (Rothman 2014). Maddow concluded that "telling jokes or being part of comedy bits not only has generations of precedent among American presidents, it really has never diminished the dignity of the office" (Rothman 2014).

This liberal-conservative conflict regarding Obama's frequent TV visits brings me to another point regarding the four political comedies, which is that they opt for the representation of liberal media and not so much of conservative networks and/or journalists. For instance, *The Campaign* features cameos of a host of real news people, the majority of whom are considered liberal and/ or left-of-center. Dobbs in *Man of the Year* may identify in his campaign as an independent candidate, but his views as a satirical news host as well as a political candidate focus on major liberal issues, such as civic and environmental rights, and equality. This choice on the part of the filmmakers is aligned with the prevailing notion that views Hollywood as a mostly liberal machine, a position echoed by several scholars, such as Mark Wheeler (2006), Haas, Christensen, and Haas (2015), and Trevor McCrisken and Andrew Pepper (2005). It also conforms with "evidence" that "suggests that in the USA, the media tends to be left-leaning," and that there is "a significant relationship between media portrayal of US politicians and political parties, and election outcomes" (McCarthy and Dolfsma 2014: 49).

Application of Hay's strategic-relational approach

Following Hay's strategic-relational approach, I discuss how the main characters' agency enters and interacts in a given political structure in these four comedies, and the kind of political philosophies and/or theories that prevail in them, ultimately constituting the cinematic point of view from which specific political issues are discussed. I finally provide the sociohistorical context of the film's release. The political structure depicted in the films is that of the election system in the United States, regulated by the Constitution, a number of amendments, and state law as the films focus on federal (presidential and congressional) elections.

Head of State

Eight days after American troops invaded Iraq on March 20, 2003, and nineteen months before the 2004 presidential election which earned George W. Bush a second term as President, Rock's *Head of State* was released in the United States and Canada before heading to screens in European countries and Australia the following fall, and released on DVD at the beginning of 2004. Directed, cowritten, and produced by one of the country's most acknowledged comic personas, *Head of State* depicts what few other films have done before; it presents the campaign and subsequent victory of an African-American candidate at the presidential elections.

Depictions of black US Presidents had been few and far between in the history of both the North American film and television industries. Yet the number of examples encountered in both media helped instruct audiences and perhaps paved the way for the reality of November 4, 2008, when Barack Obama became the first African-American to hold the supreme office of the nation. Manohla Dargis and A. O. Scott contend that the fictional representations of "[T]he presidencies of James Earl Jones in 'The Man,' Morgan Freeman in 'Deep Impact,' Chris Rock in 'Head of State' and Dennis Haysbert in '24' helped us imagine Mr. Obama's transformative breakthrough before it occurred," adding that "[I]n a modest way, they also hastened its arrival" (Dargis and Scott 2009). In particular, *24*'s fictionalized President David Palmer, writes Jenny Bahn (2012: 73), a "decisive, ethical, and competent" commander in chief "had a positive effect on the election of Obama." The term "Palmer effect," coined in 2008 by Nick Bryant, a British political journalist, was used to explain how in the writer's view President Palmer "helped create a climate of public acceptance for the notion of a black president" (Bryant 2008). With the exception of Rock's comedy, *The Man*, *Deep Impact*, and *24* operate under the rules of the dramatic mode. In addition, in the action-adventure *Deep Impact* and the television series *24*, the two black presidents are already in office and the historical significance of their victories is not instrumental to the plot.

Mays begins his narrative journey holding a public office at the municipal level, but his location at a poor and troubled Washington neighborhood, his almost makeshift office setting, and his genuine effort to help his fellow citizens—he even promises an elderly man that if the city council decides to cut a specific bus line, he will take him to work every day—depict him as more of a social worker and not a professional politician. When Senator Arnot proposes he run, Mays does not question the decision and accepts, perhaps driven by a desire to do what he can to help his fellow citizens and, most importantly, African-Americans. With the assistance of professional campaign managers, Mays enters the election structure; he abandons his casual attire for finely tailored suits and his idiolect for standard American

English, visits different states giving almost the same monotone speech, written by other people, and generally obeys every request that comes from the Party. His agency is minimal as the structure he operates in is solidly built and does not easily allow for change. Only when his brother Mitch (Bernie Mac) comes and severely reprimands him for apathy, does Mays's agency turn active. Mays decides to follow his brother's advice and, during his next speech, he ignores what he is supposed to say and instead addresses his audience as the person he used to be, the person who cared and wanted to help. His crude speech, full of Black English and even swear words, focuses on issues that concern all working people. Education, housing, work, crime, and corporation control. Mays is so angered by the injustice plaguing working people, and especially African-American working people, that his intonation rises and as he sees the concerned citizens in the auditorium respond with enthusiasm, he becomes louder and more passionate himself. This speech is the beginning of Mays's newfound strategy and the activation of his agency. He changes his clothes to reflect his racial heritage, includes black music in his new television messages, and has his brother run alongside him for the vice presidency seat. The character's agency, however fresh and challenging, does not alter the structure. After all, Mays does not want to change the election system but instead win the election using his own voice and his own agenda. Mays's strategy or, according to Hay (2002, 129), his "intentional conduct orientated to the environment within which it is to occur," may not transform the election system—but it does alter the voting choice of the electorate, thus changing the structure of the Presidency, and the country if Mays follows his program. Mays triumphantly becomes the Head of State towards the end of the film but there is no mention of his percentage, nor of the population groups that favored him or his Republican opponent. The film wraps up rather quickly with the inaugural ball and the first African-American President introducing his future wife—a young working woman he met and flirted with during the campaign—and ends with them dancing. As Haas, Christensen, and Haas (2015: 301) remark in their presentation of black political films, *Head of State* relies "on a seemingly outdated notion of race relations, with black citizens teaching whites how to loosen up, and whites bestowing political or economic power on black for self-serving purposes masked as charitable." Thus, any potential commentary on the actual change on the structure by a new agent is eclipsed as Rock chooses to treat the ascent to power of an African-American rather superficially.

Man of the Year

In 2006, Barry Levinson, the director of the emblematic political text of the 1990s, *Wag the Dog* (2007), released his political comedy *Man of the Year*, starring Robin Williams in their third collaboration after *Good Morning Vietnam* (1987), and *Toys* (1991). *Man of the Year* was released in October 2006, less than a month before the midterm elections that witnessed an important victory for the Democrats in both the House of Representatives and the Senate, and also the election of Nancy Pelosi, as the first woman to serve as the Speaker of the House. It was a time where Republican policies were often criticized as the War on Terror was not yielding the expected results and the Iraq War was still claiming American lives.

Like Mays in *Head of State*, Tom Dobbs is also presented as a man of the people, a man who voices his concern and indignation on behalf of the average citizen at governmental actions he views as detrimental to the nation's progress. He differs from Mays in that his popularity is multiplied through his job as a TV satirist, a job which brings him to millions of homes weekly, and a job that has, most likely, made him a wealthy man. When a woman in his audience, however, proposes that he runs for President, followed by a staggering eight million emails supporting his potential candidacy, he accepts the challenge and enters the political arena. A celebrity's decision to run for public office follows a long tradition in US politics, which witnessed a number of film actors helping governmental causes and/or being elected to serve the American people. From John Wayne, who "took an active role in supporting the United States' war in Vietnam," to Ronald Reagan's ascent to the presidency, Clint Eastwood's "two-year tenure as mayor of Carmel (1986–8)" (Ribke 2015: 107), and Arnold Schwarzenegger's eight-year tenure as governor of California, the United States is a nation accustomed to supporting individuals who were previously popular on the silver screen. In addition, following fictional Tom's course and the life-imitates-art adage, leading television satirist Stephen Colbert announced his candidacy for President in 2007 as his show's character. Although he dropped out from the race in November of the same year, Colbert did, in fact, begin a legitimate campaign but failed to be placed in the Democratic ballot, and reentered the race in 2012 having formed a super PAC (Political Action Committee) with colleague Jon Stewart. Stewart has not, to this date, run for public office but many media articles found the idea of him as a political figure appealing. Titles, such as "Jon Stewart, We Need You in 2016" (Davidson 2015),

"From fake news to politics—is there any way Jon Stewart will run for office?" (Rogak 2015), and "Jon Stewart Should Run for Office" (Magary 2015) prove the close relationship popular celebrities can have with political life.

Like Mays, Tom enters the presidential race without having thought of it before. As an active agent, he enters the structure not trying to alter it—he also travels around the country, participating in the debates—but because he's "fed up with party politics," as he remarks in one of the debates. His funny and satirical persona, the one that made him popular and encouraged his entrance into the political arena, is subdued in the beginning as Tom believes that the gravity of the issues does not allow for jokes. However, he soon discovers that a televised audience, comprised of the people who more likely prefer to get the news from Stewart and Colbert rather than CNN or FOX, urged him to run exactly because he could add a satirical and humorous view to serious topics.

Tom puts a number of issues on the table during the debates, mainly the great cost of presidential campaigns and the corporate interest behind donations that end up "imprisoning" politicians, terrorism and security, energy and avoidance of alternative sources of fuel, and immigration. Nevertheless, as in *Head of State*, political issues that concern especially the lower classes are mentioned—almost always with zest and including a stern attack on indifferent politicians that turn their eye away from the problem—but are not discussed. Neither Mays nor Tom, for instance, propose ways to decrease the unemployment rate, limit gun ownership, or deal effectively with security issues and illegal immigrants. Both narratives are content with underlining the misdeeds and transgressions of mostly conservative government officials without actually proposing solutions or offering alternatives. *Man of the Year*, especially, focuses also on the voting system and its potential influence on the election outcome. After all, as writer/director Levinson notes, the film was inspired by "the voting-machine error of the 2004 presidential election" (Jeffrey and Jeffrey 2006: 173), and in particular the unreliability of the Diebold voting machines, as well as the inclusion of Ralph Nader as a third, independent candidate in the race. Tom's victory comes, not as a result of the popular vote, but a computer malfunction at Delacroy, the corporation with the contract to supply its technology and facilitate the process. Despite Delacroy's employee Eleanor finding the problem, and informing her superiors, she is met with suspicion and even hostility. Her insistence, however, only leads to the following, quite revealing, castigation by the company's CEO, Stewart (Jeff Goldblum):

Here's the story: the people are voting, there's an election, and the democratic process is working. The only sour note? The people won't end up with the candidate that they voted for to be President. We can still celebrate the process. The democracy which we hold so dear will have worked. Everybody's gonna be satisfied. Perception of legitimacy is more important than legitimacy itself. That's the greater truth. Don't fuck with our democracy, undermine our way of life? Every American believes their vote counts. You wanna tell them that's not true?

By following this secondary plot, *Man of the Year* shows how the structure, according to Hay, has become so rigid and powerful that it can dictate the agents' course. Indeed, powerless Eleanor can only sit and watch as Tom wins the election and becomes President. As the film operates in the comedy mode, however, Eleanor manages to tell Tom the truth. The protagonist then decides to resign and return the seat to the person who actually won. The end finds Tom back to his TV show, with Eleanor by his side as his producer and partner for life. After all, in Tom's own words, "A jester doesn't rule the kingdom; He makes fun of the king." Interestingly, six years later, season 2 of the ABC political drama *Scandal* (2011–present) included a similar plot as the President of the United States discovers that his election was rigged by the most trusted people on his campaign. This time, however, he does not tell the truth and only hopes to get elected honestly for the second time. This televised narrative arc, perhaps inspired by *Man of the Year*'s plot, goes a step further by allowing for fraud, deception, and illegitimacy to determine the presidency, thus according agents power to tamper with the structure, with a view to changing it from within.

Swing Vote

Three months before the historic victory of Barack Obama on November 4, 2008, *Swing Vote* appeared on a limited number of North-American screens before finding its way to selected European and South-American theaters in September, while being almost simultaneously released as a DVD in Europe and South America. Starring Kevin Costner, *Swing Vote* was directed by neophyte director Joshua Michael Stern—in his second directorial endeavor—who also cowrote the screenplay with Jason Richman. What is surprising is that the film was produced entirely by Costner, which is a rarity in Hollywood, especially when it concerns an Academy Award winner and popular actor/director. As Costner told *The Telegraph*'s Tom Leonard (2008), "For six months I couldn't get anybody to make it because they said it didn't seem to have its international upside and then, finally, I decided to do it myself." Industry professionals warned him—not about the political nature of the film, since the word isn't even mentioned once in the interview—that the film was very "American" and would not travel well globally. However, Costner decided to make it "for his own country," despite the fact that the film ultimately lost money. Although Costner does not openly talk about the political nature of *Swing Vote*, I would suggest that the industry people he talked to were mainly concerned exactly with that and not with funding an inexpensive film with a major star. After all, $20 million is a small amount compared to the average budget of a Hollywood production that had reached $60 million in 2005 (Lacey 2006). The industry's hesitation corroborates most academic observations about Hollywood's unwillingness to invest in political films.

Although presidential elections provide the context of *Swing Vote*'s plot, the focus is on a working man, Bud, who finds himself in the unlikely position of being the single person to determine the outcome as his is the only vote that is missing. Implausibility may reign in this election scenario, as has already been noted by Giglio (2014: 118), but, within a comedic mode, one does have to accept certain events as real possibilities as suspension of disbelief and exaggeration constitutes conventions of comedy. Giglio may hasten to criticize most political comedies he examines for including improbable scenarios, as he is obviously in favor of cultural verisimilitude instead of generic verisimilitude, but he does make a few interesting observations regarding *Swing Vote*. First of all, the story may take place in the context of the presidential elections but the protagonist is not a candidate but a blue-collar worker. We briefly see him work at an egg factory before he is fired after being filmed drinking alcohol during his break and inadvertently destroying hundreds of eggs. Bud spends his time between being inefficient at work, trying to raise his daughter, Molly, who constantly outsmarts him, and spending time at the local bar drinking and then sleeping it off. Giglio (2014: 119) remarks: "Bud is precisely the kind of citizen Thomas Jefferson warned us about, namely, one ignorant of the issues and indifferent to the responsibilities of citizenship."

It is exactly Bud's ignorance and apathy regarding politics that triggers the plot as his daughter, who's civic-minded and sensible beyond her years, takes his place at the voting poll. Once Bud's identity is revealed, both the Republican sitting president and the Democratic candidate visit the small town of Texico, New Mexico (a traditional swing state until 2012), and the wooing of Bud begins.

The film, therefore, focuses on the voter and his/her agency. Irrespective of his abilities, knowledge, and/or will, Bud has the opportunity to change the structure of the presidency depending on his voting for the Republican or the Democratic candidate. President Boone (Kelsey Grammer) invites Bud to Air Force One, and tries to ingratiate himself with him by bringing up things he likes, such as football. On the other hand, Democratic candidate Greenleaf (Dennis Hopper) attempts to win Bud over with all his favorite things: from pulling strings to get his old music band together, to including a buffet with foods his mom used to make, and having his favorite artist, Willie Nelson, appear on a TV commercial addressing him personally. In the era of celebrity culture and, in particular, celebrity politics, Bud is transformed into the most famous individual in the United States over the course of a few hours, with the help of both traditional and digital media. The faces of the two presidential candidates are replaced by Bud's photos, as the entire nation waits during the ten-day period afforded to him by law until he makes his decision. This exposure may unsettle Bud, at first, but gradually he begins to enjoy the power it affords him. Examining celebrity politics and politicians, Kellner (2012: 5) suggests that it is exactly the superstardom status attributed to Obama during the presidential primaries and the election of 2008—the year of *Swing Vote*'s release—and his use of "media spectacle" that helped him "win the presidency" and "advance his agenda." Although Bud is not a candidate or a professional political player, he does begin to enjoy the things that accompany his transformation into the latest national media trend.

Bud's media ubiquity, however, is not used to advance his interests, i.e., help him secure a new job or money. Bud remains sociopolitically apathetic for more than two-thirds of the narrative. Instead, both presidential candidates have to denounce their political principles in order to lure Bud to their side. The sitting President declares a piece of land as a protected national reserve instead of selling it to a corporation, and announces he is in favor of gay marriage, while the democratic candidate backs down on immigration issues, because Bud would like to see fewer Mexicans entering the country to take his job, and becomes pro-life. Key conservatives' positions become liberal ones and vice versa in a comedic narrative where almost anything can happen, although I should note that both the republicans and the democrats are afforded equal political deviations and no clear political philosophy or ideology is promoted. Yet, more than *Head of State* and *Man of the Year*, *Swing Vote* underscores the lengths to which politicians will go, to win the voters' hearts and minds.

It is young Molly who provides that catalyst for the brief transformation montage of her dad. While Bud is playing cards with the President on Air Force One, and does not actually care about the unprecedented privilege that was bestowed onto him, she has been answering letters addressed to him from all over the country and about all kinds of issues, such as global warming, health insurance, job security, education, veterans issues, and the economy. It is only the fear of losing his daughter—Molly runs away towards the climax of the film—that makes Bud finally treat the situation he is in with seriousness. Just one day before the final debate between the two candidates, and two days before he has to cast his vote, a montage shows Bud reading the letters sent to him by ordinary citizens and studying facts and figures alongside Molly and Kate (the reporter) in his preparation for moderating the debate and making one of the most important decisions in his life. Although Bud's transformation into a thoughtful, knowledgeable and civic-minded person cannot happen overnight, he does appear in the debate dressed in a suit and makes a speech, before asking a question from one of the letters. The larger part of his monologue addresses the main theme of the film, the American voters:

> BUD: [...] tonight I feel ... embarrassed. I've had my chances, more than most. I've grown up in a country where ... if I decided to do more with my life than just drift and drink ... that I could be standing where ... where maybe you stand tonight. Instead, I've taken freely and I've given nothing. I'm ashamed in front of my ... daughter. And my country. I've never served or sacrificed. The only heavy lifting I've been asked is simple stuff, like ... you know ... pay attention. Vote ... For America has a ... if America has a true enemy tonight, I guess it's me.

In a nation that has seen voter turnout decreasing to less than 50 percent (1996) and has reached 60 percent or more only eight times during the twenty-five elections of the twentieth century (counting the 1900 elections), Bud's words, however sentimental and even populist, echo a significant number of American citizens. I would hypothesize that that is the reason *Swing Vote* opts for an open end, since the last images we see feature Bud just as he is about to cast his vote. Whom he chooses is not important. The fact that he makes an informed choice is paramount.

The Campaign

The Campaign is the most commercially and critically[2] successful political comedy in this election cycle and a politically timely release as it came out three months before Obama's second term in August 2012. "War has rules, mud wrestling has rules ... politics has no rules." This Ross Perot quote, from the 1998 presidential elections, is the first thing that appears on a black screen before the first scene. The viewer is, thus, immediately given the first clue regarding the fictional cosmos he/she is about to enter; the narrative will focus on the US election system, and its systemic failings. Unlike the candidates of *Head of State*, and *Man of the Year*, the two politicians in *The Campaign* are flawed. The Democrat Cam Brady is portrayed as a philandering, pretentious, and arrogant individual. He is experienced in reiterating the same public speeches, and a master at answering difficult questions by evasion and subterfuge. Despite being arrested for a DUI, and exposed in the media for sleeping around, assaulting both a baby and a dog, resignation never enters his mind or is demanded by the electorate. Instead, Cam continues his campaign by undermining his opponent through libelous TV ads, sleeping with his wife, and humiliating him in public. Marty, on the other hand, begins his narrative journey as a sweet, likeable character, and a loving family man. When his powerful dad asks him to run against Bud on the Republican ticket, sponsored by the billionaire Motch brothers—a clear reference to the Koch brothers—Marty is thrilled as he sees this step as an opportunity to enter the political arena and win the trust and respect of his father.

The Motch brothers are funding Bud's campaign but, after a sex scandal, they decide to find a new candidate to complete their new business plan; move their factories from China to the 14th Carolina district and, with the help of the elected Congressman, allow for new factories to run with the same unsafe regulations and less than meager wages they operated with in China, thus eliminating the shipping costs and increasing their proceeds. Although the Motch brothers appear in few scenes in the film, they do function as the plot catalyst. They also serve as a direct commentary on the correlation between big business and politics in the United States. Two structures, the corporate one and the political one, are either friends or foes. Corporate corruption emerges when business interests lead to introduction, alteration, and/or misuse of government politics that do not benefit the people but, rather, a few share-holders. *The Campaign* is the only film of this cycle that explicitly satirizes and criticizes the way big business influences politics, especially after 2010 and the ruling in *Citizens United v. the Federal Election Commission*, when "the Supreme Court struck down legal century-old restrictions on corporate donations to political campaigns," becoming the gravest and most "recent development in a long history of the political mobilization of business" (Phillips-Fein and Zelizer 2012, 3). The Motch brothers do not care about political affiliations. They are willing to support either a liberal or a conservative politician as long as the latter assists them in their business ventures by bending the rules or turning a blind eye to their obscure and mostly illegal practices.

Knowing that their friend, Marty's father, is of the same business-minded and immoral mentality, they easily pick the kind-hearted Marty as their candidate of choice, without him ever questioning or even meeting with them. After the first Cam–Marty public appearance resulting in the latter's humiliation, the Motch brothers send a professional campaign manager to change Marty from an effeminate, and a little weird, person to an American winner. The makeover montage that sees Marty change his hair, his clothes, his intonation, his furniture, his dogs, his wife, and his two children without having any choice in the matter is only superficially comical and anodyne as it actually underlines that Marty does not differ a lot from Cam. In fact, Marty's transformation, à la *Pretty Woman*, into a presentable and strong political candidate in the hands of a seasoned man, with the money of two other powerful men, equates his actions to those of a prostitute, like the one portrayed in *Pretty Woman* by Julia Roberts. However, Roberts's decision to sell sexual acts only impact her whereas Marty's potential agreement with the Motch brothers after an election to Congress will impact hundreds of thousands of American citizens.

Both Marty and Cam fight dirty during the campaign and libel their opponent—Cam accuses Marty of associating with terrorists because of his facial hair while Marty tries to persuade voters that Cam is a communist because he wrote a tale about a fantasy land where everything was free when he was eight. These allegations are, of course, far-fetched and part of the satirical screenplay angle but they do point to the hyperbolic and personalized stratagems political campaigns utilize in the real world. Yet, the fictional end is happy and optimistic, unlike real life. Cam wins a rigged election with the help of the Motch brothers who change sides once again, but decides to rescind and give way to Marty. Finally, the two protagonists decide to collaborate—Cam becomes Marty's chief of staff—and expose the Motch brothers' scandals before Congress. The brothers use the *Citizens United vs. Federal Election Commission* case as a shield against their sponsoring politicians, but they are ultimately apprehended once it is revealed that the campaign manager they employed was a wanted criminal.

Agency–structure relationship in the films

Hopefully, the above structural and critical analysis proves that the four films share similarities regarding both their narrative form and their mainly explicit liberal-leaning messages. I would like to close this chapter by also providing two tables (Tables 2 and 3), based on Hay's strategic-relational model that would clarify the relationship between structure and agency.

Table 2 Agent–Structure Relationship

	t	⬈	S or S_1
A	⇌	S	
		⬊	A or A_1

A: agent or strategic actor
A_1:   altered agent or altered strategic context
S: structure or strategic context
S_1:   altered structure or altered strategic context
t: transformation

An agent / strategic actor (A) enters into a political structure / strategic context (S). For instance, *Swing Vote*'s Bud (A) enters the presidential election system (S). The context is predetermined and has a number of set rules but allows for changes, however infrequently and with difficulty. Bud undergoes a transformation during the ten days he is afforded to decide between the two candidates. When he enters the voting booth, he is no longer the person we met in the beginning. Because of his interaction with the system—despite the fact his daughter was also urging him to become more civic minded—he reconsiders a number of things and in the narrative becomes a more enlightened version of himself (S_1). As Table 3 shows, the relationship between agent and structure does not end with a single interaction. "New" Bud will reenter the unchanged election system again and this contact may have a number of results, as will be discussed below.

Table 3 *Swing Vote*'s Agent–Structure Relationship

t				
A (Bud)	⇌ **S** (election system)	⟹	A_1 ("New" Bud)	⇌ **S** (same election system)

Similarly, in *The Campaign* (Table 4) both Cam and Marty change; the first decides to help people instead of serving personal and corporate interests, and the second is transformed into an active, and energetic prosecutor of injustice as a Congressman.

Table 4 *The Campaign*'s Agent–Structure Relationship

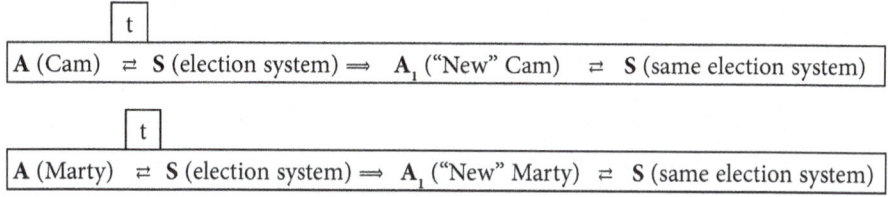

t			
A (Cam) ⇌ **S** (election system) ⟹ **A**$_1$ ("New" Cam) ⇌ **S** (same election system)

t			
A (Marty) ⇌ **S** (election system) ⟹ **A**$_1$ ("New" Marty) ⇌ **S** (same election system)

Interestingly, in the four films, it is agents, and not the structure, that change or not. The election system—that is, the laws, commissions, corporations, etc., that ensure registered voters have the opportunity to elect their President—remains unaltered. Even when the corporate corruption depicted in *Man of the Year* that assists the election of the wrong candidate, and the malfunction of a machine in *Swing Vote* that triggers the plot, are revealed—albeit to a limited number of people—the way elections are held or the percentages required for a candidate to claim victory are unaffected. Table 5 shows the possible outcomes of the agent/structure relationship.

Table 5 Agent–Structure Possible Outcome Combinations

A	⇌	S$_1$
A$_1$	⇌	S
S	⇌	A
S$_1$	⇌	A$_1$

The possibility that both agents and structure affect each other to the degree they are both altered is only 25 percent. This confirms that political strategic actors face great difficulty in altering, and/or introducing, policies that can modify the political structure. Although the possibility of a change in structure equals that of a change in the agent (50 percent), the films discussed offered a relationship model of the two that did not threaten the political status quo. Only *The Campaign*'s ending—and in particular, the end credits scenes that witnessed the Motch brothers being arrested and Cam and Marty addressing Congress about unethical corporate practices affecting politics—implied that if big business can be held accountable for their actions, in the future the political structure should, and perhaps can, act independently, and only to serve the people.

A point about the nature of structure and agents should be clarified. By definition, the two poles of this relationship are not equiponderant. Structures are slowly built over time, and are amended and solidified as strong and enduring edifices. Although political structures are constructed by agents, they cannot easily be altered by the actions of a single individual. In the comedies I discussed, for instance, the structure of the American election system is never put in question in any narrative. Questions such as: is the electoral system fair, should there be swing states or not, should we revisit the percentages a candidate needs to get elected, or the parameters of voters' and candidates' eligibility, among many others, are never posited with the possible exception of campaign financing raised in *Man of the Year* and *The Campaign*, which is anathematized as immoral but not discussed as a law amendment.

All the films take an implicit liberal stance as they promote equality, justice, and liberty for all. The narratives point to problems that US society faces, but are content with a mere observation than a representation of a way out of these social obstacles. It is interesting that no fictional candidate offers concrete solutions or presents a program based on which the voter could choose him. After all, with the exception of Cam, no fictional character decides to run for political office as a result of a personal desire. Mays, Tom, Marty, and Bud suddenly find themselves at the center of an electoral process. Mays and Tom are initially presented as socially conscious individuals—Mays is an alderman with no desire to hold office and Tom frequently castigates politicians on his show for mismanagement, corruption, and indifference to the needs of the people. Both Tom and Mays are realists in that they acknowledge things are difficult and that political change, however limited, is a tremendous task. However, their decision to run for office makes them also idealists. In political science, political idealism originating from Plato, and political realism originating from Aristotle, are "[t]he two major streams […] with which the whole Western political thought keeps marching on" (Arora and Awasthy 2007: 77). Mays and Tom constitute a mixture of realism and idealism depending on the context of particular film sequences. Bud becomes idealistic by the end of *Swing Vote* as do Marty and Cam in *The Campaign*. As Coyne (2008: 15) observes, based on his application of Arthur M. Schlesinger Jr.'s series of "paradoxes" in American history to the context of political movies, "the most clear-cut resolution [...] is in that tension between materialism and idealism. Hollywood is certainly very much a dollars-and-cents business—but, on screen, idealism wins hands down." The political comedies' happy ending—suitable to the comedy genre—is also a reminder of the optimism that generally characterizes the nation, as opposed, for instance, to the cynicism and disenchantment of the Old World. The four films do reiterate political principles inherent in the nation's liberal legacy, without actually proposing a solution to admittedly long-standing political carcinomas.

3

Political Thrillers and US Foreign Policy

As a child during the late 1970s in Greece, I grew up watching Hollywood films on the only two channels that existed before private TV licenses were allowed in the late 1980s. Although one would argue that my choice was limited—which indeed it was—I was also fortunate to get a great education on film from, primarily, the Hollywood studio era. By the time I was an adult, and private channels started broadcasting, I was already an expert in genre films from the 1930s, 1940s, and 1950s. Westerns, film noirs, war films, musicals, melodramas, horror films; I had practically seen them all. However, I was not only enjoying the films. I was also *educating* myself, mainly through the narratives' binary oppositions. The conclusions were simple but absolute: cowboys were good, Indians were bad; America was great, Russia was not; America and the Allies stood for humanity, Germany and Japan for evil. Democracy was good, communism was bad. In a way, once I reached adulthood, I knew more about US foreign policy than I did about Greek foreign policy. Although the above is a brief personal account, experience shows that most of my friends and classmates received the same education. Hollywood taught me the enemies of the United States while exalting the nation's merits. Almost two decades later, I realized Hollywood's power as I read Alan Parker's following quote: "All of our European influences have been American films because American society has been sold to the rest of the world with the greatest propaganda machine any nation ever invented—the Hollywood movie" (Palmer 1993: 9). Furthermore, in two recent studies about the representation of US foreign policy in Hollywood films, both authors underline the influence of those narratives "to defining who America's current enemies are" (Totman 2009: 1) and "in the creation of consensus and popular mentality" (Vanhala 2011: 3).

This chapter considers how the political films of the 2002–12 period represent US foreign policy, through an examination of the narrative structure and a sociopolitical contextualization of the films. "Foreign policy occupies a critical, interstitial space in world politics, produced as it is at the porous interface of domestic politics and international relations" (Brighi 2013: 10). In the United States, "the Department of State is the lead U.S. foreign affairs agency." According to its official online mission statement, the Department "advances U.S. objectives and interests in shaping a freer, more secure, and more prosperous world through its primary role in developing and implementing the President's foreign policy." In other words, the Department of State, most commonly known as the State Department, is the diplomacy hub of the executive branch of the US government which is geared towards successfully negotiating with, resolving issues, and averting crises with, foreign countries. However, diplomats and ministers are not frequently depicted on celluloid as US foreign policy is primarily represented via two established and well-recognized genres, or their hybrid union: the action genre and the thriller.[1] I argue that the combination of conventions from both generic groups with a politically charged subject gives birth to the "political thriller," which shares both semantic and syntactic elements from action films and thrillers (such as spectacular chases, location shooting, frequent use of slow motion in editing—especially to underline violence or signal the aftermath of a forceful attack—and a central conflict between good and evil) to critique or support US foreign policies and/ or their formation and execution.

The majority of political thrillers involve CIA agents, military personnel, and the Secret Service, and their struggles to eradicate a foreign threat, or a corrupt individual inside the domestic structure, which threaten stability. Naturally, all action films involving spies cannot be considered political thrillers by definition, the same way all films featuring the CIA do not focus on specific political agendas. For instance, *The Tourist* (2010), centers on Elise's (Angelina Jolie) efforts to confuse Scotland Yard as to the whereabouts of her criminal lover, who stole an enormous amount of money from an international mobster. The object of the subject/heroine's quest is her romantic interest and, as such, the film is not political. The same applies to *Duplicity* (2009), where Claire (Julia Roberts), an ex-CIA agent, and Ryan (Clive Owen), an ex-MI6 spy, vie to get hold of a secret formula, working for two enemy corporations. The comedic narrative centers on the protagonist's romantic entanglements and disperses with any critique of corporate espionage. Finally, *The Recruit* (2003), is an exploration of the dynamics between an older man and his younger apprentice. Reminiscent of the earlier *Spy Game* (2001), *The Recruit* follows the training of novice CIA agent James (Colin Farrell) under the orders and guidance of seasoned instructor

Walter (Al Pacino). Both films focus on aspects of fatherhood while in each narrative, "the relationship between handler and agent is broken by a romance, and in each there is something problematic (from the handler's perspective) about the girl" (Barrett, Herrera, and Baumann 2011: 130).

In his insightful analysis of the subgenre, Charles Derry (2001: 103) underscores that political thrillers "generally document and dramatize the acts of assassins, conspirators, or criminal governments, as well as the oppositional acts of victim-societies, countercultures, or martyrs." Due to their uniting conventions from popular genres, such as the action film and the thriller, political thrillers are not usually recognized, and/or labeled, as such by the industry or the media. However, also due to the fact that these narratives combine elements of suspense, action, and/or adventure within a political context, they appeal to a wider demographic and can therefore lead to greater profits for the industry. This hypothesis is corroborated by the corpus, as thirteen political thrillers are among the top thirty of the corpus: *Mission: Impossible – Ghost Protocol* (2011), is at the top of the corpus with a little less than $700 million worldwide, *The Bourne Ultimatum* (2007), the third film of the *Bourne* Trilogy, is at number five, having earned more than $442 million worldwide, *Mission: Impossible III* (2006), is at number seven with almost $400 million, *Live Free or Die Hard* is at number ten with a little more than $385, *Salt* is at number eleven with more than $293 million, and *The Bourne Supremacy* (2004), follows at number twelve with $288.5 million. *Bourne Legacy* (2012), is at number thirteen with $276 million, followed by *Argo* at number fifteen with $223 million, *The Bourne Identity* at number seventeen with more than $214 million, *Safe House* is at number nineteen with a little over $208 million, *The Sum of All Fears* is at number twenty-two with almost $194 million, *The Interpreter* is at number twenty-five with almost $163 million, and *Vantage Point* is at number twenty-eight with a little over $151 million. So, if one is to take into consideration the budget of the films ($145 million, $110 million, $150 million, $110 million, $110 million, $75 million, $125 million, $44,5 million, $60 million, $85 million, $68 million, $80 million, and $40 million), we can deduce that political thrillers can be quite popular narratives. After all, three popular franchises (*The Mission: Impossible films*, the *Bourne* films, and the *Die Hard* films) occupy the higher positions of the corpus, validating the popularity of action cinema on the one hand, but also pointing to the appeal of their political nature, however disguised in their narratives.

On the other hand, it is also true that similar films, that is, narratives that touch upon political subjects and/or dramatize real events, constitute less than solid investments for Hollywood, as also evidenced by the corpus: for instance, *The Kingdom* (2007) returned more than $86 million but cost $70; *Lions for Lambs* earned $63 million with a budget of $35 million; *Syriana* garnered almost $94 million costing $50 million; *In The Valley of Elah* (2007), earned $29.5 million on a $23 million budget, and *Traitor* (2008), earned over $27.5 with a cost of $22 million; while there are films which did not even reach their budget cost, such as *Green Zone* (cost: $100 million, box office: almost $95 million), and *The Cold Light of Day* (cost: $20 million, box office: $16.8 million).

A final observation is that the majority of the political thrillers are either based on novels, TV series, and/or memoirs and real events while only a handful are based on original screenplays. To best serve the analysis, this chapter is divided into political thrillers based on novels or original screenplays, and films that draw their story from real events.

Political thrillers based on fictional events

Main actors' narrative program

The analysis of the actants in the political thrillers under discussion is conducted on a macro-narrative level rather than a micro-narrative one. The reason is that the majority of the films depict several storylines which, in turn, include several characters. An analysis of all the characters, however useful, goes beyond the scope of the study, which focuses on the basic semiotic structures presented in the examined subgenres of the "disguised" political film genre. For instance, *Vantage Point*'s main subject, the attempted assassination of the American President, is told through eight different points-of-view, as witnessed by eight different characters. It is inferred that each character follows his/her own narrative program but there are stories where the subject's object does not coincide with saving the President. The narratives are rather peripheral to the central story and thus excluded from the analysis, which includes the protagonist (Subject) who saves the President (Object) and the assassins (Enemies).

On a macro-narrative level, the central conflict of political thrillers concerns a single individual against a corrupt domestic or foreign villain. Table 6 comprises the name and professional identity of the subject (primary "heroes/heroines") the helper (secondary "heroes/heroines"), the opponents (the primary and secondary villains), and all the characters' nationalities where

Table 6 Protagonists, Helpers, and Opponents in Political Thrillers.[1]

Title	Subject of action and Country of Origin	Helper and Country of Origin	Opponent 1 and Country of Origin	Opponent 2 and Country of Origin
Bourne Identity (2002)	CIA agent Jason Bourne (US)	Marie (Germany)	CIA Deputy Director Ward Abbott (US)	CIA official Alex Conclin (US)
The Sum of All Fears (2002)	CIA agent Jack Ryan (US)	–	Richard Dressler (Austria)	–
Bourne Supremacy (2004)	CIA agent Jason Bourne (US)	CIA Deputy Director Pamela Landy (US)	CIA Deputy Director Ward Abbott (US)	CIA Head Noah Vosen (US)
Bourne Ultimatum (2007)	CIA agent Jason Bourne (US)	CIA Deputy Director Pamela Landy (US)	CIA Noah Vosen (US)	CIA Director Ezra Kramer (US)
Vantage Point (2008)	Secret Service agent Thomas Barnes (US)	–	Secret Service agent Kent Taylor (US)	Veronica and Suarez: terrorists of unidentified hispanic origin
Body of Lies (2008)	CIA agent Roger Ferris (US)	Agent Hali Salaam (Jordan) CIA officer Ed (US)	terrorist Al-saleem (unidentified Middle-Eastern country)	–
Salt (2010)	CIA agent Evelyn Salt (US)	–	Agent Orlov (Russia)	CIA Sleeper agent Ted Winter (US)
Safe House (2012)	CIA agent Matt Weston (US)	ex-CIA NOC agent Tobin Frost (US)	ex-CIA NOC agent Tobin Frost (US)	CIA agent David Barlow (US)
Bourne Legacy (2012)	CIA agent Aaron Cross (US)	–	US: CIA	–

[1] To facilitate the analysis, I focus on the films with CIA agents and Secret Service agents that protect the president. Thus, the relevant information concerning two *Mission: Impossible* films and *Live Free and Die Hard* is missing from the table. However, I stress that the isotopies I discuss are shared by the great majority of political thrillers.

applicable. I should add that both heroic and villainous characters that appear sporadically and are not integral to the achievement of the main narrative goal are excluded from the table, and that is why some table cells are not filled in.

Based on the Table 6, the narrative grammar of these political thrillers is formed as follows:

> Sender of action (CIA/Secret Service) ➜ Subject of action (Jason, Ryan, Evelyn, Matt, Aaron (CIA agents) ➜ Object of action (averting a nuclear attack, an assassination, illegal acts that hurt the USA) ➜ Receiver (the American people/the citizens of the world)

With the exception of *Salt*, all the main protagonists are male. The majority are in their early to mid-thirties, while only *The Vantage Point*'s Secret Service Agent Thomas Barnes is a man in his early fifties who has recently been allowed back to active duty. Jason Bourne in the first three *Bourne* films, Aaron in *Bourne Legacy*, Evelyn in *Salt*, Matt in *Safe House*, Roger in *Body of Lies*, and Jack in *The Sum of All Fears* are all CIA agents. The almost ubiquitous presence of the CIA merits a brief discussion as the Agency has been closely collaborating with Hollywood for almost twenty years now in films that depict relevant plots. In her informative account of the relationship between the CIA and the film industry, Tricia Jenkins (2012: 2) notes that the agency "has been actively engaged in shaping the content of film and television [...] in the post-9/11 world," and that "much of what we know about Langley has been deliberately laced in the public domain by the Agency itself" (2012: 2) through the CIA's Public Affairs Office, which is responsible for all Hollywood affairs. Jenkins (2012: 5) remarks that "from 1996 to 2008, the DPA [Director of Public Affairs] oversaw the agency's entertainment industry liaison officers—Chase Brandon and Paul Barry—who were fully dedicated to assisting and influencing filmmakers and novelists."

The rogue CIA agent is a trope that has been used in many Hollywood films from the Cold War era to the present. According to Jenkins' research, the reasons behind the negative representation is, first, the stereotype of the corrupt CIA officer that has been created in earlier films and political novels, and has become a convention the viewer acknowledges right away and accepts as such, thus facilitating the screenwriting process (Jenkins 2012: 28). Second, the view on the part of the Agency that Hollywood is largely made up of liberal voices that approach the CIA with suspicion. Jenkins argues that the past negative cinematic representations led to the Agency opening its doors in the 1990s, "to help reverse its image in film and television" since, according to Paul Barry,

Hollywood's CIA representations are important to the Agency because they influence people's attitudes on their performance (Jenkins 2012: 32). Despite the Agency's efforts to change its image, the fact remains that political thrillers are fraught with corrupt individuals, and especially high-ranking officials, although there remains a slight possibility of redemption through the few characters who do not succumb to the allure of power and/or financial gain. The continuing cinematic castigation of the CIA can be attributed to the War on Terror and its consequences. On September 16, 2001, Vice President Dick Cheney appeared on the news program *Meet the Press* (NBC, 1947–present). When asked by journalist Tim Russert about the future response of the United States to the attacks, Cheney answered that aside from using what he described as "the world's finest military," the nation would "have to work the dark side, if you will," and "to spend time in the shadows in the intelligence world" (Cheney 2001). The establishment of the Guantanamo Bay detention camp in 2002, and the torture practices and subsequent human rights violation the United States were accused of (i.e., the Abu Ghraib prison case, and the case of Khalid el-Masri) were examples of the "dark side" which Cheney referred to. The public revelation and denouncement that accompanied these atrocious acts allowed for the creation of film narratives that emphasized "an America in the grip of a code of justifiable inhumanity, a democracy torn at the seams and at crisis" (Cetti 2009: 16). Thus, several political thrillers, especially before 2008, opted to portray their villain as part of the US intelligence world and create an opposition with the protagonist who questions the limits of his/her orders. Nevertheless, the films that employed a CIA consultant offered a more positive representation of the Agency. CIA operatives worked with both Ryan Reynolds and Denzel Washington in *Safe House* (Hay 2012) while in *Salt*, Angelina Jolie met with female agents to get a sense of their duties and professional behavior (Bertonado 2010). In *Vantage Point*, Dennis Quaid along with other cast members worked with "U.S. Army veteran Ron Blecker, in order to help the lead actors prepare themselves to play Secret Service agents" (Murray 2008). CIA assistance has brought forward the positive side of the Agency, although it should be stressed that they do not offer their services if they do not approve the screenplay "as in the cases of *Spy Game* (2001), or *The Bourne Identity* (2002)" (Lacey 2013).

Another trait shared by the main characters of the films is their personal life. Only Matt (*Safe House*) and Jack (*The Sum of All Fears*) have a girlfriend as the narratives begin; Jason meets and falls in love with a woman in the first film (*Bourne Identity*), only to lose her in the second installment, and Roger

Figures 19–24 (Left to right, top to bottom) Still frames from exhibition of protagonists' physical strength in political thrillers.

(*Body of Lies*) develops feelings for a nurse he meets in Jordan. Only Evelyn in *Salt* is married as the film begins but her husband is soon abducted and killed. All the protagonists, except Secret Service Agent Barnes, are employed by the CIA, are young, Caucasian, single or become single, possess exemplary physical agility and combat skills, and their mental capacities are well above average. As evidenced by the film frames in Figures 19 to 24, the narratives highlight their protagonists' extraordinary survival skills and physical abilities, simultaneously emphasizing male virility, courage, and strength—again with the exception of Evelyn, who follows a recent cinematic tradition that places women at the center of action films.

The political thriller protagonist escapes from high buildings, runs fast, trains hard, and is unafraid to face the most perilous situation with an air of

Figures 25–33 (Left to right, top to bottom) Young age vs. middle age in the *Bourne trilogy*, *Safe House*, and *Salt*.

calmness and the capacity for instant planning. Their status as CIA operatives and their rigorous training has prepared them for a life full of danger, threats, and deception. Physical virility, courage, intelligence, and strategic planning are exalted in these post 9/11 narratives, echoing the intrepid fortitude and heroism of all the actual men and women who participated in the rescue missions after the attacks on US soil, and the thousands of American soldiers who fought overseas. However, these main characters also demonstrate compassion and sensitivity, and they question not only their orders but their superiors' authority. In this way, a binary opposition is created: the young age of the protagonists, an essential ingredient of their profession, is in opposition with the maturity of their superior officers, the people who give them orders, mentor them and help them. Thus, the first narrative isotopy encountered in political thrillers is the one between young age and middle age.

The close-ups in the Figures 25 to 33 depict the protagonists of five political thrillers on the left side and their superior officers on the right, highlighting their age difference. I chose not to include all the films for reasons of economy, but I should stress that from all the political thrillers included in the corpus, only *Vantage Point* and *The Sentinel*, 2006, two films that focus on attempts to assassinate the President of the United States, star two Secret Service Agents in their fifties and sixties, portrayed respectively by seasoned actors Dennis Quaid and Michael Douglas.

At first glance, this age-related opposition can be attributed to the specific, professional roles of each character and the film industry's parameters. First, CIA field agents have to be athletic, fast, and flexible, and these abilities deteriorate as people get older. Muscle tone decreases, aerobic endurance drops and body fat increases. On the other hand, CIA superior officers, who may have been field agents in the past, have accumulated experience during the years and their professional advancement is the next logical step as they reach middle age. Second, since these films are marketed and promoted predominantly as blockbuster action thrillers, thus targeting mainly young and male populations worldwide, it is reasonable that they star young, male, and bankable A-list Hollywood stars whom the viewers admire and can easily identify with. However disguised the political nature of these "spectacular narratives," to borrow Geoff King's (2000) term, the choice of narrative plot—which is by definition political since it involves governmental institutions—and protagonists—who are operating to solve a number of crises all of which can affect the American people, and the polity—do reflect societal anxieties and can be read as implicit commentary and/or allegories of contemporary official policies and societal concerns.

In the *Bourne* trilogy (*The Bourne Identity, The Bourne Ultimatum,* and *The Bourne Supremacy*), based on the same-titled novels by Robert Ludlum, an unconscious Jason Bourne (Matt Damon), a superspy created by a CIA black operation program with the code name Treadstone, is rescued by fishermen in the Mediterranean Sea. Jason wakes up with no memory of who he is and spends the rest of the first and second films trying to uncover his true identity based on a number of clues he possesses or finds, while being monitored and pursued by the CIA. In *Salt*, CIA agent Evelyn Salt (Angelina Jolie) discovers she is in fact a sleeper agent, raised and trained in Russia, with a mission to assassinate the Russian President and cause a nuclear war between the USA and Russia. In *Safe House*, young agent Matt Weston (Ryan Reynolds) is assigned to protect international criminal and ex-CIA NOC (non-official cover) agent, Tobin Frost, after security is breached in the CIA safe house in Cape Town and the rest of his team is killed. In *Body of Lies*, CIA agent Roger Ferris's (Leonardo DiCaprio) mission as he is stationed in Iraq is to track a Muslim terrorist, following instructions by his CIA officer Ed Hoffman (Russell Crowe), who is stationed in the USA. It is easy to infer that these films have been advertised as vehicles for Damon, Jolie, DiCaprio, and Reynolds, celebrity A-list actors whose names have been associated with both critical and commercial success, and worldwide appeal. It is also customary to consider the central character of an action/thriller film—the genres under which those films were predominantly tagged as—is the hero/heroine of the narrative. A closer look, however, reveals another scenario. I would argue that Bourne, Evelyn, Roger, and Matt are, in fact, instruments in a much wider scheme and are only seemingly in charge of their fate and their personal narrative program.

In fact, my argument is corroborated by the Secret Operation Treadstone's Head, Alex Conclin (Chris Cooper), in the first film of the *Bourne* trilogy, *The Bourne Identity*. During their first encounter in a CIA safe house in Paris, Bourne and Conclin have an altercation after which Jason shouts: "Who am I?" Conclin's answer is immediate and disarming: "You are US property, you're a malfunctioning $30 million weapon." Conclin discloses more information which puts the last pieces of Jason's mind puzzle into place as he finally remembers the object of his mission and the last events that transpired before he was found floating unconscious in the Mediterranean. Bourne was supposed to assassinate the exiled African dictator Nykwana Wombosi (Adewale Akinnuoye-Agbaje), who was about to expose the CIA in a memoir. Bourne was the one who devised the plan, found the boat where Wombosi was staying, and prepared everything so that the murder would be attributed to one of the members of Wombosi's entourage. In a flashback during his confrontation with Conclin, Jason sees why he did not pull the trigger. Just as he was about to complete his mission he realized that Wombosi, who was almost asleep, had one of his children on his lap and the rest sleeping on armchairs and the couch next to him. Bourne's hesitation lasted just long enough for Wombosi's men to attack and shoot him, and perhaps cause his amnesia. Jason's inability to fulfill his order, and his subsequent memory loss, signifies the moment he stops being the means by which the CIA secretly operates around the world in an effort to maintain the supremacy of the United States.

In *Salt*, Evelyn suffers from another kind of memory loss and discovers her life has been a lie. A capable CIA field operative, she returns back to what she believes is her homeland after being tortured in North Korea during a mission, only to find out she is actually Russian, an orphan who was taken in by a Russian secret intelligence program, raised as an American, and trained to function at a specific point in the future. In the same vein, *Body of Lies'* Roger and *Safe House's* Matt are disillusioned by discovering that "all is not well" with the Central Intelligence Agency. Roger learns that his superior officer is also supervising a "side" operation in the same region, targeting the same Muslim terrorist, and Matt discovers that his boss is a corrupt official, responsible for illegal financial transactions and the death of innocent American citizens. Similar conspiracies, illegal and threatening transactions that affect both domestic and foreign policies, are encountered by the protagonists in the rest of the corpus political thrillers, such as *The Manchurian Candidate, Shooter, Vantage Point, The Cold Light of Day*, and *The Good Shepherd*. All the narratives point to a threat that is formed, cultivated, and activated in the United States by American citizens, some of whom even hold highly influential positions in the political structure. The protagonists work for either the CIA, the military, or other government agencies, but quickly find themselves in a complicated web of corruption and intrigue which they then struggle to bring to light. However, Jason, Evelyn, and the rest of the central characters operate in the context of strict parameters; they follow orders and do not act by choice. They are pawns in a strategically calculated plan to avert the world from discovering the CIA's rogue practices (The *Bourne* trilogy, *Safe House*), the level of corporate influence on American politics and corrupt politicians (*The Manchurian Candidate, The*

Shooter), and the continuing threat from both domestic and foreign powers (*Salt, Vantage Point*).

In *Shooter* (2007), retired US sniper Sergeant Bob Lee Swagger (Mark Wahlberg) is accused of attempting to assassinate the American President in a shooting that claimed the life of the Ethiopian Archbishop. It is soon revealed that the Archbishop was the target all along because he was to reveal that a US private military unit was involved in a massacre of an Eritrean village to protect the interests of American corporate oil companies, aided by Senator Charles F. Meachum (Ned Beatty). When the Senator learns about Swagger's escape, he ironically states: "There's always a confused soul that thinks that one man can make a difference. And you have to kill him to convince him otherwise. That's the hassle with democracy." The Senator's remark, however callous and perilous as it is uttered by an elected public official, speaks to the heart of the political thriller, its narrative construction, as well as part of the American ideology heritage, dubbed in its cinematic representation by Franklin (2006: 25) as "the cult of the individual." Franklin observed that since "the main focus for justice in a liberal society is the individual [...] the cult of the individual as played out in movie plots [frequently involves] a resilient resourceful individual with personal courage and ingenuity [who] overcomes the odds and succeeds without help against the grain of an oppressive environment often depicted as the government."

Foreign policy in political thrillers

Foreign policy issues in political thrillers are, first of all, visually represented by the isotopy of inside (the United States) vs. outside (a topos outside the borders). The political thrillers under discussion take place in an overwhelming number of different countries (despite some of them being filmed elsewhere because of permit difficulties and/or security reasons). The stories unfold in a great variety of locations, taking viewers to five continents (North America, South America, Asia, Europe, and Africa), more than twenty countries (among them Syria, Iraq, Jordan, Pakistan, Turkey, Saudi Arabia, the Netherlands, Spain, Italy, Germany, France, Greece, the UK, Russia, Morocco, South Africa, India, the Philippines, North Korea, and South Korea), and more than twenty cities (among them Moscow, Turin, Naples, Tangiers, Riyadh, Incirlik, Paris, London, Munich, Berlin, Mykonos, Cape Town, Manila, Seoul, Karachi, Washington, Baltimore,

New York), the community of Langley, Virginia, an unidentified mountain region in Alaska, and a few unidentified locations in the Middle East. No film's action is restricted to a single location, while the overwhelming majority of action sequences and/or missions with casualties take place outside the US borders or in very isolated areas. Although a number of political thrillers do include deaths of Americans on US soil, these most often occur in a clandestine manner; the casualties are killed in the line of duty being CIA agents or police officers, and almost no innocent citizens are ever put in danger. Only *The Sum of All Fears* includes a nuclear explosion in Baltimore, Maryland, which claims the lives of innocent citizens. However, the filmmakers opt to depict the explosion and its aftermath using mostly long, aerial shots while there is no report on the numbers of lives lost. *The Sum of All Fears* was the first mainstream narrative involving a terrorist plot to be released after 9/11, and this may be the reason its initial release date, which was quite close to the attacks, was postponed. In addition, part of the narrative of all the films takes place in Washington and/ or Langley, the places where foreign policies are planned and where decisions are taken and orders disseminated to the rest of the world. New York City also prominently features in political thrillers, with Baltimore only appearing in *The Sum of All Fears*. With the exception of *The Sum of All Fears*, which is the oldest film in the corpus, the rest of the fictional political thrillers, that is, from 2002 onwards, choose to represent the United States as a primarily safe space and almost the rest of the world as unsafe. The binary opposition between the United States and the rest of the world is pictorially signified by the use of aerial long shots or eye-level long shots, as evidenced by the following film frames shown in Figures 34 to 39.

Despite these shots being visually impressive, satisfying the viewers' desire for spectacle, they also vindicate cinema as an art and a medium, which can help us "visit" breathtakingly beautiful faraway places—whether real or technologically created. In addition, they serve to geographically underscore who the enemies and allies of the United Sates are. Russia, for instance, the great Cold War opponent, although it was actually a federation then (USSR), connotes ice and cold, although there are regions that are not always covered in snow. The shots in Figures 34 and 38 from *Salt* and *The Sum of All Fears* appeal to this commonly shared knowledge and opt for images of Russia which are easily understood. The majestic Makaryev Convent of the Russian Orthodox Church approximately 300 miles from Moscow, from *Salt*, is transformed into an isolated center for the training of sleeper agents, and the icy road from *The Sum of All Fears* connotes

Figures 34–39 (Left to right, top to bottom) Geographical isotopy in *Salt, Bourne Ultimatum, Bourne Supremacy, Bourne Identity, The Sum of All Fears,* and *Body of Lies.*

danger and suspicion as well. Interestingly, snow is represented in four out of the six pictures. Apart from its visual cue of depicting Russia or the USSR, snow in the Western tradition implicitly evokes death through relating it with winter and the temporary end of flora. What is made clear is that the iconography of open spaces outside the US borders in the majority of political thrillers implies danger and foresees difficulties, serving to construct an inhospitable "outside."

At the other end of the vast landscapes that portray an unwelcoming "outside," most political thrillers depict the "inside," using similar shots of the operation headquarters at CIA. As seen in the stills in Figures 40 to 45, the rooms are populated by a number of employees working on computers while the orders come from the standing officers who oversee the missions. Dark blues, greens, and blacks of the color palette dominate the shots and most relevant scenes; this choice, combined with the absence of windows in the majority of cases, creates a rather gloomy, secretive, and at times claustrophobic atmosphere, appropriate, however, for the work that is conducted there. In addition, the camera does not usually focus on characters—it either fragments their bodies, opts for long shots, or shows their backs turned to the screen. This fragmentation, combined with the computer blue screens that mainly orient the viewer's gaze, along with the characters', underscores America's hi-tech advancements, but also the primordial position of technology and the CIA's dependency on it for matters of national security. More importantly, however, the *mise-en-scène* that clearly prioritize the most sophisticated surveillance methods foregrounds the US position as a global big brother, a ubiquitous and omnipotent presence that watches everyone and everything 24/7 under the pretense of national and international, security.

However, despite this enormous ability to navigate the entire world in a matter of seconds from the comfort of a desk in a secure environment, these spaces do not provide the solution to these political narratives as their object— whether it's Jason Bourne, Tobin Frost, or Evelyn Salt—always manages to escape. Failure to apprehend the target, despite ample resources, is part of *Body of Lies'* thematic concerns. In the beginning of the narrative, CIA agent Hoffman, who supervises agent Ferris' mission to capture a Muslim terrorist, tries to explain to his superior officers that terrorists prefer more basic means of communication: "The enemy has figured out they're fighting guys from the future. If you live in the past, behave like it's the past and guys from the future can't see you." The use of satellites, drones, and electronic devices has been rendered inadequate since the enemy has abandoned relevant methods and chooses to communicate face to face to organize their plans. Unfortunately, Hoffman's superiors do not appreciate his briefing and the rest of the film is a struggle between an older, experienced and cynical Hoffman supervising a younger, yet more realistic (having adapted to the enemy world) Ferris, who has first knowledge not only of his target but a better grasp of the mission by having become an expert at the new rules imposed by the enemy. In his review of Ridley Scott's film, David Denby remarks that the filmmaker's main point is exactly that; the war cannot easily be won through drones, surveillance from afar, and ignorance of specific cultural sensibilities of the enemy. Denby (2008) concludes that "[t]he Americans have all the technological advantages but they don't know the people, the signs of trust and honor; they don't know which

Figures 40–45 (Left to right, top to bottom) Technological isotopy in *Bourne Identity, Bourne Supremacy, Bourne Ultimatum, Body of Lies, Salt,* and *Safe House.*

way the terrorists are going, and they can't find out." In the comedy *Man of the Year*, Tom Dobbs jokes about how NASA spent millions to develop a pen that can be used in zero gravity while the Russians solved the same problem using a pencil. This may be a joke but at its heart lies the dilemma faced by both Hoffman and Ferris in *Body of Lies*: keep using the technology which took years and billions of dollars to advance or abandon it and adapt to the new strategy which the enemy follows in order to defeat it once and for all. Despite the "happy ending" afforded to both main US characters—Ferris leaves the Agency and decides to stay in Jordan, while Hoffman continues "saving civilization", as he nonchalantly tells his wife, communicating with his assets on the phone while he eats, carpools, or watches his kid's soccer game—*Body of Lies* offers no solutions to the US–Muslim terrorism conflict but a suggestion "that the US needs to rethink its strategy and requires a new kind of agency and operative" (Kellner 2010: 248). However, it does provide commentary regarding a post-9/11 treatment of the subject of terrorism. Cetti (2009: 52–3) notes that unlike similar post-9/11 films' focus on human rights violations and torture, *Body of Lies* emphasizes the opposition between "American political arrogance and intelligence community deception in dealing with international 'friendlies' to root out the terrorist threat."

American interventionism

Examining the *Bourne* trilogy, Kellner (2010: 167) claims that it "is emblematic of anti-Bush-Cheney political thrillers," adding that the films substitute the Cold War subtext of the Ludlum's novels, and imbue them "with post-9/11 paranoia." I would add that the *Bourne* films are paradigms of American exceptionalism and interventionism that characterize the same 2000–8 administration as well as past historical events. In the DVD commentary that accompanies *The Bourne Identity*, director Doug Liman (who also served as executive producer in the next two *Bourne* films) mentions that he based the secret organization Treadstone on his father's position in the National Security Agency (NSA) during the Reagan administration, and, in particular, his role as chief counsel for the Senate's investigation of the Iran-Contra Affair. Both the Reagan and the W. Bush Administrations promoted an image of a strong United States, in a neoconservative context, fervently endorsing traditional family and religious values. George W. Bush in particular, within the context of the War on Terror, followed a course of action that favored "military force and unilateral action" instead of "diplomacy and multilateralism," and viewed "international conflicts in terms of good and evil," instead of an intricate web of power relations, whose balance relies on meticulously planned strategies (Brooks 2013: 6). Nevertheless, very few post-9/11 political thrillers, and especially those released before Obama's victory in 2008, opt for such an unequivocal binary-opposition narrative structure. This time around, the bad guys are not so bad, and the good guys are not so good.

Take exiled African dictator Wombosi in *The Bourne Identity*, for instance. Although it is not clear whether he was overthrown by the US government or placed as the head of his country by it in the first place, he threatens to reveal American involvement in the African continent, after the first assassination attempt on his life, unless the CIA helps him regain his power in a six-month period. A CIA officer who watches him on TV, says: "He was an irritation before he took power, he was a problem when he was in power and he's been a disaster for us in exile." This comment is indicative of the US's hegemonic attitude vis-à-vis smaller nations, and also of the US renewed interest in African countries during the War on Terror. This period caused a reevaluation of foreign policies as "[I]mpoverished nations with weak state apparatuses were viewed as breeding grounds for political extremism" (Schmidt 2013: 213). As Schmidt adds, "Washington again sought to strengthen military alliances, provide political assistance and training, and open military bases in dozens of African countries" (2013: 213). Wombosi is a minor character in *Bourne Identity* and functions as the trigger of Bourne's lost memory, but he is not represented as a one-sided bloodthirsty killer but rather as a political player. In addition, in his last scene, as Bourne remembers his attempt to assassinate him, Wombosi is calmly seated on a sofa, surrounded by his children. When he realizes that someone is behind him and holds a gun to his head, he simply looks up in total silence in order to protect his offspring from having to witness his murder or even be killed. Wombosi's depiction as a caring family man, an intelligent political agent, as well as a potential criminal, assists in a more complete portrait of an individual who possesses both positive and negative sides.

Bourne himself is another individual represented in grey tones, combining good and evil. As his portrait is completed in the third installment, *The Bourne Ultimatum*, the viewers realize that Jason or David Webb—his real name—was a man who volunteered for the initial Treadstone—later transformed into Blackbriar—program to become an assassin. In a flashback scene that dates to his initial training, he is asked to kill a man by the mastermind of the operation, Dr. Albert Hirsch (Albert Finney). When Jason hesitantly asks what that person did, Dr. Hirsch, angered by his reluctance, says frustratingly:

> You picked us. You volunteered. You said that you would do what it takes to save American lives. You're not a liar, are you? Or too weak to see this through? This is it. Let go of David Webb. Will you give yourself to this program?

After a short pause, Jason succumbs to all the training he had received and shoots the man he was ordered to. At that moment, he ceases to be the good guy who will save America and is transformed into a governmental instrument, a heartless killing machine that only executes orders. Jason's representation can also be read as an allegory of American soldiers who enthusiastically went to war to protect their country and democratize Iraq only to become disillusioned by their policy makers and betrayed by their country. In the *Bourne* trilogy, Jason struggles not only to find his identity but also to find the culprit behind the CIA's secret program that clearly operates outside the law. The dialogue between CIA Deputy Director Pamela Landy (Joan Allen) and Head of Blackbriar Noah Vosen (David Strathairn) about the nature of the program is revealing:

> NOAH VOSEN: [Blackbriar] is now the umbrella program for all our black-ops. Full envelope intrusion, rendition, experimental interrogation—it is all run out of this office. We are the sharp end of the stick now, Pam.
>
> PAMELA LANDY: Lethal action?
>
> NOAH VOSEN: If we have to, sure. That's what makes us special. No more red tape. No more getting the bad guys caught on our sights, then watching them escape while we wait for somebody in Washington to issue the order.

Blackbriar becomes a metonym for American interventionism worldwide, which pervades all the films in the trilogy. CIA officers are everywhere and seem to act without any spirit of cooperation, or acknowledgement that they are in a foreign land even during visible chases in broad daylight in highly populated areas. It is especially interesting to remark that the majority of the action sequences/CIA interference take place within the borders of US ally countries. Action sequences in Zurich and London leave innocent people wounded and property destroyed. The heads of Blackbriar even order CIA agents to assassinate in order to protect their illegal transactions or keep the identity of the program secret. Although Jason spares the life of two assassins (one from the CIA and one from the KGB), he does kill others to save himself or others who can help him.

In *Safe House*, Tobin Frost, the ex-CIA agent who abandoned the Agency and started selling national security secrets worldwide, presents affinities with Bourne regarding his distrust of the Agency, thus justifying his treacherous path. After acquiring a USB drive containing information on corrupt officials and illegal transactions among the CIA, the British MI6, and other national agencies, he is captured by the CIA and placed in the hands of inexperienced agent Matt. However, the filmmakers opt for a representation of a villain with a conscience. First, Tobin spares Matt's life during his first attempt to escape and consequently becomes less antipathetic. Once in the safe house, Tobin reveals that he turned to crime when he was ordered to prevent an innocent witness from appearing at a congressional hearing. He ends his monologue by telling Matt: "Everyone betrays everyone [...] I used to be innocent like you, wrap myself with the flag ..."

The role of the media

As in the political comedies discussed in the previous chapter, the fourth estate is also part of the political thriller subgenre. Its role varies from being a conveyor of critical information to the characters to assisting in the solution at the narrative's end. Television screens are present in the overwhelming majority of all political thrillers (*Bourne Identity* is the only exception I found) as can be

Figures 46–51 (Left to right, top to bottom) Media isotopy in *Bourne Ultimatum*, *Salt*, *Vantage Point*, *Body of Lies*, *Safe House*, and *Bourne Legacy*.

seen in Figures 46 to 51. Interestingly, in *The Manchurian Candidate, Vantage Point, Safe House,* and *Bourne Supremacy,* it is a news report that signals the end of the protagonist's struggle, and the film's for that matter. In *Safe House* and *Bourne Ultimatum,* it is only through media exposure of the corruption and illicit transactions of CIA high-ranking officials that the protagonists—in this case Matt and Bourne—are redeemed and allowed to live the rest of their life.

The last film of the trilogy, *The Bourne Ultimatum,* finds Bourne collecting all the information on the illegal financial transactions of Dr. Hirsch and Operation Brackbriar, and delivering them to an unnamed and unseen news outlet. A little later, Pamela Landy, Bourne's only CIA ally, watches a news report on the exposure of the covert CIA operation and the arrests of Hirsch and Vosen, while watching CIA Director Ezra Kramer (Figure 46) being taken into custody. In *Safe House,* Matt realizes that his CIA mentor is actually a criminal and that Tobin Frost, aside from saving his life, speaks the truth regarding the corruption and deceit that pervade the higher ranks of the Agency. Matt meets with CIA Deputy Director Harlan Whitford (Sam Shepard) to discuss his report of the events, which contains information that could hurt the CIA. Whitford promises Matt a promotion on the condition that he deletes the data in question, but Matt is skeptical because he wants people to know the truth. The Deputy Director defends the CIA's "lie policy," stating: "People don't want the truth anymore Matt. It's messy. It keeps them up nights." Matt understands that Whitford may be implicated in the illegal actions of his subordinates, or turn a blind eye to them, in order to let them complete their missions; thus, he refuses to change the report and decides to leave the Agency. However, he does leak the USB stick, which was passed on to him by Frost before his death, and in the next scene (Figure 50) a news report announces Whitford's arrest and the exposure of yet another political scandal. The ugly truth does come out in *The Bourne Ultimatum* and *Safe House* via the news. However, the media is not personified in these two cases. There's no special character/reporter or investigative journalist that tries to unearth what really happened, collaborating closely with the main characters. Instead, the media receives information which it deems important, and exposes the culprits to the citizens. Thus, the media assumes a significant "actant" role. As stated in the introduction, "the notion of actant is an abstract notion," and is not necessarily equated with that of a fictional character (Fontanille 2003: 150). Here, the media has the role of the subject's "helper." The main characters acquire the proof for political wrong-doing and the media helps disseminate it to the public so that the citizens be informed and, subsequently, justice be served. Finally, in both *Bourne Identity* and *Safe House*, the media is characterized as a powerful and impartial conveyor of facts and figures since it provides the solution to the conflict, thus abiding by the basic principles of journalism, impartiality, independence, and objectivity, as noted by Stephen J. A. Ward (2014: 458). Without media exposure, which acts as a kind of *deus ex machina* when everything else fails, political corruption and criminality would go undetected and dishonest individuals would continue breaking laws.

The other side of media representation is encountered in *Vantage Point*, a film that focuses on an attempted assassination of the President of the United States as witnessed from eight different perspectives, one of which is that of a US news van assigned to cover the event. Before the first explosion at the film's beginning, reporter Angie (Zoe Saldana) is describing the atmosphere at the Spanish plaza for the fictional GNN news outlet. As she starts to add that despite the positive endorsement of the plan to fight terrorism initiated by the American president to be signed by 150 countries in Spain there are also some protesters against it, her producer from inside the van, Rex Brooks (Sigourney Weaver), shuts her down. The following dialogue between the two women ensues:

> Rex Brooks: Angie, what the hell was that?
>
> Angie Jones: Not everyone loves us, Rex.
>
> Rex Brooks: Save the punditry for someone who's paid to have an opinion.
>
> Angie Jones: I'm cool with censorship, I know the American people love that.

At the end of the film, Secret Service Agent Barnes uncovers the terrorist plot, executed by a Latino couple and their Secret Service colleague, and saves the president. However, the GNN newscaster that appears at the last scene reports another story about the death of the single assassin responsible for the bombings and the attempted assassination. There is no mention of the conspiracy, the involvement of an American citizen—and, furthermore, a member of the president's Secret Service detail—nor the opposition President Ashton's counterterrorist plan faces abroad. The newscaster is not lying about the bombings, the attempted assassination, or the well-being of the president, which are indeed the facts of the news report. However, his omission and/or ignorance of the terrorist plot and the foreign contrariety to the US initiative against global terrorism result in a different news narrative disseminated to the American public. Matthew Kieran (1997: 98) explains such omissions by arguing that "an entire news structure may be geared in such a way as to preclude impartiality," and, I should add, serve a specific political agenda.

The contrasting representation of the media constitutes a direct correlation with the film's political undertone. *The Bourne Ultimatum* and *Safe House* are both films that castigate the CIA, condemn torture (*Safe House*), and are adamant about their conviction that US citizens should be made aware of all actions and decisions made by their elected officials and the government institutions they oversee and are therefore responsible for. On the other hand, despite the instances of European anti-Americanism in *Vantage Point*, the film ultimately celebrates the nation, considers it as the only world power that can initiate a plan to eradicate terrorism, and, thus, promotes a US global sovereignty. When Agent Barnes confronts his colleague-turned-terrorist, the latter tells him, as he draws his last breath, that this is a war that will never end. According to Cetti (2009: 279), this phrase implies that the "exchange between terrorists and the U.S. set in motion by 9/11 and comprising the War on Terror will never end." The author soon adds, however, that the narrative's choice to end the film by suggesting a single man was responsible for the attempted assassination, "anchors [it] firmly in the tradition of post-Kennedy era political thrillers from *The Parallax View* through to *JFK*."

Indeed, the contemporary political thriller follows a long-lasting cycle of films, and especially the paranoia thrillers of the 1970s, which, according to Scott (2011: 138), "provided the threat for an examination of American politics and society from beyond authority and accountability." Suspicion, questioning of governmental decisions, and illegality abound in the films of both eras. Ultimately, however, no political thriller of either the 1970s and, most importantly, the 2000s or the 2010s actually ends on an optimistic note. The agents' actions may reveal the intricate and corrupt governmental machinery at play (*The Bourne Ultimatum, Safe House*), the foreign or domestic threat (*Salt, Vantage Point*), and the culprits may even get arrested while the media expose them to the nation. Yet, no real catharsis takes place but only a momentary one; until the next corrupt official takes the place of the dead or incarcerated one, another foreign threat rises, or the next American plans the assassination of the president working alongside an international terrorist group. Hay's structure remains intact, however beaten and ill-constructed, and a single agent's action can only succeed in creating a very small crack.

Political thrillers and true stories

The political thrillers based on real events and/or memoirs that are included in the corpus are *Syriana* (2005), *Breach* (2007), *Fair Game* (2010), *Green Zone* (2010), *Argo* (2012), and *Zero Dark Thirty* (2012). *Argo* and *Breach* examine events of the recent past. *Argo* was directed by Ben Affleck and produced by Affleck, George Clooney, and Grant Heslov. The screenplay was written by Chris Terrio, based on retired CIA intelligence officer Antonio J. Mendez's 1999 memoir *The Master of Disguise: My Secret Life in the USA* and writer Joshuah Bearman's article "The Great Escape." The film recounts a CIA covert operation— "declassified by President Clinton in 1997" (Giglio 2014: 19)—that eventually freed six American citizens, who managed to find refuge at the residences of Canadian diplomat John Sheardon (not portrayed in the film) and Canadian Ambassador Ken Taylor, during the Iranian hostage crisis, which resulted in a total of fifty-two American diplomats and citizens being held hostage for 444 days, after Iranian students took over the US Embassy in Tehran. *Breach* was directed by Billy Ray, who also cowrote the script along with Adam Mazer and William Rotko. The film is based on the true story of Robert Hanssen, an FBI agent who was arrested for espionage in 2001 after selling a great number of national security secrets to the former USSR, and Russia after 1989. The rest of the political thrillers, released between 2005 and 2012, focus on the Middle East despite the variety of perspectives they include. Hollywood's recent interest with the region is a direct reflection of the actual politics that followed the 9/11 attacks, the War on Terror, and the Iraq War (2003–11). *Syriana*, *Fair Game*, *Green Zone*, and *Zero Dark Thirty* question, probe, and examine such issues as the reasons the United States went to war, unreliable intelligence, the media collaboration with the Bush administration propaganda agenda, the efforts to find Osama bin Laden, and the relationship between Middle-Eastern oil powers and the United States of America.

In particular, *Fair Game*, based on CIA officer Valerie Plame's memoir, *Fair Game: My Life as a Spy, My Betrayal by the White House* (2007), and her husband, retired diplomat Joseph C. Wilson's, written account, *The Politics of Truth* (2004), recounts the Plame Affair, or Plamegate, as the scandal came to be called, examining "the actual circumstances surrounding the Bush administration's casus belli" (Haas, Christensen, and Haas 2015: 248). The story relates the public identification of Plame as a CIA officer in 2003 by conservative journalist and columnist Robert Novac in *The Washington Post*. Before the

American invasion in Iraq, the CIA gathered intelligence which suggested that Saddam Hussein was potentially, yet not definitely, in possession of weapons of mass destruction (WMD). In a report, Plame suggested her husband, who was familiar with the country of Niger during his career, could be in the position to explore whether the African country was providing Iraq with uranium. As his examination revealed that such transactions could not have taken place, he wrote and published an op-ed piece in *The New York Times*, in which he openly doubted what the Bush administration considered a foregone conclusion and used as the reason for which the United States should go into war. Wilson's article angered both the CIA and the political establishment, and one immediate result was Plame's public outing by Novak in mid-July 2003, a few months into the conflict. Released six months after *Fair Game*, *Green Zone*, based on the book *Imperial Life in The Emerald City*, 2006, by Indian-American journalist Rajiv Chandrasekaran, critically examines the American plan of reconstructing Iraq and focuses mainly on the Coalition Provisional Authority (CPA—the Iraqi transitional government, formed after the invasion in March 2003 by the United States, the United Kingdom, Australia, and Poland) in the Baghdad Green Zone. US Army Chief Warrant Officer Roy Miller (Matt Damon) is looking for WMD but soon realizes that the intelligence he is provided with is inaccurate. His efforts to uncover the truth are routinely hindered by Pentagon official Clark Poundstone (Greg Kinnear) and his actions are viewed as suspect by a number of people. Nevertheless, Miller ultimately learns that Iraq has not got a WMD program and that Poundstone has known about it all along. Realizing that the whole WMD threat was just the excuse the US government needed to invade Iraq, Miller draws up a report and sends it to journalist Lawrie Dayne (Amy Ryan) as well as all the major newspaper and news outlets in the USA.

Syriana, based on specific parts of ex-CIA officer Robert Baer's memoir *See No Evil* (2003)—especially focusing on Washington's oil politics—offers a multi-focused narrative, following an ageing CIA officer operating in the Middle East, a US energy analyst residing in Switzerland, an attorney in Washington, and a Pakistani emigrant looking for work in the Persian Gulf. Released in 2005, the film's focus was extremely relevant as hurricanes Katrina and Rita "reduced the U.S. energy output by 56.6 million barrels of oil [...] driving oil up" and leading Bush to "declare in his 2006 State of the Union speech" that the USA was "seriously addicted to oil" (Beckman 2012: 128). *Syriana* examines "the nature of US elite business interests, victims and heroes, in a plotline that echoed real-life US Middle Eastern policy" (Alford 2010: 141).

Argo won the Academy Awards for Best Picture, Best Adapted Screenplay, and Best Achievement in Editing, and was nominated for four more; *Zero Dark Thirty* was nominated for five Oscars, winning the one for Best Achievement in Sound Editing, and *Syriana* won the Academy Award for Best Performance by an Actor in a Supporting Role (Clooney) and was nominated for its screenplay. The rest of the films were nominated and/or won awards in various US and foreign film festivals. *Argo* was also a surprising box office hit, as it grossed almost $232.5 million worldwide on a $44.5 million budget, reaching the 23rd spot on the US 2012 box office list. *Zero Dark Thirty*, with $132.8 million on a $40 million budget came in 32nd the same year. *Syriana* and *Green Zone* followed with profits in the area of $95 million each in their respective release years and placed in the top-100 of the domestic box office. Yet, although *Syriana* cost $50 million, *Green Zone* cost $100 million which translates into being considered a box office failure. Finally, *Breach* and *Fair Game* returned $40 million and $22 million on a budget of $23 million and $22 million respectively. According to the 2014 MPAA statistics, between 2010 and 2014, Hollywood's share from the international box office increased from 66 percent to 72 percent. Considering that the film industry's profits are today mainly dependent on how well one of their productions performs overseas, and also that all the films mentioned here did far better domestically than internationally, it is easy to conclude that political films do not appeal to a wide audience. Giglio (2014: 314) further explains that most films of this nature "draw on the type of political content that is central to America's cinematic history but irrelevant to foreign audiences." I would add that the films that returned the highest profits did so because they exploited the cultural capital of their stars. Affleck and Clooney belong to an exclusive club of stars whose name may be the only reason why an individual chooses to buy a ticket at the theater. Even in the case of *Green Zone's* commercial disappointment, I argue that Damon's presence must have increased revenue and helped it almost reach the film's cost. Finally, as the reason for the box office success or failure of a political film must take into account a number of parameters (sociopolitical circumstances, issues of censorship, the budget and production design, the cast's star power, the director and screenwriter's abilities, the marketing of the film, distribution factors, etc.), I would like to examine if the narrative structure can be added to the success/failure equation.

Another observation meriting a discussion is that these films were released from 2005 to 2012, that is, four years after 9/11 and two years after the Iraq War. A number of reasons and events account for the absence of political films per se during the first years after the attack. First, the shock and the subsequent trauma felt by the nation and its filmmakers led to other cinematic choices, lighter and escapist, in order to help the healing process. Second, the relationship between Hollywood and the US government changed. According to a CNN 2001 report entitled "Uncle Sam Wants Hollywood," President Bush sent government officials to Hollywood, in November 2001, for a meeting with studio executives, led by White House Advisor Karl Rove, to ensure some kind of cooperation on the war against terrorism and to secure the film industry's assistance.[2] As a consequence, the release of specific films was pushed back while others had to be "revisited" to adapt to the new situation. As Barker (2011: 5) explains, this meant "altering New York skylines," as was the case with *Spiderman*, "or re-editing" (an airplane hijacking scene was removed in *Collateral Damage*, 2002, while *Black Hawk Down*, 2001, was re-edited to illustrate more clearly the dichotomy between the enemy's evil persona and the benevolence of the American soldier). Additionally, TV news outlets, which had become a close ally of the Bush administration, vehemently supported the war in Afghanistan in late 2001 and promoted patriotism while spreading fear. Kellner (2003: 105) observes that, unlike foreign news and the internet "highlighted footage of Afghanistan civilian casualties and U.S. military blunders, the American television networks continued to focus on the anthrax scare, new terror threats, and invocations of the September 11 bombing."

The 2001–3 yearly box offices were dominated by the "usual suspects": fantasy (such as the *Harry Potter* films, *The Lord of the Rings* trilogy, the beginning of the *Spider-Man* franchise); animated films (such as *Shrek, Monsters, Inc., Ice Age, Finding Nemo*); the resurrection of the musical (such as *Moulin Rouge, Chicago*); and comedies (such as *My Big Fat Greek Wedding, Bruce Almighty, Cheaper by the Dozen*). Similar films dominated 2004—and every year until today for that matter—with two notable exceptions: *The Passion of the Christ* and *Fahrenheit 9/11*, a political film and a political documentary, were placed in the top twenty (number three and seventeen respectively), while causing significant public controversy. Although Haas, Christensen, and Haas (2015: 223) do not consider *The Passion* a political film, stating explicitly that "[a]lthough it reflected a distinctively traditional theological view of its subject matter, it did not pursue political themes," and was rather "a literal reenactment [...] of the death of Jesus Christ, as told by the Bible," I hold the opposite view. According to the definition of the political film I proposed in the introduction, *The Passion* undoubtedly belongs to the political film genre because its narrative structure features a subject/protagonist (Jesus) whose narrative object (salvaging human kind from sin) is situated in the political structure of a state (the power relations between the Romans, the Jewish leaders, and the Christians, which represent the new political power in Judea, and who were viewed with skepticism, if not hostility). The attainment of Jesus' object (salvation) will affect society as a whole in a positive or negative way (Christianity will create a better world through the dissemination of its key concept, love). Aside from these theoretical observations, which are analyzed further in the relevant chapter, the fact remains that in 2004 two hugely commercially successful political narratives dominated the US box office: *The Passion* and *Fahrenheit 9/11*. These two productions proved that (a) new information about "Saudi involvement in 9/11, suspicions about government and military incompetence, revelations that an invasion of Iraq had long been on the political agenda" led to reactionary films by filmmakers who resisted the media propaganda and the Bush agenda (Barker 2011: 6–7), and (b) politics could constitute a viable and profitable theme, even for mainstream Hollywood output.

Syriana was released a year after the 2004 election that saw President Bush in the White House for a second term. A film about oil politics is not a Hollywood favorite and, as the author of the memoir which provides the basis of the screenplay reveals, *Syriana* was finally produced only after Clooney and Damon gave up their salaries and billionaire entrepreneur Jeff Skoll got involved (in Alford 2010: 142), thus corroborating the difficulty political films face to get green lighted. The film was viewed as a liberal anti-Bush-Cheney narrative, which "critically engages the complexity of global politics, and the ways that US oil corporations, and intelligence and government agencies, intervene in the politics of the region, often in a destructive and utterly immoral fashion" (Kellner 2010: 164). As stated, Clooney won the Academy Award for Best Supporting Actor in 2006. However, although his speech included jokes and the traditional expression of gratitude, it also directly referred to the political nature of the film industry:

> And finally, I would say that, you know, we are a little bit out of touch in Hollywood every once in a while, I think. It's probably a good thing. We're the ones who talked about AIDS when it was just being whispered, and we talked about civil rights when it wasn't really popular. And we, you know, we bring up subjects, we are the ones—this Academy, this group of people gave Hattie McDaniel an Oscar in 1939 when blacks were still sitting in the backs of theaters. I'm proud to be a part of this Academy, proud to be part of this community, and proud to be out of touch. And I thank you so much for this.[3]

While Clooney was both attacked as smug and praised as progressive for the same speech, his words are a direct reflection of the ways Hollywood has functioned as a beacon for social critique and promotion of democratic ideals and values, ever since the birth of cinema. Although this particular Hollywood function has not led to the increase of pure political films, it is nevertheless apparent as a subtext in a staggering majority of the industry's output. The weak are always protected, justice must be served no matter what, civil rights are non-negotiable, and difference is celebrated. It is true that the narrative exploration of the above is sometimes reduced to simplistic binary oppositions; yet, I consider the dissemination of positive ideals through popular film as a plus. After all, Hollywood is part of the entertainment industry, and as such— and according to the definition of the verb "to entertain"—it aims to gratify and amuse, but also to "maintain in the mind" and "to receive and take into consideration."

However, there are authors who support that political films should go a step further than providing food for thought. Holloway (2008: 98), for instance, is critical of *Syriana*, despite finding it "smart and complex." He argues that its episodic structure "demanded the close attention of the viewer, but didn't always reward it," and, more importantly, that the multiple narrative foci reduced the film's many important subjects to "vague confirmations of half-formed truisms" (2008: 98). Among others, *Syriana* shows how the CIA can turn its back even on its own people when they cease to be of use: it includes scenes of torture in a harsh light, it speaks of blatant American intervention in the Middle East, and it uncovers illicit corporate transactions. It may be true that each of the subjects above would have been dealt with in more detail had the filmmakers opted for a single focal point but we should always bear in mind that this is a fictional narrative, a product that is sold worldwide to make a profit, while also providing enlightening information on political subjects not all viewers are knowledgeable about. Of course, as an observer and examiner of another nation's political history, and governmental policies, I do not have first-hand experience of events and situations. I can only hear about them in the news, read articles (both academic and popular), and watch relevant films and documentaries. Nevertheless, as the truth will always evade us, I have come to maintain that (a) we have to accept the limitations of fictional cinematic narratives regarding objectivity and in-depth analysis in the treatment of political subject matters, and, consequently, cease to rush to criticize possible inaccuracies, historical manipulation, and an absence of a holistic approach for a given subject, and (b) adopt a new interdisciplinary approach of examining these films, employing cinematic theory, sociology, and political science methods in order to uncover potential patterns and understand political films more fully.

Anchoring fiction to reality

Syriana, Breach, Fair Game, Green Zone, Argo, and *Zero Dark Thirty* recount events that have happened in real life using the conventions of the thriller genre. Making use of suspense, intrigue, and mystery, and adding fictional characters and/or minor events, they belong to the broader category of narrative fiction and cannot be considered as simple dramatizations of reality or documentaries. However, all the films anchor their fictional content to reality to a greater or lesser extent using news and/or archival footage, didactic voice-overs, and title cards that refer to actual historical events. Five of them choose to announce their link to reality at the very beginning of the narrative in an attempt to place the viewer in a semi-real cosmos and convince him that he/she is about to embark on a journey that has really taken place.

Narratively, the beginning of a cinematic text is paramount. Gardies (1993: 45) posits that "the beginning of films constitute a particularly important moment" as it "confirms the adopted narrative regime" and, sometimes, "fixes [...] the rules of the game." Thomas Elsaesser and Warren Buckland (2002: 47) note that film openings "pose the enigma, the dilemma, the paradox, to which the film as a whole will appear to give the answer, the resolution," and that they underline "the economy of mean(ings) with which a Hollywood opening prepares the stage and often presents (in a different form or code) the whole film in a nutshell." As I endeavor to show, the ways the political thrillers in question use "reality" in their opening segments has significant consequences for the rest of the narrative, regarding the ultimate meaning the filmmakers wish to convey to the viewers.

Before the title credits of *Zero Dark Thirty*, a title card appears with the phrase "The following motion picture is based on first hand accounts of actual events" in white letters on a black background. Then a title card reading "September 11, 2001" appears, while the viewer can only hear voices of reports and soon understands those are media journalists reporting the attacks on the World Trade Center. Media and police reports intertwine with actual calls from people in the towers—we hear an "I love you," and a distressed female voice talking to the police asking if help is on the way. The mixture of voices and the inability to listen properly conveys the chaotic circumstances of the day while reminding us of the harrowing, and still incomprehensible to some, tragedy. The strategic placement of this voice montage from 9/11 and, especially, the use of the personal calls from innocent victims, which were either messages of love to their loved ones, or filled with fear and panic, increases the emotional response of the viewers and makes them all the more eager to seek justice, if not retribution. Bigelow's choice in the beginning also makes it easier for the viewer on some level to accept the ensuing torture scenes and serves, as well, to justify US policies. *Green Zone* also begins with a black screen and voices reporting on air strikes and bombings, among loud sounds of sirens and explosions in Baghdad, in March 2003. The date is written on the screen to help pinpoint the time of the narrative, and the commencement of the Iraq War, before the last explosion sound is linked to the first scene of the film.

Fair Game begins with a cold open; that is, a scene that takes place before the credits. The scene is set in Kuala Lumpur, Malaysia. Valerie (Naomi Watts) is visiting with the nephew of a big pharmaceutical company's CEO, because the CIA suspects his uncle is in business with Arab terrorists. Valerie is there pretending she is an executive herself, seeking a joint business venture. That same night, she reveals her real identity to the young man and orders him to divulge any relevant information about his uncle, threatening him with the well-being of his brother. The credits begin and we see W. Bush and hear part of a 2002 speech regarding his efforts to convince America to go to yet another war:

> Tonight I want to take a few minutes to discuss a grave threat to peace and America's determination to lead the world in confronting that threat.

Bush's image is succeeded by another TV news report. It is 2003 and Attorney General John Ashcroft announces to the American people that the government has "raised the national threat level to 'orange,' indicating a 'high risk of terrorist attacks'" (CNN, 2003). A montage of media reports insisting on terrorizing US citizens with reports about Iraq, anthrax scares, highly likely terrorist attacks, and WMD ensues before the opening credits end and we see Valerie again. Even if the viewer is not informed about the true story, he/she understands the critique implied in the use of the archival material right from the start.

Breach also begins with a news clip of Attorney General Ashcroft, talking about the protagonist while the date, February 19, 2001, that appears on the shot, helps the viewer's orientation in time:

ASHCROFT: Sunday, the FBI successfully concluded an investigation to end a very serious breach in the security of the United States. The arrest of Robert Hanssen, for espionage, should remind us all, every American should know, that our nation, our free society, is an international target, in a dangerous world.

Argo's beginning is an almost two-minute history lesson that combines story-board panels and archival material in mainly black and white, contrasted with the colored sketches of the panel (news footage, and still photographs). The subject of the sequence is a brief history of Iran and its relationship with the USA, and the text below is narrated by a soothing female voice, reminiscent of a commonplace didactic documentary:

> This is the Persian empire, known today as Iran. For twenty-five hundred years this land was ruled by a series of kings, known as Shahs. In 1950, the people of Iran elected Mohammad Mossadegh, a secular democrat, as Prime Minister. He nationalized British and US petroleum holdings, returning Iran's oil to its people. But in 1953, the U.S. and Great Britain engineered a coup d'état that deposed Mossadegh and installed Reza Pahlavi as Shah. The young Shah was known for opulence and excess, his wife was rumored to bathe in milk, while the Shah had his lunches flown in by concord from Paris. The people starved. The Shah kept power through his ruthless internal police, the Savak. An era of torture and fear began: he then began a campaign to Westernize Iran, enraging a mostly traditional Shia population. In 1979, the people of Iran overthrew the Shah, the exiled cleric, Ayatollah Khomeini, returned to rule Iran. It descended into score settling, death squads and chaos. Dying of cancer, the Shah was given asylum in the U.S. The Iranian people took to the streets outside the U.S. Embassy, demanding that the Shah be returned, tried and hanged.

After a fade to black, we hear some voices and, once the next scene appears, we are immediately immersed in the riots that led to the 1979 hostage situation. Iranians are demonstrating outside the US embassy and an American flag is burning, while the US citizens inside the building are anxious. The first observation after the description of the films' openings is that they instantly help the viewers understand the main theme of the film, aside from familiarizing them with the time of the story's development, give or take a few years. Thus, the opening of *Zero Dark Thirty* indicates that the film will focus on 9/11, that *Breach* will examine the arrest of an American spy before 2003, that *Fair Game* will tell a story about the CIA and the time before the 2003 Iraq War, and, finally, that *Argo* will narrate the 1979–80 Iran hostage crisis. In addition, the insertion of real archival material (TV news clips, still photographs, sound bites, and documentary footage), which depicts mostly widely recognizable political figures and/or political events, leaves almost no doubt as to the political nature of the narrative. Thanouli (2013: 32) notes that in *Wag the Dog*, Levinson opens the film "from a non-diegetic level," showing a televised presidential spot, "underlining the mediated reality that lies beyond the characters' reach." By using a similar narrative stratagem (from TV news report to archival footage) in narratives that are based on true events—unlike the fictional universe of *Wag the Dog*—the political thrillers I am discussing here underscore the narrative's relationship to reality. Yet, this reality is not "beyond the characters' reach," but provides the context within which the characters will act and the plot of the film will unfold. In addition, the incorporation of archival material, which constitutes de facto historical evidence, functions as an empowering device of the story, leading to an increased emotional engagement from the viewer. In other words, this material is an "actant," providing the context of the story (the time, the place, and other useful information), replacing a possible extra-diegetic third-person narrator. *Wag the Dog* also closes with another link of the narrative to real life. Interestingly, only two out of the six political thrillers follow suit. However, most endings are strikingly similar in execution, leading to interesting conclusions regarding their sociopolitical message. The images in Figures 52 to 57 are taken from the last fictional scenes of the films.

Zero Dark Thirty, *Breach*, and *Fair Game* end with close-ups of the protagonists. *Zero Dark Thirty* follows a decade of US efforts to find Osama bin Laden that culminate in his death by Navy SEALs in May 2011. After bin Laden's demise toward the end of the film, Maya (Jessica Chastain), the CIA officer and protagonist of the film, and one of the key individuals that led to the success of the mission, boards a US military transport. She enters alone, sits down, puts her seatbelt on and asks to go home. Then, the camera closes on her face and she starts weeping before the film ends and the scene fades to black (Figure 52). In *Breach*, Eric O'Neill (Ryan Phillippe), the young FBI employee who helped uncover his superior, agent Robert Hanssen (Chris Cooper) as a traitor, is seen gathering his things from his office. While he is waiting for the elevator, the doors open and he sees his boss with two agents on his left and right sides. Hanssen seems distraught and his face is all red. The two men look at each other and Hanssen asks Eric to pray for him, with the young agent agreeing to do so. The camera zooms in on Eric's face (Figure 53), the last person we see on screen before the elevator doors close on us as well as the narrative. However, before the final credits begin, four title cards succeed one another providing the viewer

Figures 52–57 (Left to right, top to bottom) Still frames from last shots of *Zero Dark Thirty, Breach, Fair Game, Syriana, Green Zone,* and *Argo.*

with information about the outcome of Hanssen's trial, his sentence, and the consequences of his actions, as well as information about O'Neill's life.

Fair Game ends with Valerie testifying in front of a congressional committee (Figure 54) about the scandal she is implicated in. As she begins her testimony, the scene fades to black and we hear the sound of a camera shutter. While we still watch a black screen, we hear the continuation of Valerie's phrase. This time, however, as the scene fades in, we see a TV clip of the real Valerie's testimony on C-Span, while title cards on the left side provide us with more information about the investigation (how the Chief of Staff to the Vice President, Scooter Libby, was convicted, how President Bush used his executive authority to commute the sentence, how Deputy Secretary of State admitted to being a source of the leak in 2006, and how the leak was orchestrated by the White House) before the end credits roll with Valerie still testifying. Her TV clip stops with Valerie's phrase: "I loved my career because I love my country. I was proud of the serious responsibilities entrusted to me as a CIA covert operations officer."

Syriana may end with a shot of one of the main characters but, this time, it is a long shot. Attorney Bennett Holiday (Jeffrey Wright) is returning home from work at night in a Washington neighborhood (Figure 55). As mentioned, *Syriana* is a multi-focused narrative which examines how far the United States can go in order to secure petroleum. From the five different perspectives, the filmmakers opt to end their story with Holiday. Having assisted the merger of a giant US oil corporation with a smaller one that had acquired drilling rights in Kazakhstan by essentially concealing any indication of wrongdoing, Holiday stands as a symbol of a state that will bend the rules and stretch its ethics in order to obtain its object. The character began the narrative as a diligent professional but, by the end, succumbs to the powers that control the market and the government as well as solving some personal issues. Thus, despite the critique the film includes regarding oil relations between the United States and the Arab world, as well as other countries with oil resources, the ending is a rather somber realization of the continuation of corruption, betrayal, and greed. *Green Zone* ends with a shot of an oil facility in Iraq (Figure 56), as Miller is driving along the road with his team in a military convoy. In the previous scene, Miller has just emailed his report about the nonexistence of WMD in Iraq to a US media correspondent in Baghdad, as well as other journalists in the United States, since Pentagon officials and other military personnel would not tell the truth to the American people. Similar to *Syriana*, the last shot of the oil plant in *Green Zone* not only depicts an Iraqi product but directly links the 2003 American military involvement to the nation's need for petroleum.

Thus, five films begin by anchoring their narratives to real events and end by using close-ups of the "good" character, the one who solves the narrative equation and brings peace, justice, or just a temporary cease-fire, to the political and institutional conflicts that preceded it. In *Zero Dark Thirty* and *Argo*, films where the CIA was involved during production, the Agency's officers are portrayed in a positive light, unlike the political thrillers, which were based on novels. Regarding *Zero Dark Thirty*'s relationship with the CIA in preproduction, Haas, Christensen, and Haas (2015, 249) remark that "[i]n addition to arranging a meeting between the film's screenwriter, Mark Boal, and the real-life operatives most responsible for the mission's success, the CIA also provided Boal with a tour of the vault where the raid was planned," while they also shared "a mockup of the Abbottabad compound where bin Laden was killed." The authors further add that the public sensation triggered by the film led to "a U.S. Senate intelligence committee" that "investigated whether the degree of access the filmmakers enjoyed was appropriate," which ended when "the film got shut out on Oscar night" (2015: 249). Much controversy was also caused by the representation of torture, but the filmmakers publicly denied that they supported such practices. After all, I would argue that the inclusion of genuine phone calls from people who tragically lost their lives in the beginning of the film, in a way, justified and normalized the use of "enhanced interrogation techniques," as the ultimate goal was to find and punish bin Laden.

Argo's last shot (Figure 57) differs in that respect and offers an intriguing perspective. After the successful mission of the CIA, Tony Mendez (Affleck), the CIA agent who concocted the plan of having the hostages pretend they belong to a Hollywood film crew scouting locations for a science-fiction film, returns home and is lying in bed with his son. The camera then zooms out and pans on a shelf across the two characters, where the little boy rests his action figures, most of which are replicas of film characters. Then, the camera stops and zooms in on a storyboard panel from the fictional film *Argo*, which Tony decided to keep in secret, and not submit to the CIA archives, as a memento of how his idea helped save the lives of his fellow citizens. The end credits present all the characters next to photographs of the real people involved in the hostage crisis, as well as side-by-side pictures of the real events and their representation in the film, and, finally, two pictures of the iconic, yet at the time broken, Hollywood sign above the Hollywood Hills in the 1970s.[4] The astonishing similarity between the photographs of real people and events and their fictional counterparts further blurs the boundaries between fiction and reality in the digital era. In a way, the side-by-side comparisons tell us that almost no manipulation was involved in the making of this historical film, and the choice of photographs is very convincing. The last shot of the storyboard panel, combined with the photograph of the Hollywood sign, however, is a clear indication of the importance the filmmakers place in the industry and its role in a real political conflict. As Haas, Christensen, and Haas (2015: 254) note, Hollywood "looks good" in *Argo*, "especially with the acting abilities of John Goodman and Alan Arkin, who portray the Hollywood professionals who are responsible for *Argo*—from its inception, to its storyboard, casting, script, and even advertising campaign," to help Mendez be as convincing as possible as the film's producer. Indeed, a significant part of the film has Mendez consult with Hollywood people in order to prepare the plan in its most minute detail. This movie-within-the-movie trope empowers Hollywood and solidifies the role it played in the ensuing rescuing mission. It is no accident that Affleck chooses a purely cinematic shot (that of the storyboard panel) to end his narrative. Leaving the viewer with a reminder of Hollywood's involvement in the plot at the end—as many viewers can choose to leave the theater during the end credits or turn off their TV or laptop, once the credits start rolling and miss the extra information provided—Affleck underscores Hollywood's power within a narrative produced within the film industry, therefore enforcing and perpetuating its global dominance.

From G. W. Bush to Obama

Aside from *Syriana* and *Breach*, *Green Zone*, *Fair Game*, *Zero Dark Thirty*, and *Argo* were released after Barack Obama became the resident of the White House for a second term. Interestingly, my corpus does not include a single political thriller based on true events during the Bush–Cheney years which, on the other hand, witnessed the release of several political thrillers adapted from novels or based on original screenplays. The initial shock of 9/11 and the subsequent Hollywood–US government collaboration, already considered above, is the first reason why the film industry stayed away from controversial subjects and instead opted to offer its critique of US politics using entirely fictional narratives. In addition, time is a crucial factor when one films a historical event that has recently occurred, as "historical distance between events and representation, intrinsic to the historical film, brings the potential for fresh appraisals" (Hillman 2013: 328). As I have noted in the introduction, the first fictional films to focus on 9/11 were Stone's *World Trade Center*, and Greengrass's *United 93* (both released in 2006). Nevertheless, despite the directors' reputation as politically engaged filmmakers, and the subject of their films, neither can be considered a political film as both narratives choose to concentrate on the courage and heroism of ordinary people in the face of a catastrophe about which they know nothing. Consequently, it is not just a new commander-in-chief that "allowed" overtly political films in the late 2000s and 2010s, but also the passing of time, which carries a healing power and also provides suitable circumstances for such films to be produced, released, and even reap a profit. What is more, most films that are set during the Bush administration explicitly criticize its policies—whether it is oil dependency (*Syriana*), CIA corruption (*Syriana* and

Fair Game), or using a fake excuse to go into war and lying to the American people (*Fair Game* and *Green Zone*). To my knowledge, and to this date, no fictional cinematic narrative includes criticism of the Obama administration. *Zero Dark Thirty* has indeed been attacked for partisanship as the filmmakers had unprecedented "access to officials in the Obama White House, the CIA, and the Pentagon," and it has even been credited for helping the sitting President with his 2012 re-election. However, the fact of the matter is that the death of Osama bin Laden under President Obama will, in all probability, be historically considered as one of his greatest achievements (Haas et al. 2015: 248).

4

Political History Dramas and
US Domestic Policy

In the corpus, US domestic policies are predominantly represented by political dramas and/or biopics that refer to past historical events (*Good Night, and Good Luck*; *Flags of Our Fathers*; *Milk*; *The Conspirator*; *Lincoln*), two fictional dramas (*The Life of David Gale*; *The Ides of March*), and two action/thrillers (*xXx: State of the Union*; *State of Play*). Historical dramas, or "dramatic feature films," as Robert A. Rosenstone (2012: 18) labels films that "reach a wide audience and sometimes become the focus of public debate about history," dominate this subcategory in my corpus. They also constitute films that were among the best films of their release years, garnering critical acclaim, a host of awards, and accolades, while their majority also enjoyed substantial financial returns.

Good Night, and Good Luck, directed by Clooney, and cowritten by Clooney and Grant Heslov, was nominated for six Academy Awards while earning more than $54.5 million worldwide on a modest $7 million budget. *Good Night, and Good Luck* belongs to a very limited group of films that focus on the dark period of McCarthyism, and M. Keith Booker (2007: 84) argues that it is one of the finest examples of cinematic representation of this era. The film "focuses on the historic televised clash between McCarthy and distinguished CBS news commentator Edward R. Murrow that occurred after Murrow critiqued McCarthy and his methods on his *See It Now* weekly news show in March of 1954." Booker also notes that "*Good Night, and Good Luck* is as much about the rise of television as a political force in America in the 1950s, as it is about McCarthyism" (2007: 84). I agree with this remark, but I should add that insofar as Murrow, as a political subject, tries to expose Senator McCarthy to his American viewers, so that his actions are stopped and so that society is liberated from unjust witch hunts, then his is a political praxis with considerable political ramifications. Therefore, I consider Clooney's second directorial feature a political film per se, despite its obvious commentary on the importance of the television medium.

Milk won two Academy Awards (Best Actor, and Best Original Screenplay) among eight nominations, and returned $54.5 million on a $20 million budget. *Milk* is based on the real story of politician Harvey Milk, the first openly homosexual man to be elected in 1977 to public office, as a member of the San Francisco Board of Supervisors in California. The film chronicles Milk's move from New York to San Francisco, his personal life and relationships, his growing activism, his gradual entrance into politics, and his eventual victory and placement in the San Francisco Board of Supervisors. The filmmaker centers around Milk's tenacious effort to stop Proposition 6 in 1978, which aimed to ban homosexual teachers from working in California schools, and ends with his and San Franscisco mayor's assassination by Dan White, a political antagonist. In 2011 and 2012, two period films revolving around the same political figure and his time, namely President Lincoln, were released. Robert Redford's *The Conspirator*, and Steven Spielberg's *Lincoln*. While the first did not do well at the box office, with only $15 million in ticket sales on a $25 million budget, the second caused a media sensation seven months later (November 2012), garnered an impressive number of twelve Oscar nominations (it finally won two), and returned more than $275 million, while costing $65 million, thus placing it at number thirteen in the annual US box office. The contrasting reception of the two period films, crafted by well-known directors and including a stellar cast, can only be explained if one describes the perspective each filmmaker chose to satisfy his vision.

Redford's film focuses on the aftermath of Lincoln's assassination and the trial of Mary Surratt (Robin Wright), the woman who was charged with conspiring to kill the president and was executed soon after a speedy trial. Spielberg's *Lincoln*, on the other hand, involves the President's political efforts to have the Thirteenth Amendment passed, which would legally abolish slavery. Redford's point of view, and subsequent portrayal of the events after Lincoln's death, focused on a part of the Lincoln myth that is not frequently discussed, or known for that matter, and was investigatory and accusatory at times. As Kate Clifford Larson (2010: x) notes, *The Conspirator* "captures the vengeful mood of that time, and conveys an emotionally charged, fascinating story virtually unknown to Americans today." On the other hand, Spielberg maintains an admiring and almost reverent stance towards his subject throughout the film, following a cinematic tradition that depicts Lincoln as "benevolent, compassionate, honorable, sensible, good humored, and fatherly" (Hogan 2011: 58). In addition, while Spielberg's film closes with the passing of the amendment and the exhilaration felt by both those who fought for it as well as by ordinary citizens of the time, Redford's ending depicts the execution of Surratt and the other conspirators, and the disillusionment felt by Surratt's attorney Frederick Aiken (James McAvoy) with the blatant intervention of politics into the judicial system. *The Conspirator*'s ending clashes with Hollywood's long-lasting tradition of a happy ending, and can therefore be jarring to the viewer who may feel that the catharsis he/she is so used to will not come. As Walter Metz (2004, 12) notes, "classical Hollywood cinema 'tames' death, either through happy endings in which death is averted, or redemptive endings in which the characters' ultimate sacrifices are made meaningful by their ability to help others." Surratt's death marks what Catherine Russell (1995: 6) calls the "mortification" of the narrative, which she defines as follows:

> Cinematic mortification refers to the killing of the "eternal present tense" of cinematic realism, and is both an act of critical viewing and a stylistic effect of filmmaking. Narrative mortality refers to the effect of mortification on the construction of desire and temporality in narrative cinema [...] It allows cinematic narrative to move beyond the pleasure of "meaning" and toward other pleasures that lie beyond representation, beyond the end of the film and the known limits of history.

Although Russell's work focuses on Hollywood's desire for joyous endings and the various New Waves' subversion of classical norms through mortification, there are also US productions—such as *The Conspirator*—and even mainstream Hollywood films—however infrequent[1]—that choose to mortify their narrative, and show that just as in death in real life, cinematic death can be inescapable "and rarely possesses [any] transcendent meaning" (Metz 2004: 12). However, aside from *The Conspirator*, two other films of this chapter, *The Life of David Gale* and *Milk*, deal with characters who eventually die. However, these two narratives opt to structure their plot with the use of flashbacks while they begin just a little while before their protagonists die. However, in these two cases, we cannot talk about mortification. As Russell (1995: 7) observes, a conventional trope of depiction of death in classical Hollywood "is the familiar narrative structure that opens with the death to which the narrative will return." In this way, "at the end of a film, death has an ostensible authorization of 'meaning,' uniting the film's imagery into a single figuration of identity." I believe that the difference in representing historical events (using an openly positive angle in the case of Spielberg's film and adopting a critical and, at times, accusatory view in the case of Redford's film) is the main reason, combined with distribution and marketing parameters, that led to the effacement of Redford's film and the triumph of Spielberg's.

State of Play is a political thriller, based on the same-titled 2003 BBC mini-series, directed by Kevin Macdonald and adapted by Matthew Michael Carnahan and Tony Gilroy. The film follows the tradition of the 1970s investigative journalism films (*The Parallax View* [1974], *All The President's Men* [1976], *China Syndrome* [1979]) and tells the story of how DC journalist Cal McAffrey (Russell Crowe) reveals the involvement of a Congressman and old friend Stephen Collins (Ben Affleck) in the murder of the latter's female researcher, in the context of a congressional hearing on a huge corporation's mercenary activities in both the United States and abroad, and especially the Middle East. The reviews were rather positive but the film did not do well at the box office, amassing $87 million on a budget of $60 million, despite the star quality of the two main male actors. Finally, *xXx: State of the Union* (sequel to the commercial success of *xXx*, 2002) is a political action film, centering around a new agent of the special xXx program who goes to Washington to stop the plan of a military team to overthrow the US government. *xXx: State of the Union* is the only film in the corpus that is considered a very badly written and badly directed film. The average to mostly negative reviews called the film from "[s]o primitive, it must have been written in lizard blood on animal skin" (Hunter 2005), "one of the most absurd of all big-budget action movies" (Arnold 2005a), to "[l]oud, dumb and obnoxious" (O'Sullivan 2005). This film brings to mind the methods and criteria based on which theorists and researchers proceed to compile corpuses of films by genre, and in particular the question of quality. To this end, Altman (2006: 217) refers to an instructive example, a conversation between two film theorists:

> "I mean, what do you do with Elvis Presley films? You can hardly call them musicals."
> "Why not? They're loaded with songs and they've got a narrative that ties the numbers together, don't they?"
> "Yeah, I suppose. I guess you'd have to call *Fun in Acapulco* a musical, but it's sure no *Singin' in the Rain*. Now there's a real musical."

Altman uses this example to stress the dichotomy between inclusive and exclusive genre lists and to make a case for bypassing the quality criterion by semiotics, which examines structures and patterns irrespective of historical circumstances or qualitative criteria. I reiterate Altman's passage because my thesis is that, first, a theorist should not differentiate between "bad" and "good" genre examples while amassing a genre corpus, and that if a given film fits the preset criteria, exclusion should not be an option. Second, since quality is rather difficult to define—frankly, how does one measure the quality of film? Is it the production values? The awards? The actors' skills? The cinematographer's abilities? The screenplay's originality? An overwhelming audience reception? A media consensus? The questions could go on and on. Since quality criteria may change over time, a corpus can only be as objective, and complete as possible if such questions stay out of the equation. After all, the simple fact that *xXx: State of The Union* is the only film in the corpus that features an African-American protagonist, and one of the very few paradigms where the filmmakers have directly stated they intended to make a political film (Fuchs 2005), merits theoretical attention.

History manipulation and narrative consequences

With the exception of *State of Play*, *The Life of David Gale*, and *xXx: State of the Union*, which are set in the present, the rest of the films focusing on US domestic policies are historical dramas, set in different time periods. The stories of *Lincoln*, and *The Conspirator*, *Good Night, and Good Luck*, and *Milk* unfold respectively in the 1860s, the 1950s, and the 1970s. As such, they vary greatly as they all take great pains to authentically represent their narrative time. Clothes, hairstyles, settings, furniture, behaviors, as well as specific cinematography choices, lead to distinct aesthetics. After all, authenticity is one of the key elements of historical films (Stubbs 2013; Schaff 2004), and a rather debated term in the academic film of history and film.

Yet, the aura of authenticity created by these films is a significant isotopy, that creates the suitable atmosphere and corresponds to the historical and/or cultural assumptions, or the personal experience the viewers may have of the depicted era. Rosenstone (2012: 53) remarks that the history film "gives us the 'look' of the past, of buildings, landscapes, costumes, and artifacts. It provides a sense of how common objects appeared when they were part of people's lives and in daily use." Thus, the experience of the history moving picture, combined with the sound, the dialogue, the music, and the rest of the cinematic codes,

Figures 58–61 Fictional representation vs. reality.

can become a more powerful means of learning about the past than reading a descriptive passage about a specific piece of clothing in a book, or even seeing it in a museum.

Although the films cannot be compared regarding their representation of time, they do share a number of isotopies. First, they are the stories of men who defy the conventions and rules of their time, and struggle to make the world a better place for future generations through political praxis. As noted in the previous chapter, the "cult" of individualism is the basis of American ideology and constitutes the narrative core of both classical and contemporary Hollywood in innumerable representations and almost every imaginable genre. Regarding politics, Gianos (1998: 170) observes that "[w]hile scholars avoid writing of politics in terms of the actions of 'great men' (and women), the creators of fiction do not. The story is better that way." Gianos adds that there are examples of national cinemas that did not emphasize a single person as the main narrative element. The author refers to specific films of silent Soviet cinema, which rather "emphasized the collective," and "not the individual." However, Gianos rightly claims that this focus on the collective was not only ideological but was also based on technical requirements and financial limitations. As he explains, "the camera was immobile and it was easier to film groups of people, not individuals," and "early film producers were resistant to celebrate individual actors and then have to pay them more, as they eventually ended up doing" (Gianos 1998: 170). It is important that Gianos refers to the reasons behind the "collective protagonist" of earlier films because, more often than not, great cinematic movements and/or genres began their life exactly because of practical necessities and not as theoretically sound, meticulously planned, or aesthetically choreographed systems.

For instance, the first black and white film noirs of the 1940s were initially considered B movies because of their small budget, which led to their use of interior spaces with low lighting, creating an expressionist atmosphere, which was later analyzed as connotative of specific aesthetic aims, and was preserved in later noirs with much bigger budgets. Similar financial difficulties gave birth to the distinct aesthetic and documentary feel of the first Italian neorealist films during and after the Second World War. Insofar as these films were considered both critical and commercial successes, their style was maintained, thus creating a special group of films, worthy of critical and theoretical examination. Although this book does not aim at a historical study of all the parameters that give birth to genres and/or film movements, it is useful to stress the great importance of financial and production circumstances that are often neglected in film studies.

Second, as historical dramas usually invite scrutiny over erroneous representations, and historical manipulation, it is interesting to examine if and how these "mistakes" affect the narrative. President Abraham Lincoln, attorney-at-law Frederick Aiken, journalist Edward F. Murrow, and City Supervisor Harvey Milk are the main protagonists of the historical dramas that are based on real events. They are all represented as intelligent, politically proficient individuals with unquestionable integrity. Their narrative goal is a task which will have significant consequences over the nation. Lincoln wants to pass legislation to free the slaves, Aiken wants Mary Surratt to be tried fairly, Murrow wants to discredit Senator McCarthy and expose him as an unjust oppressor, and Milk wants to defeat Proposition 6, which aims to ban homosexuals from working in California's public schools. Lincoln, Aiken, Murrow, and Milk face great opposition, which narratively takes the form of a "hostile" individual. Thus, Lincoln's "enemy" is chairman of the Ways and Means Committee Thaddeus Stevens (Tommy Lee Jones), Aiken's opponents are Secretary of War Edwin Stanton (Kevin Kline) and his deputy, Judge Advocate General Joseph Holt (Danny Huston), Murrow's "enemy" is Senator McCarthy, and Milk's adversary is City Supervisor Dan White (Josh Brolin).

In his article on the historical deviations, and/or appropriations of *Lincoln*, historian Joshua Zeitz (2012) notes:

Lincoln also follows the motives and machinations of Thaddeus Stevens, the stern, steely eyed chairman of the Ways and Means Committee, a position that in the 19th century doubled as House Majority Leader. He was 'the dictator of the house'—a zealot in the cause of freedom and racial equality [...]. In life, Stevens had little patience for Lincoln, whom he viewed as a temporizing moderate. In Spielberg's movie, he is the president's sworn enemy, cautiously willing to drop his armor and work with the president to abolish slavery.

Similarly, in *The Nation*'s informative article, Richard Kreitner argues that Spielberg underestimated Stevens's contribution and remarks:

Despite the inarguable fact that the Thirteenth Amendment was made possible by principled Americans like Stevens, it is only when those principles are temporarily abandoned, or at least modified, that the film allows Stevens even a fraction of the hero-worship ritually granted to compulsive grand bargainers like George Washington, Abraham Lincoln and our own contemporary compromiser-in-chief. (Kreitner 2012)

In *The Conspirator*, Aiken has to face the stern Secretary of War Stanton, who desires a swift trial and conviction of Mary Surratt and the rest of the implicated conspirators, and Stanton's deputy, Judge Advocate General Joseph Holt. Historian Elizabeth D. Leonard, who was commissioned by the film's production company to review the screenplay, provided her criticism, writing that one of her concerns was that Surratt was portrayed "as the innocent, motherly representative of the poor, vanquished Confederacy, and the federal government—particularly through the characters of Edwin Stanton and Joseph Holt—as the purely vengeful, bullying victor, determined, for whatever reason, to continue punishing its now helpless and compliant former enemy" (Leonard 2011). Leonard notes that although the production company did take some of her suggestions under consideration and did correct specific details (such as Holt's title) or even scenes (a seduction scene between Aiken and Surratt was deleted), some problems remained, especially regarding the representation of Surratt as an innocent victim and Holt as a true villain. Leonard explains:

Along with Kevin Kline's Edwin Stanton, Danny Huston's Holt ends up playing a villain perhaps even more unsavory than John Wilkes Booth, who at least gets credit for having a moral compass, even if one disagrees with his devotion to the Confederacy. The fictionalized Holt, however, is caricatured as a grinning but cynical, malevolent scoundrel. He not only has the commissioners (and all of the key) witnesses in his pocket but also shapes the trial as he sees fit—justice be damned—for no other reason than to inflict even more punishment on this broken-hearted representative of the already subjugated South which, one is encouraged to assume, was eager for peace and reconciliation with the North.

Historian Patrick Browne (2011) also adds:

> The character of Secretary of War Edwin Stanton (who did, in fact, want this trial to be prosecuted as quickly as possible) was written as so two-dimensionally authoritarian that he might have been cartoonish were it not for Kevin Kline's salvaging of the role.

The above historians' remarks as to the possible misrepresentations of characters and events in Redford's film, as well as their acknowledgment of the things the filmmaking team got right, point to the inherent difficulties cinema faces vis-à-vis the history film. For instance, how can a cinematic secondary character, such as Edwin Stanton, achieve a three-dimensionality when he only appears in a couple of scenes? How many, and which historical sources—taking into consideration that a single historical event usually invites a great number of historical accounts, even contradictory ones—should a filmmaking team consult during preproduction? It becomes clear that almost no history film can satisfy historians in its entirety. However, I would argue that staying truthful to historical written accounts is also problematic because the truth will always evade us. What I would suggest we ask from the history film is to depict its central narrative conflict with as much historical accuracy as is afforded to its production, since the time limitations of a given film do not allow for the development of all secondary plots/events that lead up to the climax. In other words, the story Redford wanted to share with the audience was the unjust way Surratt was tried after Lincoln's assassination, and her standing in front of a military tribunal while being a civilian. And regarding this event, there is no misrepresentation but a careful reconstruction of the actual events. Of course, historians should note the possible mistakes a history film narrative includes, but also preferably bear in mind the many instances most history films actually deliver a sliver of the past to modern audiences in a way the written word cannot accomplish.

In contrast to *Lincoln* and *The Conspirator*, there are no historical changes regarding the villain, Senator McCarthy, in *Good Night, and Good Luck*. In fact, the filmmaking team even opted not to hire an actor, but include real news footage of the Senator in the film. However, *Good Night, and Good Luck* implies that Murrow and his team in his news program, *See it Now* (CBS, 1951–8), are responsible for the eventual demise of the Senator and the end of the notorious witch hunt. According to Tobias Hochscherf and Christoph Laucht (2012), the absence of sociopolitical contextualization—used to accentuate the dynamic between the honorable Murrow and the despicable Senator—reduces the film to a simplified story. Not only were there others who voiced their opposition to McCarthy's practices but the complete absence, or even mention, of significant events of the time, such as "[t]he first test of a Soviet atom bomb, […] the Rosenbergs, the 'loss' of China to Mao Zedong as well as the outbreak of the Korean War," fails to explain the general crisis the nation was experiencing, and results in a narrative that "is like a child's view of these events, untroubled by complexity, hungry for myth and simplicity" (Hochscherf and Laucht 2012).

In *Milk*, the eponymous politician is assassinated by his colleague, City Supervisor Dan White. The narrative portrays Dan as a homophobe and also alludes to him being a closeted homosexual, thus explaining his hostility towards Milk. However, after talking with White's former campaign manager, adviser and friend Ray Sloan, writer John Geluardi (2008) notes some discrepancies. "Sloan says that over the past thirty years, White has been falsely portrayed as a murderous homophobe in order to enhance Milk's legendary status as the most important gay rights leader in American history. But Sloan says White was not at all homophobic." After all, Sloan's homosexuality should have prevented Dan from forming such a close relationship with him. But, as Geluardi (2008) observes, if this was included in the narrative it would certainly create "a problem for the film's premise." Geluardi adds:

> Many historical facts about White were conveniently left out of the movie. After watching the film, you would never know that Dan White supported nearly all of Milk's gay-friendly resolutions, he willingly contributed money to fight the Briggs Initiative, and he used his influence with Board of Supervisors President Dianne Feinstein to get Milk appointed to two important committees. At the time, Milk's legislative aide Dick Pabich told a gay newspaper that White "supported us on every position and he goes out of his way to find what gay people think about things."

The above historical manipulations serve a significant narrative purpose. They enforce the personality of the central character and accentuate the binary opposition between him and his evil opponent. Of course, Lincoln, Aiken,

Murrow, and Milk are depicted as political individuals beyond reproach, regardless of their narrative adversary. However, the filmmakers' choices to omit aspects of the cinematic villains' lives have three important consequences regarding the final story and its reception: first, they simplify the narrative, transforming it into fable or a myth of the righteous individual who brings justice for all despite all odds and amidst fervent opposition. Second, the effacement of the complexities that the political decisions of this nature entail—such as whipping votes to pass a revolutionary amendment in Congress, defeat a discriminatory proposition in the City Council, insist on a fair trial while powerful members of the political establishment are against you, or expose a powerful politician through a TV show and turn a whole nation against him—reduces history itself to a series of events helmed by a single individual who is above all others. Third, the quasi-sanctification of the films' central character may lead to a false interpretation and/or representation of the real events, thus decreasing the ability of cinema to serve as a potential pedagogical tool. On the other hand, I should note that all the references regarding historical inaccuracies and/or omissions mentioned above, conclude with a final, positive assessment of the films:

Lincoln is not a perfect film, but it is an important film. (Zeitz 2012)

So, in all, a film well worth seeing. And, despite my issues with its message, I do think this is the best Civil War film made in many, many years. (Browne 2011, on *The Conspirator*)

Notwithstanding all controversy surrounding *Good Night, and Good Luck* and justified criticism directed against the tendency to represent a complex era simplistically, the film portrays some basic and timeless democratic values held in high regards by Democrats and Republicans alike. (Hochscherf and Laucht 2012)

[...] Sloan acknowledged the movie was powerful and that most of the events and characters were spot on, particularly actor Brandon Bryce's portrayal of Milk's political consultant, Jim Rivaldo, who was a close friend of Sloan's. (Geluardi 2008)

Sociopolitical relevance

Rosenstone (2012: xv) observes that "a great number of scholars from many disciplines write as if history films are not really about the past," and that their work underlines how history films use the past to comment on contemporary sociopolitical conflicts. Although Rosenstone is more interested in how history films engage with the past, he does acknowledge that history "is written or filmed in the present, and the mark of the contemporary is on every work we produce" (2012: xvi). Therefore, as parts of an ongoing cultural dialogue, the four history films of this chapter not only bring to life significant events from American history but also allude critically to specific sociopolitical circumstances that occurred during their time of production.

For instance, *Lincoln* had its premiere in October 2012 at the New York Film Festival, less than a month before the presidential election, and its limited release a few days after the election which gave Obama a second term. All this took place in a year rightly called by Haas, Christensen, and Haas (2015: 248) as "the year of the political film," since it witnessed important political narratives, such as *Argo* and *Zero Dark Thirty*, which met with universal success. In his analysis of the film, Zeitz (2012) likens the sixteenth President to Obama. Not only is Lincoln Obama's favorite President but, just like him, Obama "opened his first national campaign on the steps of the Illinois State Capitol, the building where Lincoln delivered his famous 'House Divided' speech," "served several years in the Illinois state legislature," and was "elected to one term in Congress before improbably ascending to the presidency." Zeitz (2012) notes that some historians view "Lincoln as a great conciliator," and that "Barack Obama has aspired to rise above politics and forge unity in a sharply divided polity." Based on these similarities, one could argue that Spielberg's film has a political message that transcends the historical representation of the legal abolition of slavery, aiming to unite a country traumatized by a shocking attack, terrorized by an eight-year administration that focused on spreading fear, a war that was based on fictitious evidence, and a financial crisis that threatened both domestic and global stability.

In a way, *Lincoln*'s screenwriter, Tony Kushner, corroborates the thesis above when he states:

Watching the Obama presidency through the lens of Lincoln has been a transformative thing for me. I think Barack Obama is a great president. I won't say that he's as great as Lincoln. I don't know if there'll ever be a president as great as Abraham Lincoln. But I think Obama inherited a mess as formidable as the mess that FDR inherited when he came into Washington during the Great Depression. Progressive people have not been patient enough, and thoughtful enough, in our criticisms of him. I feel it's been a blessing to be thinking about Lincoln the whole time. Lincoln reminds you that great good can come from compromise, and always from politics. (Koslow 2012)

While *Lincoln* has a positive message for both the past and the present, *The Conspirator* is more insistent on the darker aspect of politics. The representation of the intrusion of political figures in the Surratt trial, especially her being tried by a military tribunal and not a civilian one, and the instances of obstruction of justice depicted in the narrative, were viewed by some as a commentary against the Bush administration after 9/11 (see Browne [2011], Briley [2011], and Ann Hornaday [2011]). In addition, most articles and critiques directed at Redford's film focuses on the absence of the issue of slavery, the main cause of the American Civil War (Briley 2011; Grossman 2011; Scheuneman 2011). The viewer is never informed of Surratt's own slaves, nor are slaves depicted in the narrative. Nevertheless, Redford's focus is on Surratt's trial, and in particular on questions of legality, such as her right to be tried by a civilian court, the overriding of due process, and the admission of selective evidence during the trial. While Surratt was charged with conspiring to assassinate Lincoln, Redford concentrates on how politicians and the military court conspired to find her guilty. After all, as Scheuneman (2011) notes, "[O]ne year after the Mary Surratt trial, the Supreme Court ruled it unconstitutional for civilians to be tried in military tribunals, and a year after that, John Surratt was captured, tried in a civilian court, and found innocent of being involved in the assassination." *The Conspirator*'s emphasis on the murky judicial process, and its representation of political figures as one-sided, harsh, and even indifferent to law, do indeed remind the viewer of some of the tactics used during the Bush–Cheney administration. Redford may have chosen to omit aspects of the story in order to draw parallels between 1865 and the post-9/11 era, but that does not mean the film is not also an instructive part of the Lincoln myth most viewers are not even taught at school. It may not be a "happy" or redemptive story but, nevertheless, a story that should be told.

Similarly, a number of scholars (see Frank Krutnik et al. [2007], Kellner [2010], and Holloway [2008]) suggest that *Good Night, and Good Luck* is more than just one of the few films that center on the McCarthy witch hunts. The authors claim that the film draws "parallels between the post-9/11 culture of repression and that of the early Cold War era" (Krutnik et al. 2007: 17) during which the film is set. Murrow is represented as a beacon of integrity and a journalist who aims to reveal the truth, as is his ethical obligation. Kellner (2010: 28) adds that *Good Night, and Good Luck* criticizes a "rightwing extremist regime that had attempted to politicize government agencies from the Justice Department to the Environmental Protection Agency (EPA), and which imprisoned without trial those it deemed enemies under the so-called USA Patriot Act." Stating that the film can be read as an allegory regarding contemporary politics is corroborated by its director and his public comments. As Krutnik et al. (2007: 17) note, Clooney "has emphasized [...] that Murrow's principled pursuit of truth is sorely lacking today because the U.S. media has been cowed into submission by the emotive and Manichean agenda of the war on terror." Thus, the film's intent is not only to represent a cinematically underused historical period, but also to provide commentary on the gradual demise of television as a political force during the Bush–Cheney Administration.

The greatest political achievement of Milk, aside from being the first openly homosexual man to be elected to public office, was the defeat of Proposition 6. Initiated by Republican state legislator John Briggs, Proposition 6 would ban homosexual teachers, as well as individuals who supported homosexuals, from all educational facilities in the state of California. *Milk* is one of the few mainstream Hollywood films that focus on a homosexual character and his life. The film was released domestically twenty-four days after the passage of Proposition 8, which eliminated the right of same-sex couples to marry in California, thus reversing the California Supreme Court affirmation of same-sex marriage as a right protected by the Constitution in May 2008. Amidst public contestation, protests, and legal steps to overturn Proposition 8, *Milk* was transformed "from a delicate, serious-minded period biopic into something altogether more urgent and emotional: a threnody, a catharsis, a call to action" (Lim 2008), while *The Guardian*'s Henry Barnes (2009) even wondered whether an earlier release would have led to a possible defeat of Proposition 8.

A film set in the 1970s became enmeshed as the unlikely argument of a similar future debate. In a way, although *Milk* came out after the passage of Proposition 8, it followed the path of *Wag the Dog*, the film that preceded the Clinton–Lewinsky sex scandal by only a few days after its wide release, while prophesizing the President's future predicament. Thanouli (2013: 87) notes that, in this way, *Wag the Dog* provided "an interpretive framework for the real facts that took place soon after its screening," since "the distance between reality and cinema was short-circuited, rendering it impossible to draw a distinction between what is real and what is not" (Thanouli 2013: 87). Indeed, reference to *Wag the Dog* was included in the great majority of articles on the Lewinsky scandal, further blurring the borders between fact and fiction. In a similar way, *Milk* also entered the media discussion on Proposition 8, but although the film is a work of fiction, it is also a biopic which draws its narrative from real events and real people, unlike *Wag the Dog*, which was based on an entirely fictional universe. Suzanna Lenon (2013: 45) notes the number of similarities between Milk's campaign to defeat Proposition 6 and the 2000s struggle to defeat Proposition 8:

> [...] both were nationally watched campaigns and close in the polls; both figured children and schools as a central concern; both political moments featured Republican governors (Ronald Reagan, Arnold Schwarzenegger) siding with gay Californians; and both anti-Proposition 8 and anti-Proposition 6 linked support of "gay rights" with imaginings of what "America" stands for.

Lenon (2013) also includes Gus Van Sant's thoughts on releasing the film after the election for Proposition 8, and his decision not to use it as a means to influence its outcome. The author also refers to how Sean Penn denounced Proposition 8 during his Oscar acceptance speech, and mentions his and real-life Cleve Jones's work as proponents of marriage equality in California. Lenon (2013:46) concludes that *Milk* "achieved considerable meaning within the politico-legal context of Proposition 8," and "can be understood as a cultural artifact deployed to (re)mobilize political energies to support same-sex marriage, particularly in the months leading up to the 2009 Supreme Court decision that upheld Proposition 8 as constitutional."

It becomes clear that the four political history dramas can be read as both history lessons that educate audiences about past events and/or individuals, as well as serving as a sociopolitical commentary on contemporary situations. I would argue that each reading, depending on the theorist's aims, is useful and instructive insofar as we accept that a filmic narrative is in itself and irrespective of its content a historical cultural artifact that can be interpreted differently by a variety of audiences at different times. In addition, the significant number of both academic and media responses to these four recent films is indicative of the importance of the cinematic audiovisual language in today's culture—as well as the proliferation of media outlets, especially on the internet—and its placement at the heart of sociocultural debates.

Political history films as proponents of change

The most important narrative element that *Lincoln, Good Night, and Good Luck,* and *Milk* share is that they celebrate three individuals who succeeded in effecting change to the political structure. By focusing "on documented people," and setting "them amidst" important events, "the historical thinking involved" is that "individuals [...] are at the centre of the historical process" (Rosenstone 2012: 18). As was already stated above, the history films concentrate on "great men." But what makes these men great? The fact that their aspiration, determination, and ideals made it possible for the alteration of the political structure, a result that was not achieved in the examined political comedies, or the political thrillers, despite their "happy" endings. Lincoln passed a law that freed millions of slaves, Murrow exposed Senator McCarthy, thus leading to his demise and the eventual ending of the witch hunt, and Milk defeated Proposition 6, thus allowing homosexuals and their supporters to work in California schools. These political actions, the passing and cancellation of two laws, as well as a nationally televised investigation that led to the end of an era, constitute significant events in American history. Using Hay's (2002) strategic-relational theory, they also point to those rare moments where agency does affect structure. However small the change may seem, the fact that agency (collective or individual) can influence structure proves "the interaction between strategic actors and the strategic context within which they find themselves" (2002: 128).

5

Political Films From Antiquity to the Twentieth Century

This chapter comprises the last sixteen films of the corpus and includes political films that fit the criteria of the proposed definition but are labeled under different generic categories by the industry. I call these films "hidden," as their political narratives are all marketed under a variety of genres (historical dramas; epics; action/adventure; thrillers; sports movie), which further reinforces my argument about how the political film genre can only exist in Hollywood as a theoretical construction and not an industry label. However, the very existence of political narratives in a number of unexpected films, and genres for that matter, also point to the filmmakers' tendency to address political issues and their circumvention of the industry's reluctance towards politics by camouflaging their films into relatable and marketable Hollywood products.

For the purposes of this chapter, I group these films as follows:

1. Biopics: *The Passion of the Christ* (2004); *Invictus* (2009).
2. Historical Epics: This category comprises three films that derive from ancient Greek myths (*Troy* [2004]; *300* [2006]; *Alexander* [2004]) and three that are based on medieval tales (*King Arthur*, 2004; *Kingdom of Heaven*, [2005]; and *Robin Hood* [2010]).
3. British heritage and monarchy films: *The Queen* (2006); *Amazing Grace* (2006); *Elizabeth: The Golden Age* (2007); *The Other Boleyn Girl* (2008); *The Young Victoria* (2009); *The King's Speech* (2010).
4. American Jewish films: *Munich* (2005); *The Debt* (2010).

These sixteen films seem, at first glance, quite distinct in that they refer to different eras, are based on either mythic or historical events, take place from Ancient Greece to late-twentieth-century Great Britain and Germany, and none of them refer to the United States, despite being produced or coproduced by North-American companies. Interestingly, the top ten of the most commercially successful political films of the corpus includes five of the films. *The Passion of Christ*, *Troy*, and *300* are numbers two, three, and four respectively; *The King's Speech* is at number six, and *Robin Hood* at number eight. The focus of this chapter is the examination of the monarchy films—the only subgenre included in the corpus that concentrates on female protagonists—that follows the brief discussion of why *The Passion*, the historical epics, and medieval action films should be considered political cinematic narratives, and their main shared isotopies.

An unlikely political biopic: *The Passion of the Christ*

The Passion is an unlikely candidate for a corpus of political films and, therefore, merits a brief examination. Aside from being one of the most controversial films in history, it is also one of the highest grossing films in the history of the medium. On a modest budget of $30 million, *The Passion* returned almost $612 million worldwide and, to date, features among the top 100 of highest-grossing films of all time (at number ninety-eight) and one of the fifteen most profitable films (at number eight), according to boxofficemojo.com and CNBC respectively. Returning a staggering 1749 percent on its initial investment, *The Passion* is also "the highest grossing non-English language film of all time, earn[ing] over seventeen times its budget" (Bukszpan, 2010). In addition, the film has also inspired at least four academic edited collections and five monographs, which examine all possible aspects of the film from a variety of disciplines, making Mel Gibson's third directorial feature a contested academic subject as well.

However, my concern here is not the accusations leveled against Gibson's film, or his condemnation by religious circles. Instead, I argue that *The Passion* is first a political film and, second, a religious one as it follows the definitional criteria set in the introduction irrespective of its relationship to Christianity or Gibson's chosen interpretation. The film begins with Jesus's arrest and ends with his crucifixion. At the time, Judea was under Roman rule with Pontius Pilate as the Prefect, yet the Jewish community had considerable power. Caiaphas was the High Priest and he was also appointed by Rome. Through his teachings, Jesus was already seen as a new leader, someone with enough power to challenge the political structure of Judea. Both Pilate and Caiaphas objected to welcoming a new political force, and their mutual understanding led to Jesus's death. Although I am not examining the historical evidence that can shed light on whether it was Pilate or Caiaphas that actually condemned Jesus to death, I maintain that it was Jesus's increasing political capital that threatened the presumed order of Judea at the time.

Other writers have examined the political implications of Jesus's arrest and sentencing, although they do not refer to *The Passion* as a political film. Wolin (2004, 88) unequivocally states that "[t]he drama of the Crucifixion had been enacted against a political backdrop; the Lord of the Christians had been put to death at the command of a political regime." Additionally, John Meacham (2006: 5) observes that the New Testament implies that "crucifixion was a political weapon used to send a message to those still living: beware of revolution or riot, or Rome will do this to you, too." Similarly, Jay Tolson and Linda Kulman's (2006: 22) use of historical evidence that proves crucifixion was "reserved for political crimes," corroborates Jesus's part in Judea's political landscape. It becomes clear that Jesus was crucified as a result of a political conflict in order for his teaching to be contained by those who considered it a new and potentially threatening political force. The argument in favor of considering *The Passion* as a political text is further corroborated by the fact that politics and religion have long enjoyed a symbiotic yet tumultuous relationship through the centuries. As Wolin (2004, 86) remarks, "With the default of philosophy, it fell to Christianity to revivify political thought." Today, religion plays an equally significant role in the United States. "Churches, synagogues, and mosques are not only the crucial element in the religious life of many African Americans, Hispanics, Muslims, and Jews; they also have played a major role in politicizing their members and educating them in political matters" (Wolin 2004: 541). However, as Wolin observes in contrast to the nineteenth and bigger part of the twentieth century, where religious leaders help promote "democratic advances," the last decades of the twentieth century and the new millennium witnessed "a substantial segment of organized populist-Protestant religions" that "has gravitated towards a radicalism of the right" (2004: 542). The continuing influence and power of religious doctrines in the United States, combined with some of Gibson's choices, were destined to create controversy around *The Passion*, which should find a place alongside the most important political films of the first decade of the 2000s.

Ancient Greek myths and medieval tales

Both the films that originate from ancient Greek stories, and those that are based on medieval times, are labeled as historical epics and constitute the less "hidden" political films of this chapter. Based on James Chapman's notion of "presentism," that is the idea that we can draw lessons for the present from the depiction of the past in history films, Andrew B. R. Elliott (2014: 11) argues that the reasons for the return of the historical epic in the 2000s has to be hiding in the contemporary political context:

> [A]s the Cold War [the last era where the epic was highly popular before the 2000s] was replaced by a global "War on Terror," so too would new versions of past worlds emerge to critique armed incursions in the Middle East (*Kingdom of Heaven, Robin Hood*) [...], or to offer warnings based on past efforts at conquest (*Alexander*) or else actively endorse them (*300*). In the aftermath of openly falsified justifications for war in Iraq, we find attacks on unjustified warmongering (*Troy, Centurion*), or skepticism towards cynical political manoeuvring (*King Arthur*) [...], amid contentious debates about religious ideologies we find scathing attacks on fundamentalism of all stripes (*Agora, Kingdom of Heaven, King Arthur*).

Troy, 300, and *Alexander* are all about ancient Greek mythical and historical figures and their struggle for political power through conquering new lands, or defending their own. *Troy* and *Alexander* feature protagonists who go to war to increase their power—Agamemnon uses Helen's abduction as the excuse to invade Troy and finally control the whole Aegean Sea, and Alexander wants to conquer the known world in Asia to create a Hellenic Empire—while *300* sees Leonidas defending Sparta from Persian invasion. The depicted wars and battles are politically based decisions that bring change to the polity of the conquered land as well as the societies of the conquerors. In contrast to other war films, *Troy, Alexander*, and *300* make explicit that the actions of the main characters are based on political decisions, and can therefore be considered as political texts. While discussing their next step after Helen (Diane Kruger) is taken by Paris (Orlando Bloom), Agamemnon (Brian Cox) tells his brother Menelaus (Brendan Gleeson): "Peace is for the women, and the weak. Empires are forged by war," thus stating his political philosophy of imperialism. In *300*, the self-abnegation and self-sacrifice exhibited by Leonidas (Gerard Butler) and his soldiers in the Battle of Thermopylae, to defend freedom for Sparta and consequently all Greek territories is a significant political decision despite the defeat of the small Spartan army against a vastly larger enemy army. In addition, Leonidas's plan helped the Greeks prepare for the subsequent victory in the Battle of Salamina, which eventually obliged Persian King Xerxes (Rodrigo Santoro) to retreat to Asia. Finally, *Alexander* shows the Macedonian King (Colin Farrell) invade and conquer a number of countries in Asia in his imperialist plan to create a unified empire.

Troy and *Alexander* were released in 2004, and *300* in 2006. The films' insistence on military engagement, representations of well-trained, masculine bodies, and their spectacular battle sequences, can be read as Hollywood's effort to boost the morale of the nation at the beginning of the Iraq War, and to further promote the war effort. Also, in both *Alexander* and *300*, the Persian enemy is depicted as a vicious and uncultured people, following the trend of similar "representations in contemporary Western media [...] which have gained momentum since the emergence of Islamic terrorism and Western governments' declaration of a "global war on terror"" (Nacify 2012: 155). Sophia Shafi (2014: 121) adds that in *300*, "[t]he Persians are a collection of deformed hunchbacks, giants, sexual deviants, and other frights," while concluding that despite the film's setting in antiquity, "Persians represent the existential threat of Islam." Stone's *Alexander* goes a step beyond representation; when Aristotle (Christopher Plummer) is asked about the cruelty of Persians, he replies: "[...] the Oriental races are known for their barbarity and slavish devotion to their senses. Excess in all things is the undoing of men. That is why we Greeks are superior, we practice control of our senses. Moderation."

"The Untold True Story That Inspired The Legend" is one of the tag lines used for Antoine Fuqua's *King Arthur*, which is one of the first epics that follows the trend of a more realistic and darker depiction of the main character (in both epic films as well as other genres, such as superhero and sci-fi films of the twenty-first century), based more on historical research than mythos and previous cinematic representations. Irrespective of the presumed detail of characterization, setting and costumes to create authenticity, the film "follows the familiar Hollywood 'liberation' narrative, which projects political problems on to external oppressors," suggesting at the end "that military victory over the oppressors is all that is needed" (Shippey 2012: 460). Arthur (Clive Owen) is portrayed as a just Roman knight of Samartian origins, who wants to help the pagan Woads against a Saxon invasion. He therefore assumes a clear political position (in favor of freedom against slavery), and also acts on it (leading the army and fighting as a political praxis to bring peace and not as an act of vengeance or personal interest). Released in 2004, *King Arthur* can readily be interpreted as a promotion of the American war effort in Iraq and was indeed found to have "contemporary resonance" (O'Sullivan 2004) in some reviews. Its relative success at the worldwide box office—the film was budgeted at $120 million, returning more than $203.5 million—was followed by a number of similar cinematic epics in the subsequent years. In addition, the film inspired a popular video game, thus adding to the revenue through the contemporary industry practice of the tie-in.

The next two political epics were directed by Ridley Scott, also responsible for *Gladiator* (2000), the film that is considered as the point of departure for the return of the epic in the new millennium. As Jeffrey Richards (2014: 21) puts it in his chapter on Scott's "epic trilogy" (*Gladiator*, *Kingdom of Heaven*, and *Robin Hood*), "historical films have political agendas." Indeed, as my research and the analysis of the films have shown, the great majority of history films are political films that are simply distributed, recognized, and/or reviewed under different labels. Especially when films focus on globally familiar individuals (whether the film is about King Arthur, President Lincoln, or Harvey Milk), their labeling as historical dramas/biographies/epics, etc., is not only the easiest but also the most effective way for marketing and advertisement strategists. Thus, the political narrative is obscured but not erased, and is left for film critics and scholars to uncover and address.

King Arthur, *The Kingdom of Heaven*, and *Robin Hood* have all been discussed in both academia and the media as including political undertones. All three films include a male hero who becomes a leader that hopes to spread harmony and democracy in the world. The literature I encountered on these and other historical films mainly treat the narratives as stories about the past that include direct commentary on the present. For instance, Richards (2014: 26) notes that *Kingdom of Heaven* "was conceived in the aftermath of the attack on the Twin Towers on 11 September 2001 and released after the invasion of Iraq in 2003," and, as such, the author views the narrative as an examination on contemporary relations "between Christianity and Islam," and not as a story referring to medieval crusades. The same conclusion about Scott delivering a message of tolerance for the "other's" religious beliefs, and the film's relevance to contemporary sociopolitical circumstances, was drawn by scholars and media critics alike, such as Lawrence Raw (2009), Ross Douthat (2006), and William Arnold (2005b), among others.

Finally, *Robin Hood* "completes the process of proletarianization that has been going on in the Robin Hood myth since the 1970s," and Robin becomes "for the first time unequivocally a peasant" (Richards 2014: 32). The filmmaking team revisits one of the most popular medieval mythic figures in 2010 and promotes the idea of "a community of equals who fight for justice against a corrupt system" (Lewis 2013: 164). Lewis also notices the narrative's effort to respond "to early 21st-century economic and political realities" (2013: 165), as do Pete Travers (2010) and Michael O'Sullivan (2010), the latter calling it "a political attack ad paid for by the tea party movement, circa 1199." The three epics are widely considered as political commentaries of their time of release but not as political narratives, instructive of the historical events and personalities they portray. Endorsing democratic values, religious and racial tolerance, they mostly follow a liberal agenda rather than a conservative one, while exalting the integrity and justice of their male authority figures, perpetuating in essence the mythos of the true and just leader who can save his people.

Shared isotopies, shared political message

The six epics above share two major isotopies. The first is created in the actant category and is represented by the clearly defined opposition between the protagonists and the villains. Their male protagonists are the "good" guys, despite their occasional flaws (Achilles's and Alexander's arrogance, Agamemnon's imperialistic plans), while the male villains range from impertinent royals (Paris in *Troy*) to bloodthirsty savages (the Saxons in *The Kingdom of Heaven*, the Persians in *300*). Via specific narrative choices, as well as the use of costume, make-up, music, editing, and camera placement, the audiovisual text manipulates the viewers' response, "insisting" that they take the side of the benevolent protagonist(s) in an explicit good vs. evil combat. Of course, the support of the viewers is earned even before they watch the films, because the majority of the protagonists are recognizable heroes who have enjoyed great popularity throughout the centuries. The narratives, however, do not rely on this prior knowledge but enhance it through casting and narrative choices. Brad Pitt as Achilles, Russell Crowe as Robin Hood, and Gerard Butler as Leonidas, for instance, are celebrated not only as capable thespians but also as models of masculinity, and especially as men with enviable muscles and well-defined bodies—even in 2014, Pitt, Crowe, and Butler are still among the "50 Fittest Men in Hollywood," according to *Men's Health* (Morton 2014). The actors' great cultural and symbolic capital is not only measured by their worldwide appeal but underscored by their bankability at their box office. In simpler terms, and although relevant data does not exist (to my knowledge), if a film stars one of those actors, a great percentage of movie-goers will watch it irrespective of the genre, director, or review. Moreover, as A-list stars usually portray decent and well-meaning characters, viewers are even more inclined to identify with them.

Nevertheless, it is the narrative that provides the most important information about the characters and solidifies their place in it. Most of the epics discussed are advertised as presenting the "true story" of their legendary heroes, implying the filmmakers opted for a more realistic version, which does not sanctify them and is based on historical facts. Yet, all films choose to depict their heroes as visionaries and highly intelligent individuals; men with acute political knowledge, as well as fearless warriors. At the end of the narrative, there is no doubt regarding the heroes' charisma and the vast improvement of the societies they lived in because of their presence. Irrespective of the heroes' unquestionable mental and physical strength, and the democratic values they operate by and promote, the change they bring about is of a political nature. Alexander forges a new empire, changing not only the lives of the people he conquers but also Greece's future, as does Agamemnon in Troy with Achilles's assistance; Robin Hood influences King John to sign a Charter of Rights to unite the country; while Arthur forms a new political power by marrying Guinevere and becoming King of the Woads.

The second major isotopy concerns the topos of the battle and is characterized by an inside vs. outside antithesis. All the protagonists engage in battle in "an-other" place, far from the kingdom, nation, or city-state they wish to protect. Leonidas fights in Thermopylae and not Sparta, Agamemnon and the Greeks take their ships to Troy, Alexander travels to Asia from Macedonia, Robin Hood fights the French at Dover, etc. In addition, the spaces are usually far from inhabited areas, such as open spaces, fields, or deserts. This choice is not only dictated by actual war tactics but also allows filmmakers to stage and choreograph impressive battle sequences that imbue the narrative with spectacle as well as move the plot forward. Finally, on a connotative level, the transportation of the battle to another place reduces the fear and anxiety the citizens of each side feel and also appease the reaction of the viewer. It also resonates with American history and the fact that the geographical position of the United

States has not allowed the enemy to attack it on its own soil, except for Pearl Harbor and 9/11.

The six political epics promote, to a greater or lesser extent, issues of democracy and/or freedom, although these concepts did not exist in the narrative time exactly as we understand them today. As Richards (2014) notes, discussing *Robin Hood*, this is "democracy American-style." They are liberal in tone, expressing tolerance towards "other" religions (especially Scott's films), and yet they promote military intervention, or, at least, view it as a necessary evil. The epics follow the political history dramas discussed in Chapter 4 in that they also focus on the stories of "great men," as Gianos (1998, 170) remarked. The use of "great men" in political history films simplifies changes in political institutions by focusing on a prominent and charismatic personality who passes a law (Lincoln, Robin Hood), defeats one (Milk), forms a new political power (Jesus, Arthur), conquers a new country to expand his rule (Alexander, Agamemnon) or even loses a battle defending the freedom of his people (Leonidas). These acts cannot, of course, be represented in all their complexity or span of time they occurred within, and due to the limitations of a mainstream film's running time, events are simplified and portrayed as actions for which a single person is responsible. I am not suggesting the protagonists of the films are not exemplary men who did not play a significant role in changing their time's and society's status quo. However, I maintain that change in the political structure can be achieved mainly through the collaborative effect of agents. What could Alexander achieve without his army? Could Arthur defeat the Saxons without his knights or the Woads' support? Wouldn't it be impossible for Achilles to conquer Troy by himself? The answer is evident and the films do portray soldiers, advisors, and friends that the leading "great men" rely on and listen to. Yet, in the end, the impression that remains is the simplified credo that to change the world all you need is that special someone.

The heritage and the monarchy film

The heritage film is a theoretically constructed genre, originating from British film studies. It designates a group of contemporary period or costume films that share a number of semantic and syntactic elements, such as important historical or classical literary sources, impressive art and production design, and stellar casts (Vidal 2012: 1), and find their way to both wide releases and the festival circuit. Although Vidal notes that most heritage films are not based on historical events, she includes the subgenre of the monarchy film in her study, despite its originating from real people. Vidal defines the monarchy film as a narrative which "places actual royal figures at the centre of fictionalised stories," "a generic sub-cycle that has contributed greatly to establishing the heritage film as the British genre most concerned with tradition and nostalgia for the (imperial) past" (Vidal 2012: 36).

The Queen (2006), *Amazing Grace* (2006), *Elizabeth: The Golden Age* (2007), *The Other Boleyn Girl* (2008), *The Young Victoria* (2009), and *The King's Speech* (2010), are the heritage films included in the corpus. The first observation is that five out of the six are monarchy films as well. Interestingly, four out of the five monarchy films place a woman at the center of the narrative. The political film is predominantly a male genre, as I have corroborated with statistical data from the corpus in the introduction. Thus, this strong female presence in a single sub-category raises questions worthy of further analysis and constitutes the primary focus of this chapter.

In four subsequent years, from 2006 to 2009, the cinematic portrait of a British female monarch made its way to the theaters. *The Queen* (2006), *Elizabeth: The Golden Age* (2007), *The Other Boleyn Girl* (2008), and *The Young Victoria* (2009) narrated stories of strong female characters while covering a five-century historical period: from early in the sixteenth century to the end of the twentieth. What are the reasons behind this vivid interest in female rulers with unquestionable political power? In their book-length study of cinematic queens, Elizabeth A. Ford and Deborah C. Mitchell (2009: 2) argue that the sociopolitical context assisted in the production of such narratives because it also reflected an "altered political reality," along with other parameters such as Helen Mirren's and Cate Blanchett's bankability. Ford and Mitchell (2009: 2) explain that the appearance of strong women in the global political landscape, such as Angela Merkel, Benazir Bhutto, Hillary Rodham Clinton, and the increased number of women in Congress at the 2006 midterm elections, made gender equality a more tangible aim in the new millennium.

The films received mediocre (*Elizabeth: The Golden Age*, *The Other Boleyn Girl*) through positive (*The Young Victoria*) to rave reviews (*The Queen*), while *Elizabeth: The Golden Age*, *The Young Victoria*, and *The Queen* won an Academy Award each. Although *The Young Victoria* was a box office failure, the other films managed to return their initial investment, with *The Queen* becoming a box office hit in 2006. What interests me in this chapter is not a detailed gender analysis of these texts, however useful and relevant it may be, but the political power bestowed onto Anne Boleyn, Elizabeth I, Victoria, and Elizabeth II, and its use by the characters. As with the majority of films in this book, these monarchy films are not considered as political texts by either the media or the academia. Yet, their narrative structure follows a female character who acts in a political context—that of the British royal court—and aims at either saving her country from an enemy (*Elizabeth: The Golden Age*), learning how to be a ruler and governing a country (*The Young Victoria*), ascending to power to exert influence over a country (*The Other Boleyn Girl*), or politically negotiating a private tragedy (*The Queen*). Thus, all four narratives meet the definition parameters of the political film as set in the introduction.

Despite the films being made one after the other and sharing a number of similarities, they are not the product of a single filmmaking team. In fact, very few individuals worked on more than one film. A brief review revealed that writer Peter Morgan is responsible for the screenplays of *The Queen* and *The Other Boleyn Girl*, editor Jill Bilcock worked on *Elizabeth: The Golden Age* and *The Young Victoria*, and Sandy Powell was the costume designer for *The Other Boleyn Girl* and *The Young Victoria*. The directors and cinematographers are different in all the films, as well as the production companies, with the exception of the American-based Scott Rudin Productions, which coproduced *The Queen* and *The Other Boleyn Girl*. This cycle of films on female rulers in Britain corroborates Altman's (2006: 38–43) thesis about how the financial success of a given film can initiate a string of similar narratives based on the same, yet revised, formula. Applying Altman's rationale, I now look at the numbers of these four narratives. The first film of the cycle, *The Queen*, was budgeted at around $15 million and returned more than $123 million worldwide aside from also winning the Oscar for Best Actress (Mirren), and being considered one of the best films of 2006. It seems quite probable that *The Queen*'s popularity and impressive returns led to the sequel of 1998's *Elizabeth*—*Elizabeth: The Golden Age*—which had a budget of $55 million and earned a little less than $74.5 million, while getting two Academy Award nominations and winning the Oscar for Best Costume Design. Despite the mediocre course of the film, 2008 witnessed the release of *The Other Boleyn Girl*, which cost $35 million and returned almost $78 million. Lastly, in 2009, *The Young Victoria*, received the best reviews, aside from *The Queen*, and was nominated for three Academy awards, winning the Oscar for Best Achievement in Costume Design. The film had a budget of $35 million but earned a little less than $27.5 million. Another interesting conclusion to be drawn from the data is that after *The Queen*, which is set in the late 1990s, the rest of the films moved to the past, and investigated famous monarchs from the sixteenth, seventeenth, eighteenth, and early twentieth centuries.

This monarchy cycle has closed, for the moment, with *The King's Speech*, 2010, a film focused on King George VI, which features at number six in my corpus, reaching more than $414 million worldwide on a very modest budget of $15 million and winning four Academy Awards (Best Picture, Best Director, Best Actor, and Best Screenplay). *The King's Speech*'s reign (pun intended) over the female-focused monarchy films can be attributed to an aggressive marketing campaign by Weinstein Co.—who coproduced the film—which mainly repositioned it as a "buddy movie," changing its tag line from "It takes leadership to confront a nation's fear. It takes friendship to conquer your own" to "Some things never go out of style: Friendship; Courage; Loyalty" (Fritz 2011). The film accentuated the friendship that develops between the future monarch of Great Britain and his speech therapist rather than insisting on the goal of his therapy, which was to be able to rule and reach his subjects. The repositioning of the film's genre, combined with a wide US release to thousands of theaters, as well as the rave reviews that *The King's Speech* received, resulted in it being one of the most commercial films of 2010, reaching number eighteen in the US yearly box office and number thirteen in the international box office of the same year. The film's success notwithstanding, I return to the four female-centered films as they constitute the only group of political narratives with female protagonists.

The major isotopy encountered in the four films is the male vs. female opposition. *The Queen*'s focus is the story of how Queen Elizabeth II and the newly elected Prime Minister, Tony Blair, negotiate the untimely death of Princess Diana and their actions' effect on the British. In *The Other Boleyn Girl*, Anne Boleyn is in opposition with Henry VIII in her effort to persuade him to divorce his first wife and make her the queen. Elizabeth I has to confront King Philip II of Spain, who plans to conquer Great Britain and dethrone her to make way for his daughter Isabella, in *Elizabeth: The Golden Age*. Finally, in *Young Victoria*, Victoria has to constantly evade her uncle's and Belgium's King's requests, and Comptroller John Conroy's machinations, over control of the throne. Although the films include very strong male characters, the titles bear their female protagonists' names or titles while the narrative begins and ends with them, underlining at times their necessary or desired coexistence with men as shown in the next two sets of shots.

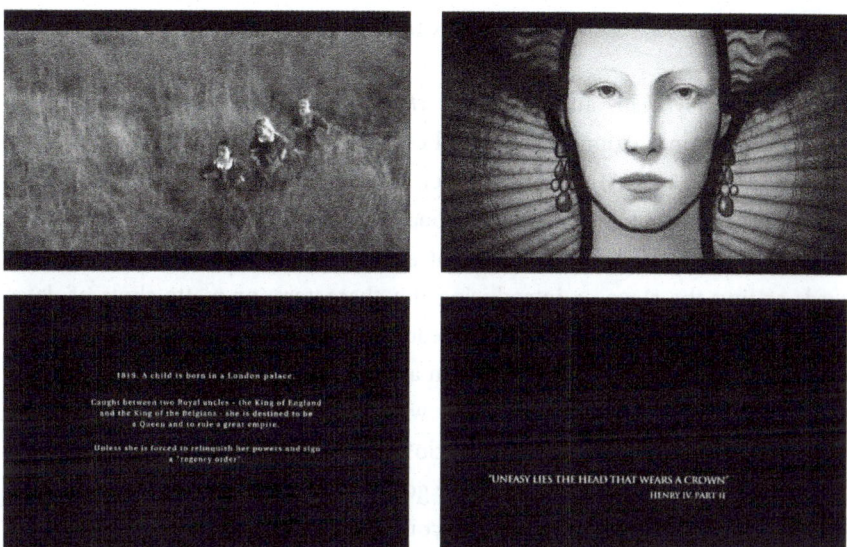

Figures 62–65 (Left to right, top to bottom) Beginning of *The Other Boleyn Girl*, *Elizabeth: The Golden Age*, *The Young Victoria*, *The Queen*.

Figures 66–69 (Left to right, top to bottom): Ending of *The Other Boleyn Girl*, *Elizabeth: The Golden Age*, *The Young Victoria*, *The Queen*.

Marriage: A political decision

The Other Boleyn Girl and *Elizabeth: The Golden Age* focus on their female protagonists from beginning to end. The former tells the story of Anne Boleyn and her ascent to the throne, as Queen Consort of Henry VIII, through her family's encouragement and her personal desire for power. *The Other Boleyn Girl* opts for an unlikely beginning of a historical drama. There are no title cards setting the stage or introducing the characters, or matte shots of dates and places in the first sequences. Instead, the viewer sees three children, two girls and a boy, running and playing in a meadow. A couple, who we presume to be their parents, is walking along with them on a nearby country path, watching over them and talking. The clothes and the chromatic palette chosen by the cinematographer accentuate the gold and brown autumn colors, and the content of their parents' discussion is contrasted with their obvious enjoyment and innocent happiness. The Boleyns, an aristocratic family, are discussing their two girls' future. However, their dialogue does not refer to what we might expect today; for instance, choosing an elementary school, an extracurricular activity, or issues of behavior, health, etc. Instead, Thomas Boleyn (Mark Rylance) announces to his wife, Elizabeth (Kristin Scott Thomas), that he has received a marriage offer, that day, for their eldest daughter Anne, but turned it down, offering their youngest Mary in her place. "Everyone improves their standing with their daughters," he continues. Before his wife expresses her opinion, Thomas explains his refusal, and states nonchalantly "I think Anne can do a lot better than a merchant's son." The story then moves forward to the day of Mary's (Scarlett Johansson) wedding while a cut takes us to the palace, where the Queen, Katherine of Aragon (Anna Torrent), delivers a stillborn. Visibly distraught, the Queen turns to her daughter and says: "No brother for you to make this country safe."

With these two initial scenes, The *Other Boleyn Girl* addresses, right from the start, the issue of marriage in what Stephanie Coontz calls "the era of the political marriage," in her detailed history of the institution which was to last until the eighteenth century. Coontz (2005: 53) notices that a shared practice between the oldest kingdoms, states, and empires created in different geographical regions is that they used marriage as "the key mechanism through which" the rulers made "alliances, and establish[ed] their legitimacy." Writing about marriage, and especially towards the end of the sixteenth century and Henry VIII's wives, Alison Weir (2007: 5) underlines:

One married for political reasons, to cement alliances, to gain wealth, land and status, and to forge between families [...] Royal marriages, of course, were largely matters of political expediency [...] Kings were expected to ally themselves with foreign powers for political and trading advantages, and had done so until 1464 when Henry's grandfather, Edward IV, had married Elizabeth Woodville, a commoner, for love alone, and caused a furore. Half a century later, a burgeoning sense of English nationalism meant that Henry VIII's marriages to four commoners passed without anyone complaining that they were not of royal blood [...] In a sense, however, these were political marriages too, since the political and religious factions at Henry's court were continually trying to manoeuvre their master in and out of wedlock.

At the time, women had to be docile servants of men, whether they were daughters or wives. *The Other Boleyn Girl* may exaggerate at times the role of Anne (Natalie Portman) as an independent woman, more akin to contemporary representation, yet a consensus has emerged among scholars (Bordo 2013; Warnicke 2003) concerning her intelligence, her successful efforts to make Henry annul his marriage and make her the Queen Consort, as well as the strong influence she exerted once she ascended to the throne. Apart from securing and increasing her family's fortune and social standing, Anne encouraged Henry VIII to finally break from the Catholic Church and become Supreme Head of the Church of England. When Pope Clement refused to annul Henry's marriage to Katherine of Aragon, the King convinced Parliament "to name him the supreme head of the church" (Joireman 2009: 95), in order to protect his lineage and the potential male heir he might have with Anne, and who would ensure the Tudor continuity. Despite the era's mores and the undisputed dominance of men, Anne's personality and influence, however limited, cannot be erased. Anne may have failed in producing a male heir to Henry and ended up beheaded, accused of treason, adultery, and incest, but the film ends by implying she was vindicated after all, even after death. The last freeze frame shows a young girl, approximately the same age Anne was at the beginning, running in the fields, and below her name appears (Figure 66); it is Elizabeth, daughter of Anne and Henry, who was soon to rule England for more than four decades.

Elizabeth: The Golden Age begins with a variation on the title cards that accompany many historical and heritage films. Six shots of historical figures and events in stained glass windows succeed one another, while each shot is accompanied by a written phrase introducing the place, the setting, and the main characters of the narrative that is about to unfold. The viewer, therefore, learns that "the year is 1585", and "Spain is the most powerful empire in the world. Philip of Spain has plunged Europe into holy war. Only England stands against him, ruled by a protestant queen." Figure 63 is a close-up of Queen Elizabeth I (Blanchett), while below appears the title of the film. The film concentrates on the last period of her reign, characterized by "the trial and execution of Mary, Queen of Scots, and by the outbreak of war with Spain and her ally, the French Catholic League" (Guy 1995: 1). A recurring theme of the plot, apart from Philip and Mary's threat instigated by the Spanish plan to assassinate her, is again the issue of marriage. The Virgin Queen is advised continually to marry one of her suitors to safeguard her kingdom and even prevent Spain's attack. As Guy (1995: 3) notes, Elizabeth's acceptance of long courtships by royals all over Europe lies at the center of her politics and constitutes her "most effective tool of policy." Guy adds that her "dithering, prevarication, and generally dismissive behavior [...] provided Elizabeth with her weapons of political manipulation and manoeuvre. In order to beat her male courtiers at their own game, she changed the rules and capitalized on the power granted to her by virtue of her gender" (1995: 3).

The film may take liberties with history, but its central facts (the war with Spain, Mary Stuart's execution, the assassination plot) did take place. What is interesting, however, is that most reviews (Stevens 2007; Dargis 2007; Morris 2007) concentrate on the lavish production values, and particularly the love triangle that emerges between the Queen, Bess (Abbie Cornish), her lady-in-waiting, and Sir Walter Raleigh (Clive Owen), and Elizabeth's rage when she discovers that Bess and Walter are married and expecting their first child. However, Elizabeth's narrative program from the beginning of the film is to guard against the Spanish as well as all the domestic threats, and usher in a new era of peace for England. Indeed, the ending finds the Queen forgivingly blessing Bess and Walter's child, and the last shot filmed from above (Figure 67), shows her alone, creating a full circle from her close-up at the beginning. While the camera circles around Elizabeth, the viewer reads the on-screen text, informing him/her that "The loss of the Armada was the most humiliating defeat in Spain's naval history," that "Philip died ten years later leaving Spain bankrupt," and that "England entered a time of peace and prosperity."

The romantic angle in *The Young Victoria*, between Victoria (Emily Blunt) and her future husband, Prince Albert (Rupert Friend), is more prominent than in both *The Other Boleyn Girl* and *Elizabeth: The Golden Age*. The film begins with a title card (Figure 64) that provides the necessary information about the time (early to mid-eighteenth century), the birth and upbringing of Victoria, her mother's (Miranda Richardson) and Sir John Conroy's (Mark Strong) failed efforts to have Victoria sign a regency order, yielding all power to them, and ends with Victoria's coronation in 1838 as the film title appears. The narrative, then, moves back to the year before to explore Victoria's journey to her wedding, and its political implications. Even though the Queen does marry Prince Albert out of love, this still occurs in the strict context of a political alliance. First of all, her uncle, King Leopold (Thomas Kretschmann), is the one who asks the Prince to visit Victoria and "make her smile," as he believes that a marriage is the only way to keep his niece safe. In other words, and despite Victoria's and Albert's mutual affection for each other, their introduction is part of a political decision to safeguard the future of the British monarchy.

After King Leopold's encouragement, Albert is tutored before and during his courtship concerning Victoria's likes and dislikes, the political figures of importance, as well as his main opponent for the future Queen's heart. In an intriguing sequence, Albert learns to dance while his instructor, Baron Stockmar (Jesper Christensen), King Leopold's primary physician and trusted adviser, asks questions about political friends and foes. Once a name is pronounced, the viewer is transported to the person, with the assistance of parallel editing, as they are announced before the King's gala for his birthday. A brief yet concise political lesson ensues:

STOCKMAR:	Present Prime Minister?
ALBERT:	Melbourne.
STOCKMAR:	Lord Melbourne. Liberal leader who'll probably be in power when the Princess succeeds. He may be troublesome.
ALBERT:	Why?
STOCKMAR:	Because he puts the interests of England above those of Europe.
ALBERT:	Which is bad?
STOCKMAR:	Which is not useful to us. He wouldn't spill one drop of British blood to save a foreign throne.
ALBERT:	But why would he want to save a foreign throne if it wasn't in England's interest?
STOCKMAR:	That is just the kind of thinking your uncle Leopold is afraid of. Which is why he is content to find his niece as the future Queen of England.

ALBERT:	The Duke of Wellington.
STOCKMAR:	In the public mind, the leader of the Conservative Opposition is their pet hero, Napoleon's conqueror, the grand old Duke of Wellington.
	The next Tory Prime Minister will be Sir Robert Peel.
ALBERT:	Which side does Victoria favour?
STOCKMAR:	She's a liberal. Above all, she favours Lord Melbourne. And he'll take full advantage of it. Lord Melbourne will make her fall in love with him. It's his method.
ALBERT:	Don't underestimate Victoria.
STOCKMAR:	Don't underestimate Melbourne.

The film does depict the development of Victoria and Albert's relationship, from courtship through marriage to ruling England, yet almost equal screen time is devoted to how the nineteen-year-old Victoria learns to be queen and to avoid the people who desire to undermine her, as well as the political context of the time. The film ends before Albert's death at forty-two, showing the loving pair in a close-up (Figure 68), while the ensuing title cards explain that "Victoria and Albert reigned together for twenty years, and together they would champion reform in every part of their expanding empire."

The political nature of the film was observed and assessed positively by some reviewers (Gleiberman 2009; Smith 2009), yet others claimed it was only the backdrop for the romantic story. Dargis (2009), for instance, notes that "There's a political dimension to Leopold's matchmaking, but those details are immaterial to the romance that develops and deepens." Yet, had it not been for King Leopold, Albert might have never met Victoria in the first place. Although *Elizabeth: The Golden Age*, *The Other Boleyn Girl*, and *The Young Victoria* are set in a clearly defined political context, and incorporate explicit political strategies as part of the narrative—something that films that are more easily associated with politics provide in fewer doses, such as some political thrillers and comedies—the consensus is that they belong to the historical drama and/ or romance genres. Vidal (2012: 36) may rightly note that some monarchy films "also lend themselves for exploration of moments of political crisis," but her focus is on the construction of identity through these films and therefore her exploration of the narratives' political significance is limited. I would argue that the proposed narrative-based construction of the political genre is a valuable way to trace the existence of political films in genres that are produced, marketed, and/or recognized as belonging to other generic categories.

If we apply Hay's strategic-relational theory to these films, marriage becomes the means by which the agents (Anne and Victoria in this case) can affect the structure (the British monarchy system). By marrying Henry VIII, Anne Boleyn succeeds in not only becoming Queen Consort but also persuading the King to proceed to a schism between the Vatican and the Anglican Church. However little influence Anne's request to defy the Pope may have had on Henry's decision, the fact is that it did play a part. Thus, in the case of *The Other Boleyn Girl*, an agent does help bring change to the structure. To clarify a little further, I'll return to the political comedies I discussed in Chapter 2. In *Head of State* and *Man of the Year*, Mays and Tom run for President. Although both films are easily defined as political comedies, in none of them is the structure affected in any way. Moreover, neither Mays nor Tom provide the viewer or their potential fictional voter with a detailed plan of how they will improve the living conditions for the average citizen, but limit their speeches to broad accusations against low wages, environmental pollution, and political corruption. The political thrillers of Chapter 3 also underscore the dominance of the structure when confronted with agents. Despite his efforts, for example, Jason Bourne can only expose the CIA's covert operations and flee the country. In his confrontation with a powerful structure, it is the agent who retreats, even if he is at least able to strike a blow. As *The Bourne Legacy*, the fourth installment shows, the CIA's new covert program is already in place despite the previous scandal.

The fourth film with a female royal protagonist is Stephen Frears's *The Queen*. The narrative concentrates on how Elizabeth II (Mirren) and the new Prime Minister Tony Blair (Michael Sheen) negotiate the death of Diana in August 1997 in a freak accident in Paris. While Queen Elizabeth initially resorts to treating the tragic event as a private matter, since Diana had already divorced Prince Charles in 1996 and was therefore not part of the royal family, Blair opts to address Diana's death publicly and consequently witness his popularity rise even more. Vidal (2012: 36) notes:

> The film's concern with the overlap between the private and the public in an era of mass-mediated events is dramatized via the negotiation between two ideological positions and political agendas: the Queen's inflexible upholding of the traditional values of duty and emotional restraint is contrasted with Blair's strategic management of the media frenzy surrounding Diana's death.

The Queen has been examined in academia as a paradigm of the new biopic that addresses the political and cultural present (Sheehan 2013); as a heritage/

monarchy film (Vidal 2012); as a reflection of women's progress in the field of politics; and as Hollywood's strategy to boost the star system of its golden age (Ford and Mitchell 2009). It has not, however, been discussed as a political narrative, as industrial terminology and marketing strategies (biopic, Helen Mirren as "acting royalty") and specific academic interest (gender representation, genre studies) divert attention. *The Queen* is not a dramatization of a monarch who finds herself in a personal predicament. Instead, I would claim that Diana's death is the pretext of Frears's exploration of the crisis in British monarchy at the time. After all, the narrative begins with Shakespeare's quote from *Henry IV*: "Uneasy lies the head that wears a crown" (Figure 65), connoting that the monarchy will be in turmoil as the plot evolves.

A series of sensational royal divorces in the early 1990s, the fire at Windsor Castle in 1992, which was initially going to be restored via taxation (a decision quickly abandoned because of public outrage), and the intimate revelations about Diana and Charles after the publication of Andrew Morton's biography *Diana: The True Story* in 1992, led to a distrust in the monarchy. However, according to Andrzej Olechnowicz (2007: 286), "[t]he fluctuations in support for the monarchy [...] were undoubtedly extreme and dangerous, but not unprecedented or terminal." Although the Queen has no "formal political role" in Britain's constitutional monarchy, she is still considered "a considerable asset in terms of [...] relations on the international scene," while domestically she wields "considerable symbolic, even moral authority and be widely revered as a unifying figure" (Gordon 2010, 30). Thus, her decision to treat Diana's fatal accident as a private matter, her physical absence from the capital—the Royal family was at Balmoral Castle in Scotland in August—and subsequent media silence, combined with Blair's opposite decision, led to a clear political victory for the latter and an initial defeat for the former. Newspaper headlines, such as the *Daily Mail*'s "Has the House of Windsor a heart?" *The Express*'s "Show us you care," and the *Sun*'s "Where is our queen? Where is her flag?" expressed the public's dissatisfaction with their monarch's apparent inertia (Thompson 2007). The film insists on the impact of this public condemnation of the Queen, who seems genuinely perplexed and astonished by the reaction. Part of a dialogue between her and the Queen Mother (Sylvia Syms) expresses her confusion and, more importantly, her political thought-process:

ELIZABETH II: [...] There's been a change, some shift in values. When you no longer understand your people, mummy, maybe it is time to hand it over to the next generation.

THE QUEEN MOTHER:	Don't be ridiculous. Remember the vow you took?
ELIZABETH II:	I declare that my whole life, rather it be long or short, shall be devoted to your service.
THE QUEEN MOTHER:	Your whole life. That is a commitment to God, as well as your people.
ELIZABETH II:	But what if my actions are damaging the crown?
THE QUEEN MOTHER:	Damaging it? You're the greatest asset this institution has. One of the greatest it has ever had. The problem will come when you leave […].

The Queen is obviously more worried about how her reaction affects her subjects than her own emotional status. And that is a politically driven stasis, ruminating over how one's actions influence a whole nation. This is why Elizabeth II finally succumbs to the public's demand and agrees to a televised address a day before the funeral, where she expresses her gratitude for the love and prayers people have shown. The nation's collective anger is assuaged and faith in the monarchy will slowly be restored. Frears also underscores the role Blair plays in defending the Queen to the media and persuading her to return to London from Balmoral Castle. By doing so, the filmmaker comments on the relationship between the two worlds: that of government politics, with executive, legislative, and judiciary power, and that of monarchy politics, with more of a symbolic power to withhold national unity. At the end of the film (Figure 69), Frears unites these two political forces by having the Queen and the Prime Minister strolling in a garden, discussing the agenda of the newly formed government. *The Queen* begins with a Shakespearean quote as reminder of the monarchy's struggles, but ends by inferring that these troubles, at least in the twenty-first century, can be overcome through compromise and, most importantly, through cooperation with the government as well as support by the citizens. A perfect circle is complete as *The Queen* opens and closes with political statements that imply the real nature of the narrative, despite the marketing and distribution practices that dictate a "safer" approach.

6

Behind the Scenes of the Disguised Political Film Genre

In their respective monographs Giglio (2014) and Haas, Christensen, and Haas (2015) include the criterion of "intent" in their search for the political film. The latter uses the criterion as a narrative feature, as observed in the introduction, whereas the former finds intent outside of the narrative, that is the production side. Giglio (2014: 30) uses intent as one of two criteria (the other being audience effect) in his "two-tier test to identify political films." For Giglio, intent means an explicit purpose of delivering "a political statement" that begins at the production level of a film. This political intent takes the form of clear relevant statements in media interviews and articles, made by the filmmakers involved, who, as Giglio notes, include "the producer, director," and "film studio." Giglio continues his reasoning by mentioning a number of political documentaries, such as Leni Riefenstahl's *Triumph of the Will* (1935), and the Frank Capra war series *Why We Fight* (1942–45), which were commissioned by political forces and whose political intention cannot be doubted. However, when the author moves to fiction films, he does not cite a single director, producer, or studio executive who states that a specific film was made to transmit a political message. Although Giglio acknowledges the difficulties that arise regarding "the definition of intentionality" and partially explains that the reason behind those obstacles is "the fact that filmmaking is a collective enterprise, especially when a film is made under contract for a studio" (2014: 30), I find the inclusion of the criterion of intent problematic, at least as far as it concerns fiction features, as it is not based on actual journalistic material (that is, interviews with filmmakers). Moreover, as I have already mentioned, the criterion of intent is quite difficult to prove without systematic research and wide industry knowledge. However, as the internet today provides the theorist with a great amount of information, I go beyond the films discussed in the previous chapters and search for the "intent" in interviews by directors, writers, and/or actors.

Although Giglio includes producers, directors, and film studios in his list of film individuals who provide the intent—I believe that by "film studio," Giglio means studio executives—I think it would be useful to include the writer(s) during the research because their work is paramount to the overall categorization of the final film, despite, of course, the many compromises that usually take place between preproduction and actual exhibition. Finally, I am also looking at interviews by actors.

Based on the statistical data drawn from the corpus and presented in the first chapter, this chapter includes media interviews and articles on directors, writers, and actors, mostly associated with the genre. Since the making of a film requires significant capital, I think the examination of the individuals linked to the political film of the corpus can yield helpful insights regarding the state of political films in contemporary Hollywood.

The first part of the research involves those directors more frequently associated with the political films that appear in the corpus, and have directed more than one film. These are: Ridley Scott, Paul Greengrass, Robert Redford, Oliver Stone, Steven Spielberg, Doug Liman, George Clooney, and Antoine Fuqua. Among them, Stone, Redford, and Greengrass are generally considered by both the public and the media to tackle political themes and I assumed that their long careers and acknowledged talent and abilities would not make them hesitant regarding the political nature of their film work. Before I started searching for interviews by Stone, Redford, and Greengrass regarding their post-9/11 political films, I searched for potential feature articles that concentrated on their oeuvre to date, using their names and the keywords "political director," "political filmmaker," and/or "political film." The search yielded more than 600,000 pages for Greengrass, more than five million pages for Stone, and more than eleven million pages for Redford. Yet, I was genuinely surprised as no article that focused on these three directors' relationship with political films was found in media outlets, online newspaper editions, or popular film entertainment sites (such as *Vulture*, *HitFix*, the *A.V. Club*) despite the filmmakers' well-known political views, activism, and prior film credits. I note that I stopped the search after investigating the first five Google pages, each comprising ten different entries/websites that include all the keywords I used in the search. I consider it, therefore, possible that an article may exist, for example, on Stone being a political filmmaker if one is to look up all the five million websites. Nevertheless, it is also a fact that the first result page on Google contains not only the most recent and most-read entries, but also the page that comprises the greater number of the keywords of a given search, if not all of them.

The next step was to find interviews with the directors that discuss the political films that are included in the corpus. These interviews are, of course, part of the film's promotion strategies and are used to encourage the media to publish relevant articles, interviews, and/or stories online or in print, and thus create a discussion around the film which will consequently lead people to the theaters. What I want to stress here is that during the promotional period of a given film, directors, as well as writers and actors, aside from being artists also become "products," parts of the industry's assembly line; in other words, they are transformed into means of profit maximization. After all, even if film is considered as pure art, it does have to sell in order to ensure the artist's and the crews' livelihood. Ridley Scott offers part of the truth of a Hollywood director's job description (Hiscock 2010):

> We make movies and we try to sell them. There's no other way around it. To say it's all about pure art is nonsense; it's about how do you sell your movie. I don't care if it's a high budget or a low budget movie, if I don't sell it there's no point in making it.

Scott's frank statement is, and should be accepted as, a reality for every filmmaker, irrespective of the funds he/she may acquire, the industry he/she works in, or the kind of films he/she makes (i.e., art films as opposed to mainstream ones). There is also another aspect worthy of discussion in Scott's assertion. Filmmakers create art but also operate as businesspeople and, in particular, sales people when it comes to promoting their work (of art). Thus, it should be no surprise that directors also hesitate to openly discuss the political intentions included in their film for fear of alienating potential viewers/buyers.

The above hypothesis was confirmed in a number of interviews given by Greengrass, Redford, and Stone. In a *Variety* interview, Scott Foundas (2013) views Redford's acting and directorial choices as "a panoramic portrait of a nation at a constant moral and political crossroads" from the 1860s to the War in Iraq. Yet Redford himself calls his last political film, *The Company You Keep* (2013), "a classical drama" while, although he admits that the Washington portrayed in *The Conspirator* may mirror the post-9/11 capital as well, he does not refer to the political nature of the film, insisting instead on its historical aspect (Grant 2011). Only while talking about *Lions for Lambs*, which is one of the most explicitly political films in his filmography, does Redford talk about politics, although, once again, there is no labeling of the film as political. When asked why he hadn't made such a film at another time, Redford replies:

> [...] I'm always interested in the political theme. Have been since 1970. I did the *Candidate*, I did *All the Presidents Men*, *Quiz Show*, there are various films that are about power of media and film, but times have changed so drastically since I started doing it, its like there's always a new film to be made about the new condition [...] You would've thought after Watergate that all those people that did those dirty tricks for Nixon and lied and cheated [...], that would never happen again. It is! Only worse. So you say, "that's an interesting film to make, not about what's happening, about the factors underneath that's happening [...] That's why Tom Cruise represents something about winning. Winning, winning, winning. That's very American. Both good and bad. And her [Meryl Streep] representing a category that was much stronger 30 years ago. After Watergate, the press was at its highest point, now look [...] (Sciretta 2007)

Redford is not the only political filmmaker that avoids labeling his films as such. Oliver Stone, a director known for his liberal politics and cinematic representations of politically troubled times in American history, but also seminal political figures, like John Fitzgerald Kennedy and Richard Nixon, does not even use the word "politician" in his promotional interviews about *W.*, his George W. Bush biopic (see David Sigerson [2008] and Ebert [2008]). "In the end," he writes to Roger Ebert, "this is centrally the story of a man, more than a formal, broad history" (Ebert 2008). Although it is true that *W.* is a biopic, in that it follows the life of the forty-third President from his college years to the Oval Office, its political nature cannot be denied, and one would expect that Stone would be the first to acknowledge it publicly. Steven Spielberg, on the other hand, does not consider *Lincoln* a biopic but rather a "Lincoln portrait" (Fleming 2012). He also admits that he did not release the film during the 2012 elections because he did not want it "to be a political football." However, as the film was screened for both the Democratic White House and Republicans in Washington, Fleming Jr. asked the director about those Lincoln qualities he would like the politicians who watched it to "walk away with." Spielberg replied:

> Lincoln's leadership is based on a number of precepts but my favorite one is that he acted in the name, and for the good, of the people. In that sense, the two great things he did at the end of his life, to end slavery and the Civil War, was for the good and in the name of the people. He put people ahead of politics, even though he was artful at using politics to be able to accomplish his task. (Fleming 2012)

In other words, even though *Lincoln* is clearly a film with political resonance, Spielberg evades its direct relationship to politics and his diplomatic answer manages to place the president's human side above his political actions. Even Greengrass, writer/director of *Bloody Sunday* (2002)—which focuses on the British-Irish conflict and the massacre of 1972—and *United 93* (2006), the first dramatization of the 9/11 attacks, avoids admitting that the two *Bourne* films he directed (*Bourne Supremacy* and *Bourne Ultimatum*) have any relationship with the post-9/11 world or reveal any political concerns. Instead, he states:

> You know, the thing is when you come to a Bourne movie, you're coming to have some fun. That's honestly the truth of it, I mean me personally. It's a Saturday night movie. I'm not being facetious here, I'm being honest ... I don't come to a Bourne movie to make any kind of statement. (Weintraub 2007b)

Clooney is one of the most politically active actors/directors/writers in Hollywood today and a supporter of the Democratic Party. As Giglio (2014: 7) notes, "Obama received considerable financial support from such A-list stars as George Clooney, Tom Hanks, Barbra Streisand, and Denzel Washington" during both his campaigns. Clooney is also very outspoken about his beliefs and has even been accused of being a traitor when he publicly condemned the 2003 American invasion of Iraq, an unpleasant incident which, according to David Sterritt (2012: 224) can, in part, explain the motivation behind his future film choices.

Clooney and Grant Heslov, friends for over thirty years, have been owners of Smokehouse Productions since 2006. With an Oscar for Best Picture (*Argo*, 2012), the duo has consistently chosen films that underscore a specific political agenda (*The Men Who Stare at Goats*, *The American*, *The Ides of March*), although they have also produced melodramas (*August: Osage County*) and are currently producing a Jodie Foster thriller, *Money Monster*, which is scheduled for a 2016 release. In 2014, Clooney and Heslov's company signed a two-year deal with Sony in order to "develop and produce comedy and drama series for broadcast, cable and digital platforms" (Kenneally 2014). Despite their focus on political subjects, the duo appeared in a *Hollywood Reporter* (2015) article, entitled "The 30 Most Powerful Film Producers in Hollywood." Although Clooney and Heslov's production company does not yield the same profits as Platinum Dudes (Michael Bay, Brad Fuller, and Andrew Form) or Jerry Bruckheimer Films, the critical and commercial success of *Argo* and the appeal of *The Ides of March* has made the producing duo a force to be reckoned with in contemporary Hollywood.

Clooney openly explains that the use of politics in his filmography stems from his personal background. His great grandfather was a mayor, his father a respected anchorman and his upbringing involved political discussions and the development of "a social and political conscience" which, in addition to the sociopolitical upheaval of the 1960s and 1970s—the Civil Rights Movement, the second feminist wave, the anti-Vietnam protest—solidified his political views (Sullivan 2011). However, in an *Interview* discussion with noted television writer and producer Norman Lear (2015), *Good Night, and Good Luck* is mainly portrayed as a film about journalists, despite the political discussion the two men have regarding how the media today portray Iraq and the Bush administration post-9/11 policies.

In a 2006 Guardian interview, Emma Brockes acknowledges the political nature of Clooney's *Good Night, and Good Luck*, and *Syriana*, two films that "tackle corruption in the American government." Yet, the actor/filmmaker and known political activist does not admit his cinematic political intent. Vocal though he is about politics in his personal life, as a filmmaker, Clooney does not state he is a political filmmaker or that his films are political narratives. In a number of interviews for both *Good Night, and Good Luck*, and *The Ides of March* (Emma Brockes [2006], Rebecca Murray [n.d.], among others), and even features, such as Alex Bilmes's (2014) piece for *Esquire*, discussion of Clooney's politics is restricted to his actions as an American citizen and not as a member of Hollywood's elite. Similarly, Ben Affleck discusses *Argo* and Iranian politics with *Rolling Stone*'s Sean Woods (2012), but calls the film a drama that focuses on Tony—the main character—and the CIA, and avoids its labeling as a political narrative.

Ridley Scott is more adamant about the industry's hesitation to sell films as political, and I would add the directors' subsequent omission of relating their work to politics in their interviews. Furthermore, Scott acknowledges that the long-lasting narrative stratagem of clearly defined binary oppositions in films between the good and the bad guys cannot easily be subverted and/or revised, because the US audience does not welcome it. As Lindesay Irvine (2005) writes, Scott "agrees that [*Kingdom of Heaven*'s] even-handed treatment of Muslims and Christians did not help its fortunes at the US box office." The director openly admits that "they [the studios?] should have sold it far more on the basis of religion and politics. And they didn't. They skirted. They were nervous about it." The result was that "only 25% of the film's takings were in the States." Yet, the director remarks that the film was warmly received in the Arab world, and that a number of Islamic groups wrote and thanked him "for a very understanding film about Muslims" (Irvine 2005).

Simple and politically correct narratives and spectacles are the main ingredients, which Hollywood's multi-billion-dollar industry seeks in its products in the twenty-first century. Scott may still get the substantial budgets he needs to make what I define as political narratives, but the majority of his films almost invariably include spectacular action sequences, thus delivering one part of the equation "simplicity/action." His consistent worldwide commercial success—his lifetime gross total is more than $1.3 billion—allows him not only to delve into the subject matters he wants, but to acquire the necessary capital to do so.

Another reason why filmmakers opt to not want to publicly mix politics with their films is the backlash they may face. For instance, *Munich* resulted in Spielberg, a well-known pro-Israeli director and one of the most powerful men in Hollywood, to being called "no friend of Israel" because the film does not overtly take a side. In a telephone interview with Ebert (2005), Spielberg explains:

> This film is no more anti-Israel than a similar film, which offered criticism of America is anti-America. Criticism is a form of love. I love America, and I'm critical of this administration. I love Israel, and I ask questions. Those who ask no questions may not be a country's best friends.

Munich's writer, Tony Kushner, defended the screenplay in a *Los Angeles Times* article, where he writes:

> "Munich" is not me or my politics masquerading as a movie. It's been shaped with remarkable generosity by Steven Spielberg into a historical fiction informed by several perspectives, including mine [...] I think it's the refusal of the film to reduce the Mideast controversy, and the problematics of terrorism and counterterrorism, to sound bites and spin that has brought forth charges of "moral equivalence" from people whose politics are best served by simple morality tales. We live in the Shock and Awe Era, in which instant strike-back and blow-for-blow aggression often trump the laborious process of analysis, investigation and diplomacy. [...] In the film, the Palestinian-Israeli conflict is presented not as a matter of religion versus religion, or sanity versus insanity, or good versus evil or civilization versus barbarism or Judeo-Christian culture versus Muslim culture, but rather as a struggle over territory, over geography, over home. (Kushner 2006)

In a way, Kushner reiterates Scott's rationale about *Kingdom of Heaven* and Hollywood's disinclination to allow complicated political and historical matters treated with complexity, and its insistence on simplification and clarity. *Munich*'s controversy notwithstanding, Spielberg and Kushner both continue their successful careers. On the other hand, there is one filmmaker who did not. Mel Gibson was accused of racism and anti-Semitism after the controversy that followed in the weeks after the release of *The Passion of The Christ*. The result was that Gibson, with five Academy Awards and a lifetime box office of more than $2.1 billion, has not worked for or with a Hollywood studio for eleven years. In 2014, Allison Hope Weiner, one of the journalists who, as an employee of *EW* and *The New York Times*, had participated in the public condemnation of Gibson, wrote a lengthy article on *Deadline* entitled "A Journalist's Plea On 10th Anniversary Of 'The Passion Of The Christ': Hollywood, Take Mel Gibson Off Your Blacklist" (Weiner 2014). At the time of the writing of this chapter, late August 2015, Gibson remains persona non grata.

Another interesting observation drawn from the corpus is that the majority of political thriller directors are not American. Britons Greengrass, Scott, and Pete Travis, Australian Phillip Noyce, and Swede Daniel Espinosa dominate the contemporary political filmography, having directed the most commercial and artistically successful films. Online reviews suggest that often it is the US production companies that choose a director to make a specific film. But, what makes the directors accept the invitation, especially a novice one, apart from the appeal of helming a Hollywood film and the substantial paycheck? Seasoned Australian Noyce (*Salt*)—also known for past political thrillers such as *Patriot Games* (1992), *Clear and Present Danger* (1994)—provides this last piece of the puzzle. When asked by *The Hollywood Reporter*'s Gregg Kilday about his decision to return to Hollywood after a ten-year absence, he answers:

> I made three films in 10 years, and each one of the production processes was followed by a year and half of travel to the four corners of the earth [...] a lot of effort helping distributors find audiences. After 10 years as a town crier, saying "Please come and see my movie," I really was glad for the prospects of having the colonizing genius of Hollywood doing the town-crying for me. The studio system is such an effective proselytizer. (Kilday 2012)

Noyce's elegant answer is indicative of Hollywood's global domination. Therefore, it comes as no surprise that directors associated with the tradition of European political film and a left ideological agenda (such as Greengrass and Costa-Gavras) do not hesitate to become part of the US film industry. *Vantage Point*'s British director Pete Travis shares that he loves movies that the literature calls paranoid thrillers (*Cinema.com* n.d.), such as *Three Days of the Condor* and *The Parallax View*, yet his film is less radical and does not actually question American policies or the War on Terror. Although Travis' filmography includes overtly political narratives, such as TV film *Omagh*, which examines a 1998 bombing in Northern Ireland (Levy 2008), and the director claims one of his influences is Paul Greengrass (who cowrote *Omagh*'s screenplay), *Vantage Point*—his first American feature—is much less complicated regarding its narrative treatment of terrorism, while Travis does not mention the word "political" in the online interviews I consulted.

Similarly, when asked about the political relevance of his first American feature and the conflict surrounding the sharing of classified information, *Safe House*'s director, Swede Daniel Espinosa, prefers not to associate the film with the sociohistorical circumstances and opts for a generalized reply. Espinosa explains that what first appealed to him in the script was the exploration of the "Master/Apprentice" dynamic between his two leads:

> I just think we're at an interesting place in history because we have a perspective of ourselves as living in a democratic society, and we have to make a decision: should we allow the government and those that we elect as responsible for us to make these decisions without letting us know what's really going on and why [...] It's the whole WikiLeaks issue, and there's no judgment on that in the film, but we have to make a decision, (Weinard 2012)

The reluctance on the part of both seasoned and novice directors to publicly discuss the political nature of the narratives can be explained on the one hand by the economic parameters explicitly voiced by Scott as well as the potential backlash filmmakers can face—as in Spielberg's case. Contemporary political films, it seems, are still deemed unwanted or even suspicious by the industry, which operates in a strictly defined capitalist market with no apparent interest in producing complex narratives that can open up discussions on issues of vital importance.

Following the majority of the aforementioned directors' reluctance to discuss politics as a significant narrative element of their films, writer Grant Heslov avoids the political intent of his films. When asked about the statement he wanted to make about the present moment with *Good Night, Good Luck*, he answers that:

> [t]he political aspect of the film was secondary to us. We knew that there would be a lot of political hay out of this. That really wasn't our goal. For us it was strictly about the state of journalism. (Jacobson 2005)

Heslov even denies the political intent in *The Ides of March*, a film that cannot easily be mistaken as anything else other than a political narrative, and reveals that the political label does not offer either a marketing or distribution advantage; in fact, when Jack Giroux (2011) wonders about whether the film was pitched to foreign buyers as a narrative "about a guy losing his morals," Heslov agrees and adds that what they tried to sell was a film about "a guy who starts off as a true believer, for all the right reasons, and then at the end still gets his guy elected, but sort of compromises everything and sells his soul, but still might have gotten the right guy elected."

Contrary to Heslov's evasive answers, Matthew Michael Carnahan, writer of *The Kingdom*, *Lions for Lambs* and *State of Play*, and holder of a degree in international relations and political science, does not shy away from the political motivations behind his work:

> I've been fascinated with politics as far back as I can remember. We grew up a poor Irish, democrat family from Michigan so the politics seemed to kind of run in the blood. I have early memories of talking politics, talking about Jimmy Carter's presidency at the dinner table. My dad the republican and my mom the democrat, I have always had this abiding love of government, politics and the idea that someone can remain true and heaven forbid, even righteous, and still be able to navigate the treachery or our system. (Brevet 2007)

Carnahan even admits that his screenplay for Redford's *Lions for Lambs* is "a call to action," the action being that the American citizens understand the futility of the world in Iraq and "becom[ing] cognizant of that" (Sommers 2007).

In a personal and revealing account of the writing process for *Frost/Nixon* and its meaning on *The Telegraph* in 2009, British Peter Morgan (*Frost/Nixon*, *The Other Boleyn Girl*, and *The Queen*) explains the film's resonance with its contemporary political landscape and his conviction of its political nature despite his initial intention of writing a character study, that first became a stage play in 2006, before its adaptation for the big screen. During the promotional campaign for *Frost/Nixon*, Morgan observed first-hand the industry's avoidance of the film's political intentions:

> It's a boxing match. It's a character study. It's a comedy. It's a suspense piece. It's a courtroom drama. In the run-up to the American release in late-December, all of us connected with the project were flying from coast to coast selling it in anything other than political terms.

The effort to promote a film as anything but political is evident in most interviews, and explains the absence or scarcity of this label in the media and the databases I consulted for the compilation of the corpus. For instance, Doug Liman, director of *Fair Game*, which is based on a true political scandal, says that "I don't see *Fair Game* primarily as a political movie. It's obviously a film that has a lot of politics in it, but our interest in this was to make an emotional film about what these people went through" (Wise n.d.a). Similarly, in another interview, Liman is asked if *Fair Game* is part of a contemporary trend that includes other political/spy thrillers, such as *Green Zone* and *Nothing But The Truth* (2008). Again, he offers a rather evasive answer, but this time acknowledging *Fair Game* as a political film:

> I think it's in the spectrum of "It's a really great movie." And a lot of other movies that have been about the war or dealt with the war have not been great movies. In fact, they've been motivated more by politics than by story, and that's been a turn-off to audiences. This is sort of the first political movie that's been made where I feel like the commitment was there from the first moment to story and character, and not to politics. (Vanairsdale 2010)

Morgan's classification of his work also shifted, but his written account leaves no room as to his motivation whereas one cannot be sure what prompted Liman, an otherwise very vocal filmmaker, to disavow the political intentions of *Fair Game*. Morgan finally admits that *Frost/Nixon* is a political film when the economy collapses in 2008 and Barack Obama becomes President. It is only then that he writes:

> And that's where *Frost/Nixon* suddenly does become political. Because before it's a character piece, or a gladiatorial fist-fight, or a thriller, a courtroom drama, or comedy—before it's anything—*Frost/Nixon* is a play about accountability and the prosecution, conviction and atonement of an elected public servant who violated the cherished principles of democracy and broke the law. Its central narrative is the unlikely securing, by a rank outsider, of a conviction where the political and judicial processes failed, and the achievement of a catharsis for the people in whose name the transgressions were enacted. (Morgan 2009)

Writers, it seems, are more vocal about the political intentions of their films, even though they are not as "interesting" media subjects as the stars or directors of the film, because their work usually ends as filming begins. Yet, it is important that at least one member of the filmmaking team admits that political films are part of Hollywood's production and distribution system, despite all efforts to conceal such intentions.

A common thread in the majority of interviews I read is that although their content, and especially the journalists' introductions, includes the words "political" and "politics," as do some of the questions, the filmmakers' and actors' answers rarely refer to these terms directly. For instance, Katie Curic (2004) begins her interview with *The Manchurian Candidate* stars and director by stating that the film "is a political thriller, for a political season." Yet neither the director Jonathan Demme nor the protagonists Denzel Washington and Meryl Streep openly discuss the overt political context of the narrative. Finally, Curic writes that "[w]hile these three agree, *Manchurian Candidate* doesn't have an ideological agenda, they admit it's no coincidence it's set against the backdrop of an election." In particular, Washington is especially opposed to even uttering a phrase that may be connected to politics and when interviewed by Jennifer Krieger (2008) for the same film, he dismisses all potential political criticism included in the film and concludes that the point of a film is to make people think. On the other hand, Naomi Watts may not get upset during interviews promoting *Fair Game*, but opts to designate the film as a story "about truth and lies" (Wise n.d.b). Interestingly, a number of politically active actors also shy away from referring to the political nature of the films they star in. In respective interviews on *Milk* (Rich 2008; Balfour 2009), *Green Zone* (Eisenberg 2010; Weintraub 2010), *Lincoln* (Wilcox 2012) and *Breach* (Weintraub 2007a), Sean Penn, Matt Damon, David Strathairn, and Chris Cooper do not talk about the political nuances of the narratives they are involved with despite their otherwise being quite known for their political activism and views.

Strikingly, even director Kathryn Bigelow, whose *Zero Dark Thirty* even became a subject of a congressional hearing in Washington DC, steers clear of explicit political discussions in the media. In a *Telegraph* interview with David Gritten (2013), there is no mention of the words 'politics' or 'political' as the article focuses mainly on the accusations against the director made after the film's release, and Bigelow's vehement denial of being "pro-torture" (Gritten 2013). Bigelow does not publicly refer to her film as political in either *The New York Times* (Barnes 2012), *Time* (Winter 2013), *The Economist* (2013), or *The Guardian* (Brockes 2013). In fact, Brockes finds this so surprising that she comments on it, and writes that "[h]er assiduously neutral position on the politics of the film brings to mind, ironically, a politician." Bigelow's screenwriter, Mark Boal, follows suit in his media engagements (Alex Rees 2013; Hayden 2013) and evades relevant questions.

It becomes clear that even those filmmakers who clearly engage in political narratives tend to evade talking about their film's political relevance, choosing to promote their films as an entertainment product and leaving all political resonance to be extracted and discussed by the viewers. It would be very easy to accuse these individuals of fearing the industry or caring more about increasing their bank accounts. However, I find that their promotional tactics are indicative of a rational separation that occurs between their artistic and political intentions and their professional identity, as either actors/directors/writers, from their function as promoters/salespeople of a specific product (their film). After all, it is the film that has to succeed financially, not only to enable the filmmakers to enjoy their stardom and earn substantial amounts of money but also to allow them to continue making the same kind of political narratives. The success of these films should always be considered as a part of a much larger industry upon which hundreds of thousands of families are dependent—suffice it to say that the Los Angeles entertainment industry has an "annual employment of 130,900 jobs in 2014" (Verrier 2015).

In a *New York Times* interview, Scott explains the difference between a director and a studio executive: "One studio head said to me, 'I make movies I don't even want to see.'" In contrast, Scott's retort is: "I only want to make movies that I want to see" (Carr 2010). However self-evident the above reasoning may seem, it does lie at the heart of the commercialization vs. art debate. Is the industry selling films as products or works of art? While the answer is not within the scope of this book, it does put into perspective the large gap that exists between the business side and the artistic/talent side. Generally, and with minor exceptions, Hollywood executives want to sell as many tickets and tie-in products as they can, and when they find a formula that works (i.e., superhero films and appealing franchises) they will exhaust them until the next "big thing" comes along. As Liman, *The Bourne Identity*'s director, says bluntly: "They're [the studios] spending money to make something that's a cookie-cutter product. You know, just copy someone else's movie and get on with it" (Fear 2014). At the same time, directors, writers, and actors are artists who want to convey ideas, emotions, values, and sometimes talk about serious subjects through their art. While the former avoid controversy and focus on simplicity and spectacle, the latter tackle thorny issues and do not shy away from complicated and disputed questions.

7

Epilogue: Beyond the Corpus

The genesis, development, and endurance of a film genre are based on a number of factors. Industrial parameters, artistic inspiration, audience taste, and sociohistorical context are all entangled in the creation and continuation of groups of films that share similar characteristics. However, as I have shown, a genre can also be constructed theoretically if a specific group of films has not already been labeled as such by Hollywood or the media for whatever reasons. Although the corpus on which I base my research covers the years between 2002 and 2012, I would like to underscore that political films do not disappear after 2012, the year that Haas, Christensen, and Haas (2015, 248) dub as the "the year of the political film." So, before I make some final observations about the disguised political film genre, I would like to briefly discuss some newer additions, released between 2013 and 2015.

As noted in Chapter 2, comedy is not the industry's preferred mode for criticizing political affairs, as only fifteen comedies were part of the corpus, which spans ten years. This is corroborated by Hollywood's output since, after the release of the last political comedy in the corpus (the 2012 *The Campaign*), no political mainstream comedy was released, with the exception of two releases in 2015: The spy-comedy *The Man from U.N.C.L.E.* and the late-October distribution of *Our Brand is Crisis*. The former, a UK–USA coproduction, was based on the NBC television series with the same title that ran from 1964 to 1968 and was directed by Briton Guy Richie, a filmmaker known for highly stylized scenes and action sequences as well as a preference for mixing action with comedy. Unlike its contemporary spy comedies that spoof James Bond (the *Johnny English* films, for instance), *The Man from U.N.C.L.E.* does not ridicule its spy-protagonists but rather uses comic touches to lighten the subject and cause laughter in sequences that, if reserved for a dramatic spy thriller, would have the viewers on the edge of their seat. More importantly, the film, which is set in the 1960s, offers the possibility of cooperation between the US and the

USSR in an effort to prevent a criminal organization from obtaining nuclear power. Thus, CIA agent Solo (Henry Cavill) teams up with KGB spy Illya (Armie Hammer), as well as East-German Gaby (Alicia Vikander)—whose father, a renowned nuclear scientist, has gone missing and is thought to be helping to create an atomic bomb for private interests.

Our Brand is Crisis is the latest addition to the political filmography of producers Clooney and Heslov and their company, Smokehouse Pictures. The film is a fictional version of the 2005 documentary of the same title by Rachel Boynton, which "followed the work of James Carville's political consulting firm as it worked Gonzalo Sánchez de Lozada's campaign for president of Bolivia in 2002" (Watercutter 2015). Interestingly, the protagonist in the initial script was written for a male character, specifically Clooney, and was reworked when Sandra Bullock "expressed interest" (Watercutter 2015).

Although I mentioned that only two political comedies were released after 2012, I would be remiss if I did not briefly refer to the controversy that surrounds the political satire *The Interview* (2014), one of the rare cases of this generic form produced by a major studio. The film, directed by Evan Goldberg and comedian Seth Rogen, and written by Dan Sterling based on a story by Goldberg, Rogen, and Sterling, follows celebrity TV host Dave Skylark (James Franco) and his producer Aaron Rapoport (Rogen), who have been recruited by the CIA in their attempt to assassinate North Korea's dictator Kim Jong-un. *The Interview* was scheduled for release by Sony at Christmas 2014. However, in late November, the company had its electronic network shut down due to a large-scale hack by "a group calling themselves Guardians of Peace (#GOP)" (Albright 2015). Unreleased films were made available online, while employee and executives' email correspondence became the subject of public scrutiny as unflattering conversations and industry individuals were scorned. The GOP threatened Sony to not release *The Interview* by implying terrorist actions in the theaters that were to show the film. Despite the controversy and the public insistence on protecting the freedom of speech and art and on releasing the film, Sony decided to cancel its US wide release and opted for online rent or purchase streaming of *The Interview* before becoming available on Netflix in January 2015.

The relative shortage of political comedies in Hollywood can be attributed to two reasons. First, the theme of American presidential elections, which is recycled in many similar narratives, does not seem to strike a chord with the international audience. Especially if one considers that a substantial percentage of moviegoers are young adult males, it can be safely hypothesized that their interests lie outside the realm of political campaigning, disputes among candidates, political strategizing, and elections. Second, the 2010s witnessed an impressive proliferation and popularity of political comedy content on US television screens, as was noted in Chapter 2. Jon Stewart's and Stephen Colbert's shows and *Real Time With Bill Maher* (HBO, 2003–present), among others, not only use comedy to denounce and/or satirize policies and politicians but have managed to influence the political perception of part of their audience as well as the US government itself. According to *Politico*'s Darren Samuelsohn, whose 2015 article reveals that Stewart had secretly visited the White House twice during the Obama administration, the comedian has actual political power that goes well beyond his television show and his potential impact on his fans' political thought and/or action. Among Stewart's actual contributions to US political life, Samuelsohn finds that he "is widely credited with changing how the government treated military veterans and Sept. 11 first responders and for the cancellation of a hyperpartisan CNN talk show" (Samuelsohn 2015). Furthermore, the wide dissemination of online outlets that create unprecedented space for news, as well as increasing demand for it, use short videos taken from shows—usually the most radical, inflammatory, or surprising for one reason or another—as their main subject and create a whole new meta-discourse around a specific line the comedian used, its subtexts, etc. In a 2014 *Washington Post* article featuring the twelve most memorable political sketches of the year, Jamie Fuller observes that the "number of political sketches being produced on a weekly basis" is indeed "insane" (Fuller 2014). No film was mentioned in this list, not only because Fuller chose television as the medium from which to draw his data but simply because no political film comedy had been released that year. It could be argued that since TV talk shows and their comedian hosts' political commentary have created an undeniable new trend in communicating and managing political news, the film industry sees no reason to produce similar narratives. After all, according to Jason Zinoman (2012), the obvious "left-wing, opinionated and earnestly engaged" discourse of the majority of talk shows, and I would add the sometimes fiery and explicit way in which political commentary is expressed, cannot find its way in Hollywood political comedy. The industry's inherent conservatism regarding political matters, and its profit-making target, end up diluting scripts that could potentially contribute to creating a meaningful political comedy. Finally, a late night talk show, broadcast three to five times per week, is afforded by definition the opportunity to comment on news that has just happened. This sense of immediate critique is lost in a cinematic narrative whose journey from inception to release may take years.

As mentioned in Chapter 3, political thrillers are usually marketed as action/adventure films or spy thrillers. Despite involving spies, governmental institutions such as the CIA, and political figures from both the United States and foreign nations, their political character is concealed in their marketing and promotional campaigns as well as in most media reports. Aside from the *Bourne* franchise that began its course in the 2000s, *Jack Ryan: Shadow Recruit* (2014), marks the fifth film with the same spy character protagonist, portrayed by four different actors since the 1990s. In addition, two other film franchises released their fifth installment in 2013 and 2015: *A Good Day to Die Hard* (2013), and *Mission: Impossible—Rogue Nation* (2015). The former, which catapulted Bruce Willis to stardom back in 1988, was relatively successful worldwide (on a $92 million budget, it generated close to $305 million despite moderate to negative reviews), while the latter reinvigorated the *Mission* franchise and solidified the recently problematic appeal of Tom Cruise, with more than $650 million worldwide on a $150 million budget, as well as a host of favorable reviews. It would be interesting, although not a target of this book, to examine these two series' course from the late 1980s and mid-1990s, respectively, to the 2010s, and to study their commentary, or lack thereof, on the contemporary political landscape diachronically. Nevertheless, a few observations should be made. The first *Die Hard* film in 1988 is considered a conservative text, "dictated" by the Reagan era. It is a narrative that focuses on a true masculine hero, and belongs to what Yvonne Tasker (1993) has labeled as "muscular cinema" of the 1980s and early 1990s, designating a group of films that celebrate and commodify the body builder's male body in big-budgeted action films starring such actors as Sylvester Stallone and Arnold Schwarzenegger. Aside from the film's gender representations, Deron Overpeck also notes that *Die Hard*'s "representational politics are so conservative that they hearken back to World War II: even the primary villains are Germans and Japanese" (Overpeck 2007: 199), despite, of course, differences in their contemporary motivation. Interestingly, the script of the 2013 installment reimagines Reagan's "evil empire," and casts Russians as the villains against John McLane and his son-turned-CIA agent Jack (Jai Courtney) in a narrative that was criticized for its lack of ingenuity and blatant use of violence.

Mission: Impossible—Rogue Nation, on the other hand, may also insist on US hegemony over global matters through Ethan Hawke, the agent of the secret organization Impossible Mission Force (IMF), which is disbanded in this fifth installment. Yet, its script is more attuned to global politics as Ethan has to uncover the Syndicate, an international terrorist consortium, with the help of an MI6 female agent. Irrespective of reviews and box office, it is obvious that both franchises propagate American exceptionalism despite their rather simplistic plotlines and insistence on spectacular action sequences. After all, what stays in the end with the viewer is the fact that both John McLane (Willis) and Ethan Hawke (Cruise), both patriotic Americans, save the day yet again. With total earnings of $1.4 billion (*Die Hard* films) and $2.7 billion (*Mission: Impossible* films), this powerful, however latently imbued in the narrative, message of US supremacy will continue to be spread as the sixth installment of both franchises has already been announced in the media. The political thrillers above share the same isotopies discussed in Chapter 3. They center on virile male characters, although not as young as Bourne, and position the threat outside the US borders, while the villains are older male figures. In other words, aside from reusing the myth around their charismatic heroes, most political thrillers of the 2010s seem to follow the same formula.

However, a difference is noted in two 2013 political thrillers which focus on the character of the president. *Olympus Has Fallen* was released in March. It was directed by Antoine Fuqua who, according to the corpus, has also directed two more political films between 2002 and 2012 (*Shooter* and *King Arthur*), and was based on an original screenplay by Creighton Rothenberger and Katrin Benedikt. *White House Down*, directed by Roland Emmerich (the name behind such survival blockbusters as *The Day After Tomorrow* [2004], and *2012* [2008]) and written by James Vanderbilt, was released in June. Both films performed relatively poorly with both viewers and critics. *Olympus Has Fallen* cost $70 million and returned more than $161 million worldwide, placing thirty-sixth in the US top-100 of 2013. *White House Down* cost $150 million and earned a little over $205 million, featuring at number forty-six of the top 100. The two films share a number of narrative similarities. The White House is overtaken in both cases by terrorists (*Olympus Has Fallen* opts for a foreign enemy while *White House Down* chooses a domestic threat), and eventually saved by two seemingly indestructible government employees: former secret service agent Mike Banning (Gerard Butler) in *Olympus Has Fallen* and newly appointed Capitol policeman John Cale (Channing Tatum) in *White House Down*. President Asher (Aaron Eckhart) and President Sawyer (Jamie Foxx) in *Olympus Has Fallen* and *White House Down* respectively, are virile male figures and quite active in the plot, although Asher's capture by the terrorists limits the possibility of him reacting as the absolute masculine hero that Sawyer is allowed to be in *White House Down* since he evades the threat and teams up with Cale to save the innocent hostages.

Haas, Christensen, and Haas place both films in a cycle of disaster and apocalyptic films that were featured in theaters during the same period (such as the 2012 releases *The Road, Contagion, World War Z*, and the 2013 *Battleship*). The authors argue that although new cinematic technology allows for relevant narratives to be filmed with unprecedented verisimilitude, the conventions of the disaster genre also "translated the political anxieties and widespread calamities marking the new century" (2015: 364). Haas, Christensen, and Haas note that, in a way, the 1990s and the 2000s underscore the demise "of the 'American experiment,' with the United States unable and/or unwilling to play its Second World War and postwar superhero role on the world stage. Specifically, "Russia's seizure of Crimea in Ukraine"; the threat of a "debt default in 2011 and 2013"; the ambiguous end of "two wars on foreign soil"; the "intractable yet amorphous war on terror"; the widening "gap between the rich and everyone else"; and the "dysfunctional federal legislature" are the defining traits of the time and lead to these two films that actually depict the destruction of the White House, the symbol of the American government, thus underlining the fact that to start anew, you sometimes have to leave your past behind (2015: 365).

Although *Olympus Has Fallen* and *White House Down* present narrative structures that follow the political thrillers discussed in Chapter 3, there is a significant difference. Both films choose to bring the threat inside the United States and, in particular, the center of the government, one of the most recognizable symbols of the nation globally. Thus, they avoid the isotopy between the "inside" (the United States) and the "outside" (outside the borders), shared by the rest of the films in the same group that preceded them. According to Haas, Christensen, and Haas (2015: 365), "[u]nleashing destruction and firepower within the Capitol's dome suggested at best that politically the United States should turn away from foreign matters and mind the home front, an isolationist tendency also embraced by libertarians and extended to the continuing tumult in Iraq and Syria." I would also add that placing the threat inside the US borders, and in particular the seat of the government, is, first, allowed by the historical distance of 9/11, and second, can serve as a warning of American interventionism abroad. *Olympus Has Fallen* and *White House Down* are cautionary tales regarding global politics, and question American hegemony and even American political arrogance by having the White House itself "broken into" without serious difficulty, and by capturing members of the cabinet. It would be interesting to see if this change persists in the future.

The Butler (2013), *12 Years a Slave* (2013), and *Selma* (2014), are three history films that were released in two consecutive years, garnering critical acclaim and many awards. The three films center on African-American men, covering a time period from the mid-1800s to the 1960s, and address issues of racial discrimination and civil rights struggles. Yet, I only consider *Selma* as a political text because, according to the proposed definition, it is the only film that revolves around a character who acts in a political context and whose actions have important ramifications for the whole society and, in particular, the US African-American community. *The Butler*, loosely based on the real life of Eugene Allen, narrates the life of Cecil Gaines (Forest Whitaker) who was a White House butler for thirty-four years and served under eight Presidents. Although Cecil becomes witness to many historical events, from Brown vs. Board of Education, the 1963 March on Washington, and the Vietnam War to the inauguration of Obama, the film cannot be considered a political text per se, since the narrative concentrates on Cecil's everyday routine and his family life, amidst the events of his long life and career. Similarly, *12 Years a Slave* is a biopic of Solomon Northup and is based on his memoir of the same title, which was first published in 1853. Northup was a free-born African-American, who was kidnapped in Washington and sold into slavery in 1841. The book and the film focus on his life as a slave and his twelve-year struggle to have his freedom restored. *The Butler*, *12 Years a Slave*, along with other films, such as *42*, 2013, a biopic of legendary baseball player Jackie Robinson, are important narratives that focus on racism and the lives of African-Americans who have been distinguished by history. Yet, as I noted in the introduction regarding similar films, such as *Crash*, *The Great Debaters*, *The Freedom Writers*, *The Help*, and *Django Unchained*, their subject of inequality, racial discrimination and racial tension, and civil rights struggles is limited within the boundaries of each protagonist's narrative program and never enters the political arena.

On the other hand, *Selma* is the only recent black-themed film with a clear political subject as it depicts the 1965 voting rights marches from the town of Selma, Alabama to Montgomery, a protest that, once realized, ultimately had a significant role in the Voting Rights Act being passed a little later. Written by Briton Paul Webb and directed by Ava DuVernay (her third feature film), *Selma* focuses on Dr. Martin Luther King's efforts to convince President Johnson to pass the law allowing African-Americans the right to vote, the failed attempts to march from Selma to Montgomery, and Dr. King's endurance and negotiations. As with most history films, *Selma* was criticized for inaccuracies despite being praised in general as an important production. Fred Mazelis and Tom Mackaman (2015) find that the film's weaknesses have mainly to do with the absence of the wider "historical and political context," and the rather erroneous—according to them and several historians—depiction of President Johnson as the "villain." Similarly, in a *New York Times* article that cites several historical sources, it is underscored that Dr. King and Johnson were partners and not the adversaries *Selma* clearly depicts:

> It is true, historians say, that Johnson was hesitant to introduce a voting rights bill so soon after the passage of the Civil Rights Act. But Professor May noted that on Dec. 14, 1964, Johnson directed his attorney general, Nicholas Katzenbach, to begin drafting such a bill—a fact the film does not mention, he said, (Schuessler 2014).

This particular representation of the LBJ–Dr. King relationship created a controversy around the film in almost the same way that *Zero Dark Thirty* was vehemently attacked for its depiction of torture and *Argo* for not acknowledging the pivotal role Canada played in freeing the American hostages from Tehran in 2012. As my analysis in Chapter 4 shows, almost no history film can escape media articles or academic essays emphasizing some sort of fallacy regarding the depicted historical events. Especially when the cinematic narrative revolves around major and/or disputed events, when even historians are also divided in their interpretation, fictionalized history films will remain suspect of distorting and/or misrepresenting facts and people. Yet, for the purpose of this monograph, *Selma* remains an important political text, not only because it is "the first major feature film about King" (Banks 2015) but because it brings to life a series of events (the marches) not known widely beyond the US borders, thus teaching the global audience while reminding the American one.

The years 2013 and 2014 witnessed the continuation of what I call in Chapter 5 "hidden" political films. *300*'s sequel, *300: Rise of an Empire*, was released in 2014, the same year Scott released the biblically-themed *Exodus: Gods and Kings*. Both films were moderately successful; the former made $337.6 million worldwide on a $100 million budget and the second earned $268 million costing $145 million. As was observed, Scott is among the few directors who has helmed similar political narratives (in the 2002 to 2012 period covered by the corpus, he directed *Robin Hood* and *Kingdom of Heaven*, as well as the overtly political *Body of Lies*). Although most of his films have been scrutinized regarding historical accuracy, *Exodus: Gods and Kings* caused a media controversy over whitewashing the characters. Scott was accused of casting "white actors in the lead roles, despite depicting events taking place in the Middle East and North Africa." The director explains that this choice "was predicated on the need to attract financial backing" (Child 2014), and has already clarified that:

I can't mount a film of this budget, where I have to rely on tax rebates in Spain, and say that my lead actor is Mohammad so-and-so from such-and-such. I'm just not going to get it financed. So the question doesn't even come up. (Nick Allen 2014)

Despite Scott's explanation, which is indicative of Hollywood's production practices since the birth of the industry, as well as the contemporary neoliberal market—irrespective of the ethical implications of such a structure—the backlash did not end. Whitewashing still complicates matters in Hollywood for an overwhelming percentage of non-white actors; yet it is only recently, and because of the widespread of online outlets, that controversies begin even at the time of a film's production. I should add that it is not only films of a political nature that are scrutinized but all productions that seem to ignore the problem of race. Along with *Exodus: Gods and Kings*, Cameron Crowe was also targeted with whitewashing his romantic comedy *Aloha* (2015), by not casting Asian-Pacific Islanders and, thus, he was accused of "'insulting' Hawaiian culture" (Lee 2015).

However, I would argue that the controversy over Scott's whitewashing of *Exodus: Gods and Kings* obscures the political theme of the film. The narrative follows Moses (Christian Bale) as the Hebrew who revolts against Ramses in Egypt to free the rest of his enslaved community. In his interesting article on the film, Ryan McMaken (2014) considers it "moderately successful," "[a]s an exercise in political and military themes." Although McMaken finds that the narrative and its subject would have been better served if there were a clear protagonist, he is one of the few writers who do acknowledge Scott's focus on political behavior, thought, and action.

Chapter 5 also included the examination of the monarchy film and specifically the films that focused on female British queens. The industry tried to continue the trend in recent years, but both *Diana* (2013), and *Grace of Monaco* (2014), failed with both viewers and critics, despite the films' production values and star-studded cast. *Diana* was a European coproduction, directed by acclaimed German director Oliver Hirschbiegel (*The Downfall* [2004], *The Experiment* [2001]), and based on Kate Snell's book *Diana: Her Last Love*, 2000. Starring Naomi Watts as the Princess of Wales, the film explores her secret love affair with Pakistani heart surgeon Hasnat Khan and concentrates on romance rather than Diana's under-examined political power. Costing $15 million and generating a little over $21 million, *Diana* was mainly considered as a dull oversimplification of a royal's life (Gant 2013; Merry 2013). The generally negative response to the film even led its star, Watts, to call it a "sinking ship" and note that "there were problems [with the film] and it ended up taking a direction that was not the one I was hoping for" (Miller 2014). *Grace of Monaco*, an international coproduction, had a similar journey to *Diana*. Also helmed by a young yet acclaimed director, Frenchman Olivier Dahan (*La Vie en Rose* [2007]), the film opened the Cannes Film Festival in 2014. Unlike *Diana*, *Grace of Monaco* includes the former-Hollywood star-turned-royal's political involvement during a crisis between Monaco and France in the 1960s. Yet, a number of alleged disputes between its director and the distributors (The Weinstein Company, TWC), regarding some editing that TWC requested from Dahan, Harvey Weinstein's absence from the Cannes premiere, combined with the Monaco royal family's criticism of the production (Hammond 2014), led to the film earning only $26.5 million worldwide on a $30 million budget, and not being distributed in the United States. A year after its premiere, US viewers had the chance to watch *Grace of Monaco* on Lifetime (Hipes 2015), a private cable channel that mostly caters to female-centered shows and TV films.

Summarizing the disguised political film genre

This monograph is aimed at defining the political film in contemporary Hollywood using a methodology deriving from semiotics in a theoretical context informed by film genre, political science, and sociology. The study has allowed me to arrive at the following six main conclusions regarding the genre:

1. **The disguised political film genre can only exist as a theoretical construction and repeats a specific narrative structure.**
   The data used in the monograph were drawn from a comprehensive corpus of approximately 200 films that were initially viewed to determine the surface narrative grammar of the texts using semiotic tools. This allowed

me to propose a clear definition of the genre as a film whose story can take place in the past or the present, follow the dramatic or comedic mode, originate from real or fictional events—or a combination of both—with a subject/protagonist whose narrative object is situated in the political structure of a state, and its attainment will affect society as a whole in a positive or negative way. Based on this definition, I proceeded by excluding more than a hundred films from the corpus to arrive at an inclusive list of films that I feel represent the disguised political film produced in contemporary Hollywood. The overwhelming majority of the films I viewed were marketed under different generic labels (action, adventure, spy films, etc.), while most popular online databases do not include political films in their categorization. These observations undoubtedly substantiate Hollywood's antipathy towards the genre and its successful actions to be disassociated with similar films. Thus, I conclude that the political film genre can only exist as a theoretical construction, a category produced through academic analysis. This construction initially examines the structure of the texts and then combines the results with the cultural context and the industrial factors of the films to discuss the interaction among them and study the potential functions of similar texts.

2. **The disguised political film genre is a male-centric genre.**
   As far as both its narrative and production sides are concerned, the contemporary political film in Hollywood focuses on male protagonists and is also predominantly helmed by male filmmakers. With the exception of the monarchy films I examine in Chapter 5, which revolve around female royal figures, most subgenres of the disguised political film genre are focused on male stories, which are mainly directed and produced by male filmmakers. However, Bigelow's *Zero Dark Thirty*, a film starring Jessica Chastain, and *Salt*, a political thriller whose screenplay was conceived for a male star but had to be rewritten once Angelina Jolie expressed interest, alongside revisionist epic films, such as *Robin Hood* and *King Arthur*, that include secondary yet strong female characters, may be considered as a sign of change regarding the blatant gender disparity that reigns in Hollywood both in front of, and behind, the camera.

3. **The disguised political film genre is mainly associated with specific genres.**
   According to the corpus categorization, there are a couple of popular genres that steadily produce political narratives despite their being marketed under

different labels; namely the action thriller and the epic. It is ironic that entire franchises, such as the *Bourne* films, the *Mission: Impossible* series, the *Die Hard* franchise, or the *Jack Ryan* films, which have, combined, resulted in almost $6.5 billion in admissions worldwide, are continuously produced and marketed by the film industry as anything but political narratives despite their obvious narrative structure that perpetuates the myths of either the benevolent United States or the lonely American agent who can finally bring justice to the world.

4. **The political film genre deals predominantly with issues of foreign policy.**

The majority of the disguised political films in the corpus focus on issues of foreign policy, and present the duality between good and evil as an isotopy of Americans (good) vs. foreign threat (evil). On the one hand, a conflict is a necessary ingredient of the classical narrative whose rules these films obey. On the other hand, the foreign threat is a trope that is dictated by each sociocultural landscape, and expresses the anxieties and fears of each time period. Just as Russian villains appeared in films during the Cold War—although they still remain part of various contemporary narratives—post-9/11 films use Middle-Eastern characters to depict evil. Finally, I would suggest that the relative scarcity of films that focus on domestic policies is also dictated on the one hand by the unwillingness on the part of some filmmakers to discuss problematic and even traumatic events, and, on the other, by the difficulty of raising capital for such films that usually do not resonate with the global audience.

5. **The disguised political film genre conveys a predominantly liberal agenda.**

With rare exceptions (such as *American Sniper*, *Act of Valor*, the *Die Hard* films, *Troy*, and *300* that are mostly conservative and promote a militarist culture), the disguised political film genre is mostly liberal in nature. Films such as *Syriana*, *Lions for Lambs*, *Milk*, *The Kingdom*, *Good Night, and Good Luck*, *State of Play*, *Green Zone*, *Body of Lies*, *Fair Game*, *Lincoln*, *Head of State*, *Man of the Year*, and *Traitor* may be critical of US policies but also promote liberalism, associated with "a regulatory state, civil liberties and rights for minorities, equality, and secularism," as well as the "so-called free market economy" (Kellner 2010: 3).

6. **The disguised political film genre does not question American exceptionalism as evidenced by its narrative structure.**

Irrespective of the conservative or the liberal ideology promoted in the political narratives of the corpus, and the frequent castigation of older and contemporary policies that the American government implements, the political films do not question American exceptionalism, a consumerist laissez-faire ideology, nor interventionism, which has been popularized by Alexis de Tocqueville's seminal *Democracy in America* since the 1840s. Even though most political thrillers, for instance, represent corruption as part of many US governmental institutions, such as the CIA, the Secret Service or the Pentagon, US military intervention in foreign territories, execution of dangerous missions in ally cities, or organization of operations with no regard for international laws are almost never questioned. The United States remains, therefore, a beacon of freedom and prosperity despite its moments of crises, while no actual critique of the political system as a structure is undertaken in these narratives. Whether we examine a historical drama film, an epic, an action thriller, or a comedy, the structure of the disguised political narrative follows the same pattern, solidifying the structure and leaving the agent almost powerless in Hay's strategic-relational theory. Despite their ultimate victory or defeat and fictional, or not, nature, Jason Bourne, Abraham Lincoln, Harvey Milk, Tony Mendez, Robin Hood, Leonidas, Alexander the Great, Tom Dobbs, Cam Brady, and Marty Higgins remain solitary agents who, despite challenging the structure and sometimes achieving their goal, do not actually propose a new or improved system. For instance, Jason Bourne may uncover an illegal, covert CIA program and corrupt officers, but nowhere in the films does he support a potential shutdown of the intelligence agency or a radical reorganization. Similarly, Tom Dobbs castigates the government for not protecting the environment but does not offer an alternative proposal. Viewed from this perspective, the disguised political films seem content to point out the mistakes of the nation's political structure while implying that there is nothing wrong with the structure, which only suffers from the misdeeds of "evil" individuals.

Complicated, multilayered, conservative, and progressive, controversial or not, the political film in contemporary Hollywood remains one of the strongest repetitive narratives, alongside romantic and horror plots, despite its necessary disguise and obligatory camouflage. And it is exactly this mask political films must wear (the mask of the thriller, that of the epic, etc.) that is cleverly used by those filmmakers who want to comment on political issues, working within a capitalist system while trying to affect minor cracks. And, finally, it is this disguise that will allow us to watch Hollywood political films for years to come.

Notes

1. Introduction

1   Indicative titles include "How Obama Seized the Narrative" (Morphos 2012), "Media's Obama Narrative Collides with Reality" (Smith 2012), and "Obama's 2012 Victory: The Demographic Becomes the Narrative" (Sheets 2013). There is even a Pew Research study on the master narratives of the 2012 presidential campaign (n.a. 2012).

2   See, among others, Robin Toner (1992), Thomas Edsall (1999), Alison Mitchell (2000), Jarrett Murphy (2004), and Claire Cain Miller (2008).

3   In his study of the political film, M. Keith Booker (2007, 215) claims that in the beginning of the new millennium "American political film seems to have taken a decided step backward in critical power [...] even as the political problems facing America have grown more and more pressing." Booker adds "The first six years of the new century have seen virtually no genuine interrogation, within fictional films, of recent events such as the 2003 invasion of Iraq and other contemporary policies of the Bush administration" (2007: 215). I would argue that the 9/11 attacks, which halted the release and/or production or even canceled films with plots that could be considered controversial at the time, along with the War on Terror, the enforcement of the Bush administration agenda, the film industry's well-established antipathy toward films with disputable stories and political implications, and the absence of historical distance between the major historical events, only delayed the release of political narratives in the period Booker examines.

4   As evidenced by data provided by boxofficemojo.com regarding domestic grosses, forty-five out of the fifty most commercially successful political documentaries of all time, that is, an impressive 90 percent, were released in the 2000s and 2010s.

5   This claim is also supported by most authors on the subject (see, among others, Haas, Christensen, and Haas [2015], Kellner [2010], Davies and Wells [2002], and Neve [1992]). Michael Coyne (2008: 8) makes a distinction, however, stating that "While underlying political messages are virtually all-pervasive in American movies, however, there has been relatively little sustained critical attention paid to that corpus of narratives dealing primarily with US politics per se."

6   The approach adopted by IMDb and Netflix follows the academic thesis, outlined by Janet Staiger, that claims that no such thing as a "pure" genre exists and that the

overwhelming majority of films are an amalgam of at least two generic categories. There are, of course, a number of films on IMDb that are labeled under a single category/genre. I find that the majority of these films belong to the past (i.e., *High Noon* [1952], under Western although there are also contemporary titles that are listed under a single label (i.e., *Boyhood*, 2014, under Drama) and old titles that belong to more than one categories (i.e., *Frankenstein* [1931], is a Horror/Sci-Fi film, and *Stagecoach* [1939], an Adventure/Western).

7   The only method I haven't used is the "idealist method" which involves "find[ing] a film and judg[ing] other films against the pattern and conventions in that film" (Staiger 2003: 187).

8   For science fiction films, see, among others, Keith M. Johnston (2011), Natalia Voinova (2013), and Steven Sanders (2008). For horror films, see, among others, Jon Towlson (2014), Reynold Humphries (2005), and Barry Keith Grant and Christopher Sharrett (2004). For Westerns, see Janet Walker (2001). For gangster/crime films, see Jonathan Munby (1999).

9   It should be noted, however, that *United 93* is a rather anti-Hollywood film in that "it is ordinary people who are the self-organizing protagonists who stand in for their fellow citizens and take heroic action," (Kellner 2010: 104) following a cinematic tradition that dates back to the beginning of the medium's history and specific national cinematographies, such as the Soviet cinema of the 1920s.

10   Another exception would be the 2014 biopic *Selma*, which represents the 1965 Selma to Montgomery voting rights marches. However, the film was released after 2012 and is not included in the final corpus.

11   I should note that in recent years, comic book adaptations have begun a new tradition of lending stories and characters to film, resulting in a great number of tent-pole blockbusters, which are integral to the viability of the industry but also assist in the evolution of film technology through the constant technological advances that are needed to realistically depict the spectacular sequences that appear in the comic books.

12   Since my focus is on Hollywood films and the representation of US politics, I have to note that the James Bond films released between 2002 to 2012 (*Die Another Day* [2002], *Casino Royale* [2006], *Quantum of Solace* [2008], *Skyfall* [2012], and *Spectre* [2015]) are excluded from the corpus due to the fact that Bond is a British agent working for British Intelligence.

2. Political Comedies

1   These, and all other images, are taken by the author from the films' DVDs.

2   Based on the reviews on metacritic.com and rottentomatoes.com.

3. Political Thrillers and US Foreign Policy

1   US television, on the other hand, has recently begun concentrating on the State Department via two new shows, *Madam Secretary* (CBS, 2014–present), and *The Brink* (HBO, 2015).

2   This meeting serves as a prime example of the Hollywood–politics relationship and is frequently noted in the relevant bibliography (See, among others, Barker [2011], Matthew Alford [2010], Michael Silk [2012], Sara E. Quay and Amy M. Damico [2010], Douglas Kellner [2010], and Jack Shahee [2008]).

3   This part of Clooney's speech was taken from the official Academy Award site.

4   By the late 1970s, the Hollywood sign was almost in ruins despite being declared a cultural historic monument in 1973. The first "O" had disintegrated, resembling a "U," the third "O" had tumbled down the mountain, and the bottom of the second "L" was set on fire. Hugh Hefner "held a successful fundraising party at the Playboy mansion" in 1978 as "part of a drive by entertainment industry celebrities and the Hollywood Chamber of Commerce to restore" the monument, and the new sign was finally "unveiled at a diamond jubilee gala in 1978" (Grainge 2008: 3).

4. Political History Dramas and US Domestic Policy

1   Hollywood films with unhappy endings that utilize death as "a violent means of condemning 'closure'" of the film "as a narrative and historical event" (Russell 1995: 3), and not as a punishment or cathartic resolution, are indeed a rarity, but they do exist. Among others, this group of films includes *One Flew Over The Cuckoo's Nest* [1975], *The Mist* [2007], and *Atonement* [2007]. I should note, however, that contemporary US television has been incorporating a great number of "unexpected" deaths of main protagonists (i.e., *Game of Thrones* [HBO, 2011–present], *Dexter* [Showtime, 2006–13], *The Good Wife* [CBS, 2009–present], *Grey's Anatomy* [ABC, 2005–present], *Vampire Diaries* [The CW, 2009–present], to name but a few shows), and not just because the actors involved wanted to leave or there were conflicts between them and the show's producers, and/or writers.

Bibliography

Albright, Dann (2015), "2014's Final Controversy: Sony Hack, *The Interview* & North Korea," *Makeuseof*, January 3. Available online: http://www.makeuseof.com/tag/sony-hack-the-interview-north-korea/ (accessed November 6, 2015).

Alford, Matthew (2010), *Reel Power. Hollywood Cinema and American Supremacy*, New York: Pluto Press.

Allen, Nick (2014), "'I can't cast Mohammad so-and-so from such-and-such' says Ridley Scott," *The Telegraph*, November 28. Available online: http://www.theguardian.com/film/2014/dec/09/christian-bale-defends-ridley-scott-exodus-whitewashing (accessed October 30, 2015).

Altman, Rick (2003), "A Semantic/Syntactic Approach," in Barry K. Grant (ed.), *Film Genre Reader*, 27–50, Austin, TX: University of Texas Press.

Altman, Rick (2006), *Film/Genre*, London: BFI.

Arnold, William (2005a), "'XXX2' is a Triple Threat to Good Cinema," *Seattle Post Intelligencer*, April 28. Available online: http://www.seattlepi.com/ae/movies/article/XXX2-is-a-triple-threat-to-good-cinema-1172040.php (accessed July 27, 2015).

Arnold, William (2005b), "Magnificent Visuals and a Rousing Tale Sweep Aside 'Kingdom's' Flaws," *The Seattle Post-Intelligencer*, May 5. Available online: http://www.seattlepi.com/ae/movies/article/Magnificent-visuals-and-a-rousing-tale-sweep-1172618.php (accessed August 12, 2015).

Arora, N. D. and S. S. Awasthy (2007), *Political Theory and Political Thought*, Delhi: Har Anand.

Baer, Robert (2003), *See No Evil*, New York: Cornerstone Digital.

Bahn, Jenny (2012), "Barack Obama or *B. Hussein*? The Post-Racial Debate in *Boston Legal*," in Nicholas A. Yanes and Darrais Carter (eds), *The Iconic Obama, 2007–2009: Essays on Media Representations of the Candidate and New President*, 63–84, Jefferson: McFarland.

Balfour, Brad (2009), "Q & A: Sean Penn and Gus Van Sant Pour Out Their Hearts About Milk," The Huffington Post, March 23. Available online: http://www.huffingtonpost.com/brad-balfour/q-a-sean-penn-and-gus-van_b_168715.html (accessed August 17, 2015).

Banks, Alicia (2015), "'Selma' Controversy Grows Over LBJ Clash With Martin Luther King on Civil Rights," *The Wrap*, January 2. Available online: https://www.thewrap.com/selma-controversy-grows-over-lbj-clash-with-martin-luther-king-on-civil-rights/ (accessed October 28, 2015).

Barker, Martin (2011), *A "Toxic" Genre. The Iraq War Films*, London: Pluto Press.

Barnes, Brooks (2012), "As Enigmatic as Her Picture. Kathryn Bigelow on 'Zero Dark Thirty,'" *New York Times*, December 27. Available online: http://www.nytimes. com/2012/12/30/movies/awardsseason/kathryn-bigelow-on-zero-dark-thirty. html?pagewanted=all (accessed August 17, 2015).

Barnes, Henry (2009), "Could Gus Van Sant's Harvey Milk Movie Have Killed off Proposition 8?" *The Guardian*, January 9. Available online: http://www.theguardian. com/film/filmblog/2009/jan/09/gus-van-sant-harvey-milk-proposition-8 (accessed April 9, 2016).

Barrett, Oliver Boyd, David Herrera, and James A. Baumann (2011), *Hollywood and the CIA: Cinema, Defense and Subversion*, London: Routledge.

Beckman, Karen (2012), "Movies, Terror, and The American Family," in Timothy Corrigan (ed.), *American Cinema of the 2000s. Themes and Variations*, 125–46, New Bunswick: Rutgers University Press.

Beinart, Peter (2014), "The Majesty of the Presidency Is Overrated," *The Atlantic*, March 12. Available online: http://www.theatlantic.com/politics/ archive/2014/03/the-majesty-of-the-presidency-is-overrated/284384/ (accessed June 18, 2015).

Bertonado, Helena de (2010), "Angelina Jolie's Spy Advisor," *The Telegraph*, August 16. Available online: http://www.telegraph.co.uk/culture/film/starsandstories/7934530/ Angelina-Jolies-spy-advisor.html (accessed April 9, 2016).

Bilmes, Alex (2014), "George Clooney: The Full Interview," *Esquire*, January 4. Available online: http://www.esquire.co.uk/culture/features/5480/the-george-clooney-interview/ (accessed August 15, 2015).

Booker, M. Keith (2007), *From Office to Ballot Box. The American Political Film*, Westport, CT: Praeger.

Bordo, Susan (2013), *The Creation of Anne Boleyn. A New Look at England's Most Notorious Queen*, New York: Houghton Mifflin Harcourt.

Brevet, Brad (2007), "Carnahan's 'Kingdom' of 'Lions' and 'Lambs,'" *Rope of Silicon*, September 24. Available online: http://www.ropeofsilicon.com/interview_ carnahans_kingdom_of_lions_and_lambs/ (accessed August 16, 2015).

Brighi, Elisabetta (2013), *Foreign Policy, Domestic Politics and International Relations: The Case of Italy*, Oxford: Routledge.

Briley, Ron (2011), "'The Conspirator': Film and Historical Truth," *History News Network*, February 6. Available online: http://historynewsnetwork.org/ article/135526 (accessed April 9, 2016).

Brockes, Emma (2006), "I've Learned How to Fight," *The Guardian*, February 10. Available online: http://www.theguardian.com/film/2006/feb/10/georgeclooney (accessed August 15, 2015).

Brockes, Emma (2013), "Kathryn Bigelow: Under Fire," *The Guardian*, January 12. Available online: http://www.theguardian.com/film/2013/jan/12/kathryn-bigelow-zero-dark-thrity (accessed August 17, 2015).

Brooks, Stephen (2013), *American Exceptionalism in the Age of Obama*, New York: Routledge.

Browne, Patrick (2011), "'The Conspirator.' A Review," *Historical Digression*, May 26. Available online: http://historicaldigression.com/2011/05/26/the-conspirator-a-review/ (accessed August 1, 2015).

Bryant, Nick (2008), "Ten Quick Lessons from the US election," *BBC*, November 8. Available online: http://news.bbc.co.uk/2/hi/americas/7717578.stm (accessed June 3, 2015).

Bukszpan, Daniel (2010), "The 15 Most Profitable Movies of All Time," *CNBC*, September 10. Available online: http://www.cnbc.com/2010/09/10/The-15-Most-Profitable-Movies-of-All-Time.html (accessed August 3, 2015).

Carr, David (2010), "English Legends: That Robin Guy and Sir Ridley," *New York Times*, May 7. Available online: http://www.nytimes.com/2010/05/09/movies/09ridley.html?_r=0 (accessed August 15, 2015).

Cetti, Robert (2009), *Terrorism in American Cinema: An Analytical Filmography, 1960–2008*, Jefferson: McFarland.

Chambers, Claire (2015), "Gender," in Catriona McKinnon (ed.), *Issues in Political Theory*, 258–281,e

Cheney, Dick (2001), "Transcript of The Vice President Appears on Meet the Press with Tim Russert," *The White House*, September 16. Available online: http://georgewbush-whitehouse.archives.gov/vicepresident/news-speeches/speeches/vp20010916.html (accessed April 8, 2016).

Child, Ben (2014), "Christian Bale Defends Ridley Scott Over *Exodus* Whitewashing," *The Guardian*, December 9. Available online: http://www.theguardian.com/film/2014/dec/09/christian-bale-defends-ridley-scott-exodus-whitewashing (accessed October 30, 2015).

Cinema.Com (n.d.), "*Vantage Point*: Pete Travis Interview". Available online: http://cinema.com/articles/5829/vantage-point-pete-travis-interview.phtml (accessed July 17, 2015).

CNN (2001), "Uncle Sam Wants Hollywood," November 9. Available online: http://edition.cnn.com/2001/SHOWBIZ/Movies/11/09/hollywood.war/index.html?eref=sitesearch (accessed July 18, 2015).

CNN (2003), "Ashcroft, Ridge, Mueller Announce Threat Level Increase," Friday, February 7. Available online: http://edition.cnn.com/2003/US/02/07/threat.transcript/ (accessed July 21, 2015).

Cohen, Rich (2010), "Angelina the Conqueror," *Vanity Fair*, August. Available online: http://www.vanityfair.com/news/2010/08/angelina-jolie-201008 (accessed July 18, 2015).

Coontz, Stephanie (2005), *Marriage, a History. How Love Conquered Marriage*, London: Penguin.

Courtés, Joseph (1991), *Analyse Sémiotique du Discours*, Paris: Hachette.

Coyne, Michael (2008), *Hollywood Goes to Washington. American Politics on Screen*, London: Reaktion Books.

Curic, Katie (2004), *"Manchurian* Cast Talks Politics," *Dateline NBC*, July 25. Available online: http://www.nbcnews.com/id/5489846/ns/dateline_ nbc-newsmakers/t/manchurian-candidate-cast-talks-politics/#.VabJopOqqko (accessed April 8, 2016).

Dargis, Manohla (2007), "Elizabeth: The Golden Age (2007)," *New York Times*, October 12. Available online: http://www.nytimes.com/2007/10/12/movies/12gold. html?ref=movies (accessed August 10, 2015).

Dargis, Manohla (2009), "Poor Little Royal Girl: A Melancholy Monarch," *New York Times*, December 17. Available online: http://www.nytimes.com/2009/12/18/ movies/18young.html?ref=movies (accessed August 10, 2015).

Dargis, Manohla and A. O. Scott (2009), "How the Movies Made a President," *New York Times*, January 16. Available online: http://www.nytimes.com/2009/01/18/ movies/18darg.html (accessed June 3, 2015).

Davidson, Amy (2015), "Jon Stewart, We Need You in 2016," *The New Yorker*, February 11. Available online: http://www.newyorker.com/news/amy-davidson/ jon-stewart-need-2016 (accessed June 9, 2015).

Davies, Philip, John Davies, and Paul Wells (eds) (2002), *American Film and Politics from Reagan to Bush Jr.*, Manchester: Manchester University Press.

Debord, Guy (1967), *La société du spectacle*, Paris: Buchet-Chastel

Denby, David (2008), "Good Fights. 'Body of Lies' and 'Happy-Go-Lucky,'" *The New Yorker*, October 13. Available online: http://www.newyorker.com/ magazine/2008/10/13/good-fights-2 (accessed July 12, 2015).

Derry, Charles (2001), *The Suspense Thriller: Films in The Shadow of Alfred Hitchcock*, Jefferson: McFarland.

Douthat, Ross (2006), "Boringus Maximus," *Slate*, June 27. Available online: http:// www.slate.com/articles/news_and_politics/summer_movies/2006/06/boringus_ maximus.html (accessed August 12, 2015).

Ebert, Roger (2005), "A Telephone Call With Steven Spielberg," *Chicago Sun Times*, December 25. Available online: http://www.rogerebert.com/interviews/a-telephone-call-with-spielberg (accessed August 15, 2015).

Ebert, Roger (2008), "Oliver Stone: The XYZS of 'W,'" *Chicago Sun Times*, October 15. Available online: http://www.rogerebert.com/interviews/oliver-stone-the-xyzs-of-w (accessed August 15, 2015).

Edsall, Thomas (1999), "Study Disputes Clinton 1996 Campaign Strategy," *The Washington Post*, May 22. Available online: http://www.washingtonpost.com/ wp-srv/politics/campaigns/wh2000/stories/ads052299.htm (accessed August 18, 2015).

Eisenberg, Eric (2010), "Interview: *Green Zone's* Matt Damon Talks About Getting His Ass Kicked," *Cinema Blend*, March 3. Available online: http://www.cinemablend.

com/new/Interview-Green-Zone-s-Matt-Damon-Talks-About-Getting-His-Ass-Kicked-17520.html (accessed December 14, 2015).

Elliott, Andrew B. R. (2014), "Introduction: The Return of the Epic," in Andrew B. R. Elliott (ed.), *The Return of the Epic Film: Genre, Aesthetics and History in the Twenty-first Century*, 1–18, Edinburgh: Edinburgh University Press.

Elsaesser, Thomas and Warren Buckland (2002), *Studying Contemporary American Film. A Guide to Movie Analysis*, London: Arnold.

Fear, David (2014), "No 'Tomorrow': Doug Liman on the Blockbuster That Almost Broke Him," *Rolling Stone*, June 6. Available online: http://www.rollingstone. com/movies/news/no-tomorrow-doug-liman-on-the-blockbuster-that-almost-broke-him-20140606 (accessed August 15, 2015).

Fleming, Mike Jr (2012), "Mike Fleming's Q&A With Steven Spielberg: Why It Took 12 Years To Find 'Lincoln,'" *Deadline*, December 6. Available online: http://deadline. com/2012/12/steven-spielberg-lincoln-making-of-interview-exclusive-383861/ (accessed August 15, 2015).

Fontanille, Jacques (1999), *Sémiotique et littérature, Essais de méthode*, Paris: PUF.

Fontanille, Jacques (2003), *Sémiotique du discours*, Limoges: Pulim.

Ford, Elizabeth A. and Deborah C. Mitchell (2009), *Royal Portraits in Hollywood: Filming the Lives of Queens*, Lexington, KY: University Press of Kentucky.

Foundas, Scott (2013), "Robert Redford Keeps 'Company' With America," *Variety*, April 11. Available online: http://variety.com/2013/film/news/robert-redford-keeps-company-with-america-1200349040/ (accessed August 15, 2015).

Franklin, Daniel P. (2006), *Politics and Film. The Political Culture of Film in the United States*, Oxford: Rowman and Littlefield Publishers.

Fritz, Ben (2011), "The Business Behind The Show," *LA Times Blog*, January 25. Available online: http://latimesblogs.latimes.com/entertainmentnewsbuzz/2011/01/ kings-speech-may-be-recut-for-lower-rating-gets-new-ad-campaign-following-oscar-nominations.html (accessed August 9, 2015).

Fuchs, Cynthia (2005), "XXX: State of the Union: Special Edition (2005)," *PopMatters*, August 24. Available online: http://www.popmatters.com/review/xxxx-state-of-the-union-special-dvd/ (accessed July 30, 2015).

Fuller, Jaime (2014), "12 of the Most Memorable Political Sketches of 2014," *Washington Post*, December 24. Available online: https://www.washingtonpost.com/ news/the-fix/wp/2014/12/24/12-of-the-most-memorable-political-sketches-of-2014/ (accessed October 24, 2015).

Gant, Charles (2013), "Film Review: 'Diana,'" *Variety*, September 6. Available online: http://variety.com/2013/film/reviews/film-review-diana-1200601753/ (accessed November 2, 2015).

Gardies, André (1993), *Le récit filmique*, Paris: Hachette.

Geluardi, John (2008), "White Lies," *SF Weekly*, December 3. Available online: http:// www.sfweekly.com/2008-12-03/news/white-lies/ (accessed July 31, 2015).

Genette, Gérard (1972), *Figures III*, Paris: Seuil.

Gianos, Phillip L. (1998), *Politics and Politicians in American Film*, Westport, CT: Praeger.

Giglio, Ernest D. (2014), *Here's Looking at You: Hollywood, Film and Politics*, 4th edn., New York: Peter Lang.

Giroux, Jack (2011), "Interview: Grant Heslov Discusses The Dark and Cynical 'The Ides of March,'" *Film School Rejects*, October 9. Available online: http://filmschoolrejects.com/features/interview-grant-heslov-the-ides-of-march-jgiro.php#ixzz3i96ERvah (accessed August 15, 2015).

Gleiberman, Owen (2009), "*The Young Victoria*", *Entertainment Weekly*, December 30. Available online: http://www.ew.com/article/2009/12/30/young-victoria (accessed August 10, 2015).

Glitre, Kathrina (2006), *Hollywood Romantic Comedy. States of the Union, 1934–1965*, Manchester: Manchester University Press.

Gordon, Richard (2010), Repairing British Politics: A Blueprint for Constitutional Change, Oxford: Hart Publishing.

Grainge, Paul (2008), *Brand Hollywood: Selling Entertainment in a Global Media Age*, New York: Routledge.

Grant, Barry Keith, and Christopher Sharrett (eds) (2004), *Planks of Reason: Essays on The Horror Film*, Oxford: Scarecrow.

Grant, Meg (2011), "Robert Redford, Unedited," *AARP*, March/April. Available online: http://www.aarp.org/entertainment/movies-for-grownups/info-01-2011/robert-redford-unedited.3.html (accessed May 18, 2016).

Grant, Moyra (2003), *Key Ideas in Politics*, Cheltenham: Trans-Atlantic Publications.

Gray, Jonathan and Jeffrey P. Jones (2009), "The State of Satire, The Satire of State," in Jonathan Gray and Jeffrey P. Jones (eds), *Satire TV. Politics and Comedy in the Post-Network Era*, 3–36, New York: New York University Press.

Greimas, Algirdas Julien (1986 [1968]), *Sémantique Structurale*, Paris: PUF.

Gritten, David (2013), "Kathryn Bigelow interview for *Zero Dark Thirty*: The Director on the Trail of Terrorism," *The Telegraph*, January 18. Available online: http://www.telegraph.co.uk/culture/film/9809355/Kathryn-Bigelow-interview-for-Zero-Dark-Thirty-The-director-on-the-trail-of-terrorism.html (accessed August 17, 2015).

Grossman, James (2011), "Historians and *The Conspirator*: Using Film to ask Big Questions," *Blog Historians*, April 13. Available online: http://blog.historians.org/2011/04/historians-and-the-conspirator-using-film-to-ask-big-questions/ (accessed August 1, 2015).

Gunter, Barrie (2015), *The Cognitive Impact of Television News: Production Attributes and Information Reception*, New York: Palgrave Macmillan.

Guy, John (1995), "Introduction. The 1590s: The Second Reign of Elizabeth I?" in John Alexander Guy (ed.), *The Reign of Elizabeth I: Court and Culture in the Last Decade*, 1–19, Cambridge: Cambridge University Press.

Haas, Elizabeth, Terry Christensen, and Peter J. Haas (2015), *Projecting Politics. Political Messages in American Films*, New York: Routledge.

Hammond, Pete (2014), "Cannes: Harvey Weinstein Defends Actions On Grace Kelly Movie, Says Monaco Royal Family Has A 'Legitimate Problem' With The Film," *Deadline*, May 16. Available online: http://deadline.com/2014/05/ cannes-harvey-weinstein-defends-actions-on-grace-kelly-movie-says-monaco-royal-family-have-a-legitimate-problem-with-the-film-731660/ (accessed November 2, 2015).

Hay, Carla (2012), "Denzel Washington & Ryan Reynolds Reveal the Dangers of Filming 'Safe House,'" *Examiner*, February 10. Available online: http://www. examiner.com/article/denzel-washington-ryan-reynolds-reveal-the-dangers-of-filming-safe-house (accessed July 12, 2015).

Hay, Colin (2002), *Political Analysis. A Critical Introduction*, New York: Palgrave Macmillan.

Hayden, Eric (2013), "*Zero Dark Thirty* Screenwriter: I Should Be Able to Write 'Bin Laden Was Killed by Aliens' If I Wanted," *The Hollywood Reporter*, February 16. Available online: http://www.hollywoodreporter.com/news/zero-dark-thirty-screenwriter-i-422016 (accessed August 17, 2015).

Hill, Steven (2014), "Why Does the US Still Have So Few Women in Office?" *The Nation*, March 7. Available online: http://www.thenation.com/article/why-does-us-still-have-so-few-women-office/ (accessed August 6, 2015).

Hillman, Roger (2013), "Sounding the Depths of History: Opera and National Identity," in Robert A. Rosenstone and Constantin Parvulescu (eds), *A Companion to the Historical Film*, 328–348, Hoboken, NJ: Wiley-Blackwell.

Hipes, Patrick (2015), "'Grace Of Monaco' Finally Gets Its U.S. Release—On Lifetime," *Deadline*, April 7. Available online: http://deadline.com/2015/04/grace-of-monaco-lifetime-network-premiere-date-set-1201406096/ (accessed November 2, 2015).

Hiscock, John (2010), "Ridley Scott Interview," *The Telegraph*, April 29. Available online: http://www.telegraph.co.uk/culture/film/7651823/Ridley-Scott-interview. html (accessed August 14, 2015).

Hochscherf, Tobias and Christoph Laucht (2012), "*Good Night, and Good Luck* (2005)," *Film & History*, November 15. Available online: http://www.uwosh.edu/ filmandhistory/controversial_films/films/goodNightGoodLuck.php (accessed July 31, 2015).

Hogan, Jackie (2011), *Lincoln, Inc.: Selling the Sixteenth President in Contemporary America*, Plymouth: Rowman & Littlefield.

Holloway, David (2008), *9/11 and the War on Terror*, Edinburgh: Edinburgh University Press.

Hollywood Reporter (2015), "The 30 Most Powerful Film Producers in Hollywood," *The Hollywood Reporter*, April 13. Available online: http://www.hollywoodreporter. com/person/george-clooney-grant-heslov (accessed August 7, 2015).

Hornaday, Ann (2011), "Robert Redford's *The Conspirator* and The Lost Union Cause," *The Washington Post*, April 14. Available online: http://www.washingtonpost.com/lifestyle/style/the-conspirator-and-the-lost-union-cause/2011/04/14/AFhcYjeD_story.html (accessed August 1, 2015).

Humphries, Reynold (2005), *The American Horror Film: An Introduction*, 3rd edn., Edinburgh: Edinburgh University Press.

Hunter, Stephen (2005), "'xXx': A Capital Offense," *The Washington Post*, April 29. Available online: http://www.washingtonpost.com/wp-dyn/content/article/2005/04/28/AR2005042801719.html. (accessed July 27, 2015).

Hutcheon, Linda (2006), *A Theory of Adaptation*, New York: Routledge.

Irvine, Lindesay (2005), "$225 Isn't Bad, I Guess," *The Guardian*, October 6. Available online: http://www.theguardian.com/film/2005/oct/06/features.lindesayirvine (accessed August 15, 2015).

Jacobson, Harlan (2005), "Grant Heslov Interview," *Film Comment*, September/October. Available online: http://www.filmcomment.com/article/grant-heslov-interview/ (accessed August 7, 2015).

Jakobson, Roman (1981), *Selected Writings III: Poetry of Grammar and Grammar of Poetry*, The Hague: Mouton.

Jeffrey, Rus D. and Sandra L. Jeffrey (2006), *Frame by Frame: 2006: a Family-friendly Guide to the Movies*, Lincoln: iUniverse.

Jenkins, Tricia (2012), *The CIA in Hollywood: How the Agency Shapes Film and Television*, Austin, TX: University of Texas Press.

Johnston, Keith M. (2011), *Science Fiction Film: A Critical Introduction*, London: Berg.

Joseph, Sarah (1988), *Political Theory and Power*, New York: E. J. Brill.

Joireman, Sandra Fullerton (2009), *Church, State, and Citizen: Christian Approaches to Political Engagement*, Oxford: Oxford University Press.

Kaklamanidou, Betty (2013), *Genre, Gender and the Effects of Neoliberalism: The New Millennium Hollywood Rom Com*, London: Routledge.

Kaklamanidou, Despoina (2006), *When the Novel Met The Cinema*, Athens: Aigokeros, (in Greek).

Kellner, Douglas (2003), *From 9/11 to Terror War: The Dangers of the Bush Legacy*, Lanham: Rowman & Littlefield.

Kellner, Douglas (2010), *Cinema Wars. Hollywood Film and Politics in the Bush-Cheney Era*, Malden: Wiley-Blackwell.

Kellner, Douglas (2012), *Media Spectacle and Insurrection 2011. From the Arab Uprisings to Occupy Everywhere*, New York: Bloomsbury.

Kenneally, Tim (2014), "George Clooney's Smokehouse Pictures Enters Overall Deal With Sony Pictures Television," *The Wrap*, June 9. Available online: http://www.thewrap.com/george-clooneys-smokehouse-pictures-enters-overall-deal-with-sony-pictures-television/ (accessed August 7, 2015).

Kieran, Matthew (1997), *Media Ethics: A Philosophical Approach*, Westport, CT: Praeger.

Kilday, Gregg (2012), "Q&A: 'Salt' director Phillip Noyce," *The Hollywood Reporter*, July 20. Available online: http://www.hollywoodreporter.com/news/q-a-salt-director-phillip-25761 (accessed July 17, 2015).

King, Geoff (2000), *Spectacular Narratives. Hollywood in the Age of the Blockbuster*, London: I.B. Tauris.

Koslow, Jessica A. (2012), "Tony Kushner Explains How He Adapted *Lincoln* For The Age of Obama," *LA Weekly*, November 5. Available online: http://www.laweekly.com/arts/tony-kushner-explains-how-he-adapted-lincoln-for-the-age-of-obama-2371100 (accessed August 1, 2015).

Kreitner, Richard (2012), "Why American Politics Still Needs Radicals," *The Nation*, December 10. Available online: http://www.thenation.com/article/lincoln-thaddeus-stevens-and-why-american-politics-still-needs-radicals/ (accessed July 30, 2015).

Krieger, Jennifer (2008), "Denzel Washington Interview for *The Manchurian Candidate*," The Cinema Source, January 28. Available online: http://www.thecinemasource.com/blog/interviews/denzel-washington-interview-for-the-manchurian-candidate/ (accessed July 17, 2015).

Krutnik, Frank, Steve Neale, Brian Neve, and Peter Stanfield (2007), "Introduction," in Frank Krutnik, Steve Neale, Brian Neve, and Peter Stanfield (eds), *"Un-American" Hollywood. Politics and Film in the Blacklist Era*, 3–18, New Brunswick, NJ: Rutgers University Press.

Kuhn, Annette and Guy Westwell (2012), *Oxford Dictionary of Film Studies*, Oxford: Oxford University Press.

Kushner, Tony (2006), "Defending 'Munich' to my Mishpocheh," *Los Angeles Times*, January 22. Available online: http://articles.latimes.com/2006/jan/22/opinion/op-kushner22 (accessed August 16, 2015).

Lacey, Liam (2013), "The CIA's Image in Films Has Never Been Shinier," *The Globe and Mail*, February 21. Available online: http://www.theglobeandmail.com/arts/film/the-cias-image-in-films-has-never-been-shinier/article8935790/ (accessed July 15, 2015).

Lacey, Rose (2006), "Hollywood's Most Expensive Movies," *Forbes*, December 18. Available online: http://www.forbes.com/2006/12/18/movies-budget-expensive tech media-cx_li_1214moviebudget.html (accessed June 22, 2015).

Lagopoulos, Alexandros Ph. and Karin Boklund-Lagopoulou (1992), *Meaning and Geography: The Social Conception of the Region in Northern Greece*, New York: Mouton de Gruyter.

Lagopoulos, Alexandros Ph. and Karin Boklund-Lagopoulou (2014), "Social Semiotics: Towards a Sociologically Grounded Semiotics," Keynote Speech at 12th World Congress of Semiotics, Sofia, New Bulgarian University, September 16–20.

Larson, Kate Clifford (2010), *The Assassin's Accomplice: Mary Surratt and the Plot to Kill Abraham Lincoln*, Philadelphia, PA: Basic Books.

Lasswell, Harold (1936), *Politics: Who Gets What, When and How*, New York: McGraw-Hill.

Lear, Norman (2005), "George Clooney," *Interview*, October. Available online: http://www.interviewmagazine.com/film/george-clooney/#_ (accessed August 15, 2015).

Lee, Benjamin (2015), "Cameron Crowe's New Film *Aloha* Accused of 'Whitewashing' Hawaii," *The Guardian*, May 26. Available online: http://www.theguardian.com/film/2015/may/26/cameron-crowes-new-film-aloha-accused-of-whitewashing-hawaii (accessed October 30, 2015).

Lenon, Suzanne (2013), "White as Milk: Proposition 8 and the Cultural Politics of Gay Rights," *Atlantis*, 36 (1), 44–54. Available online: http://journals.msvu.ca/index.php/atlantis/article/viewFile/3185/2568 (accessed August 2, 2015).

Leonard, Elizabeth D. (2011), "A Historian's Review of 'The Conspirator,'" *Civil War 150*, May 11. Available online: http://uncpresscivilwar150.com/2011/05/elizabeth-d-leonard-a-historians-review-of-the-conspirator/ (accessed July 31, 2015).

Leonard, Tom (2008), "Kevin Costner: 'I Always Rail Against Anything that's Unfair,'" *The Telegraph*, September 30. Available online: http://www.telegraph.co.uk/culture/film/starsandstories/3561444/Kevin-Costner-I-always-rail-against-anything-thats-unfair.html (accessed June 22, 2015).

Levy, Emanuel (2008), "*Vantage Point* with Director Pete Travis," *Emanuel Levy.com*, February 8. Available online: http://emanuellevy.com/interviews/vantage-point-with-director-pete-travis-3/ (accessed July 17, 2015).

Lewis, Jacob (2013), "Ridley Scott's Robin Hood and the Political Evolution of the Greenwood," in Mary K. Leigh and Kevin K. Durand (eds), *Marxism and the Movies: Critical Essays on Class Struggle in the Cinema*, 164–84, Jefferson: McFarland.

Lim, Dennis (2008), "Harvey Would Have Opened It in October," *Slate*, November 26. Available online: http://www.slate.com/articles/arts/culturebox/2008/11/harvey_would_have_opened_it_in_october.html (accessed August 1, 2015).

Madrigal, Alexis C. (2013), "How Netflix Reverse Engineered Hollywood," *The Atlantic*, January 2. Available online: http://www.theatlantic.com/technology/archive/2014/01/how-netflix-reverse-engineered-hollywood/282679/ (accessed February 2, 2015).

Magary, Drew (2015), "Jon Stewart Should Run for Office," *The Concourse*, February 11. Available online: http://theconcourse.deadspin.com/jon-stewart-should-run-for-office-1685171725?rev=142366648642 9&utm_campaign=socialflow_deadspin_twitter&utm_source=deadspin_twitter&utm_medium=socialflow. (accessed June 9, 2015).

Marsh, David (2010), "Meta-Theoretical Issues," in David Marsh and Gerry Stoker (eds), *Theory and Methods in Political Science*, 212–231, New York: Palgrave Macmillan.

Mazelis, Fred and Tom Mackaman (2015), "The Historical and Political Issues in

Selma," World Socialist Web Site, January. Available online: https://www.wsws.org/
en/articles/2015/01/20/selm-j20.html (accessed October 28, 2015).

McBeth, Mark K. and Randy S. Clemons (2011), "Is Fake News the Real News? The
Significance of Stewart and Colbert for Democratic Discourse, Politics, and Policy,"
in Amarnath Amarasingam (ed.), *The Stewart/Colbert Effect: Essays on the Real
Impacts of Fake News*, 79–98, Jefferson: McFarland.

McCarthy, Killian J. and Wilfred Dolfsma (2014), "Neutral Media? Evidence of Media
Bias and its Economic Impact," *Review of Social Economy* 72 (1): 42–54.

McCrisken, Trevor and Andrew Pepper (eds) (2005), *American History and
Contemporary Hollywood Film*, Edinburgh: Edinburgh University Press.

McFarlane, Brian (1996), *Novel to Film*, Oxford: Clarendon Press.

McMaken, Ryan (2014), "Terrorism and Police States in Exodus: Gods and Kings,"
Mises Institute, December 30. Available online: https://mises.org/library/terrorism-
and-police-states-exodus-gods-and-kings (accessed October 30, 2015).

Meacham, Joh (2006), "Who Really Killed Jesus?" in Paula Fredriksen (ed.), *On The
Passion of the Christ: Exploring the Issues Raised by the Controversial Movie*, 1–16,
Berkeley: University of California Press.

Merry, Stephanie (2013), "Naomi Watts Stars in Melodramatic yet Dull
'Diana,'" *The Washington Post*, October 31. Available online: https://www.
washingtonpost.com/lifestyle/style/naomi-watts-stars-in-melodramatic-yet-dull-
diana/2013/10/31/ff3b1efc-422d-11e3–8b74-d89d714ca4dd_story.html (accessed
November 2, 2015).

Metz, Walter (2004), *Film Criticism: Film History and Contemporary American Cinema*,
New York: Peter Lang.

Miller, Claire Cain (2008), "How Obama's Internet Campaign Changed Politics,"
New York Times, November 7. Available online: http://bits.blogs.nytimes.
com/2008/11/07/how-obamas-internet-campaign-changed-politics/?_r=0 (accessed
August 18, 2015).

Miller, Julie (2014), "Naomi Watts Admits the Princess Diana Movie Was a
'Sinking Ship,'" *Vanity Fair*, April 1. Available online: http://www.vanityfair.com/
hollywood/2014/04/naomi-watts-princess-diana-movie-sinking-ship (accessed
November 2, 2015).

Mitchell, Alison (2000), "The 2000 Campaign: The Strategy; Shifting Tactics, Bush Uses
Issues to Confront Gore," *New York Times*, September 17. Available online: http://
www.nytimes.com/2000/09/16/us/2000-campaign-strategy-shifting-tactics-bush-
uses-issues-confront-gore.html (accessed August 18, 2015).

Morgan, Peter (2009), "*Frost/Nixon:* Peter Morgan on a Change of Perspective," *The
Telegraph*, January 14. Available online: http://www.telegraph.co.uk/culture/film/
starsandstories/4223232/FrostNixon-Peter-Morgan-on-a-change-of-perspective.
html (accessed August 16, 2015).

Morphos, Evangeline (2012), "How Obama Seized the Narrative," *Reuters*, December

17. Available online: http://blogs.reuters.com/great-debate/2012/12/17/how-obama-seized-the-narrative/ (accessed August 16, 2015).

Morris, Wesley (2007), "'Elizabeth' II Surrenders to Soapy Camp," *The Boston Globe*, October 12. Available online: http://www.boston.com/ae/movies/articles/2007/10/12/elizabeth_ii_surrenders_to_soapy_camp/ (accessed August 10, 2015).

Morton, David (2014), "50 Fittest Men in Hollywood," *Men's Health*, October 6. Available online: http://www.menshealth.co.uk/building-muscle/get-big/50-fittest-men-in-hollywood#image-1 (accessed August 13, 2015).

Munby, Jonathan (1999), *Public Enemies, Public Heroes: Screening the Gangster from Little Caesar to Touch of Evil*, Chicago: The University of Chicago Press.

Murphy, Jarrett (2004), "Why Bush Won," *CBS*, November 3. Available online: http://www.cbsnews.com/news/why-bush-won-02-11-2004/ (accessed August 18, 2015).

Murray, Rebecca (2008), "Dennis Quaid Discusses the Action Thriller 'Vantage Point,'" *About.com*, February 17. Available online: http://movies.about.com/od/vantagepoint/a/vantagedq21408.htm (accessed July 13, 2015).

Murray, Rebecca (n.d.), "George Clooney Discusses His Film, 'Good Night, and Good Luck,'" *Movies About*. Available online: http://movies.about.com/od/goodnightandgoodluck/a/goodnight100105.htm (accessed August 15, 2015).

Nacify, Hamid (2012), "Accented Filmmaking and Risk Taking in Postcolonial Militancy, Terrorism, Globalization, Wars, Oppression, and Occupation," in Mette Hjort (ed.), *Film and Risk*, 143–64, Detroit, MI: Wayne State University Press.

Neale, Steve ([1990] 2003), "Questions of Genre," in Barry Keith Grant (ed.), *Film Genre Reader*, 160–184, Austin, TX: University of Texas Press.

Neve, Brian (1992), *Film and Politics in America: A Social Tradition*, London: Routledge.

O'Connell, Michael (2012), "Presidential Debate Hits 32-Year Record in Gross Ratings," *The Hollywood Reporter*, October 4. Available online: http://www.hollywoodreporter.com/live-feed/obama-mitt-romney-presidential-debate-ratings-record-376575 (accessed June 9, 2015).

O'Sullivan, Michael (2004), "Long Live This 'King,'" *The Washington Post*, July 9. Available online: http://www.washingtonpost.com/wp-dyn/articles/A36591–2004Jul8.html (accessed August 12, 2015).

O'Sullivan, Michael (2005), "Ice Cube's Overblown 'XXX' Factor," *The Washington Post*, April 29. Available online: http://www.washingtonpost.com/wp-dyn/content/article/2005/04/28/AR2005042800673.html (accessed July 27, 2015).

O'Sullivan, Michael (2010), "Movie review: 'Robin Hood' stars Russell Crowe and Cate Blanchett," *The Washington Post*, May 15. Available online: http://www.washingtonpost.com/wp-dyn/content/article/2010/05/13/AR2010051301793.html. (accessed August 12, 2015).

Olechnowicz, Andrzej (2007), *The Monarchy and the British Nation, 1780 to the Present*, Cambridge: Cambridge University Press.

Otterbeing, Keith F. (2004), *How War Began*, Austin, TX: Texas University Press.

Overpeck, Deron (2007), "Movies and Images of Reality," in Stephen Prince (ed.), *American Cinema of the 1980s. Themes and Variations*, 188–209, New Brunswick, NJ: Rutgers University Press.

Palmer, William J. (1993), *The Films of the Eighties*, Carbondale, IL: Southern Illinois University Press.

Phillips-Fein, Kim and Julian E. Zelizer (2012), "Introduction," in Kim Phillips-Fein and Julian E. Zelizer (eds), *What's Good for Business: Business and American Politics since World War II*, 3–15, Oxford: Oxford University Press.

Plame, Valerie (2007), *Fair Game: My Life as a Spy, My Betrayal by the White House*, New York: Simon & Schuster.

Quay, Sara E. and Amy M. Damico (2010), *September 11 in Popular Culture: A Guide*, Santa Barbara: ABC-CLIO.

Rancière, Jacques (2011), *The Politics of Literature*, Cambridge: Polity Press.

Raw, Lawrence (2009), *The Ridley Scott Encyclopedia*, Lanham: Scarecrow Press.

Rees, Alex (2013), "*Zero Dark Thirty*'s Mark Boal on Torture, Women in Hollywood and the End of the War on Terror," *GQ*, January 25. Available online: http://www.gq-magazine.co.uk/entertainment/articles/2013–01/23/mark-boal-zero-dark-thirty-war-terror-torture-interview (accessed August 17, 2015).

Ribke, Nahuel (2015), *A Genre Approach to Celebrity Politics: Global Patterns of Passage from Media to Politics*, New York: Palgrave Macmillan.

Rich, Katey (2008), "Sean Penn On The Life And Death Implications Of *Milk*," *Cinema Blend*, November 25. Available online: http://www.cinemablend.com/new/Sean-Penn-On-The-Life-And-Death-Implications-Of-Milk-11010.html (accessed December 14, 2015).

Richards, Jeffrey (2014), "Sir Ridley Scott and the Rebirth of the Historical Epic," in Andrew B. R. Elliott (ed.), *The Return of the Epic Film: Genre, Aesthetics and History in the Twenty-First Century*, 19–35, Edinburgh: Edinburgh University Press.

Rogak, Lisa (2015), "From Fake News to Politics—Is There Any Way Jon Stewart Will Run for Office?" *Salon*, February 12. Available online: http://www.salon.com/2015/02/12/from_fake_news_to_politics_is_there_any_way_jon_stewart_will_run_for_office/ (accessed June 9, 2015).

Rollins Peter and John E. O'Connor (eds) (2008), *Why We Fought. America's Wars in Film and History*, Lexington, KY: The University Press of Kentucky.

Rosenstone, Robert A. (2012). *History on Film/Film on History*, 2nd edn, New York: Routledge.

Rothman, Noah (2014), "Maddow Reviews All the Times US Presidents Appeared on Comedy Shows," *Mediaite*, March 13. Available online: http://www.mediaite.com/tv/maddow-reviews-all-the-times-us-presidents-appeared-on-comedy-shows/ (accessed June 18, 2015).

Russell, Catherine (1995), *Narrative Mortality. Death, Closure, and New Wave Cinemas*, Minneapolis, MN: University of Minnesota Press.

Samuelsohn, Darren (2015), "Jon Stewart's secret White House visits," *Politico*, July 28. Available online: http://www.politico.com/agenda/story/2015/07/jon-stewarts-secret-white-house-visits-000178 (accessed October 26, 2015).

Sanders, Steven (ed.) (2008), *The Philosophy of Science Fiction Film*, Lexington, KY: University Press of Kentucky.

Schaff, Barbara (2004), "Still Lifes—Tableaux Vivants: Art in British Heritage Films," in Eckart Voigts-Virchow (ed.), *Janespotting and Beyond: British Heritage Retrovisions Since the Mid-1990s*, 125–134, Tubingen: Gunter Naar Verlag Press.

Scheuneman, Stacy (2011), "Movie Review: *The Conspirator*," *The Yale Herald*, April 21. Available online: http://yaleherald.com/arts/movie-review-the-conspirator (accessed August 1, 2015).

Schmidt, Elizabeth (2013), *Foreign Intervention in Africa: From the Cold War to the War on Terror*, New York: Cambridge University Press.

Schubart, Rikke and Anne Gjelsvik (2013), "Introduction. Know Your Enemy, Know Yourself," in Rikke Schubart and Anne Gjelsvik (eds), *Eastwood's Iwo Jima: Critical Engagements With Flags of Our Fathers and* Letters from Iwo Jima, 1–14, New York: Wallflower.

Schuessler, Jennifer (2014), "Depiction of Lyndon B. Johnson in 'Selma' Raises Hackles," *New York Times*, December 31. Available online: http://www.nytimes.com/2015/01/01/movies/depiction-of-lyndon-b-johnson-in-selma-raises-hackles.html (accessed October 28, 2015).

Sciretta, Peter (2007), "Interview: Robert Redford," *Slashfilm*, November 8. Available online: http://www.slashfilm.com/interview-robert-redford/ (accessed August 15, 2015).

Scott, Ian (2011), *American Politics in Hollywood Film*, 2nd edn., Edinburgh: Edinburgh University Press.

Shafi, Sophia (2014), "Muslim Monsters," in Jeffrey H. Mahan (ed.), *Media, Religion and Culture: An Introduction*, 121–35, New York: Routledge.

Shahee, Jack (2008), *Guilty: Hollywood's Verdict on Arabs After 9/11*, Northampton: Olive Branch Press.

Shapiro, Michael J (2009), *Cinematic Geopolitics*, London: Routledge.

Shear, Michael D. (2015), "Jon Stewart Met Privately With Obama at White House." *New York Times*, July 28, 2015. Available online: http://www.nytimes.com/2015/07/29/us/politics/jon-stewart-secretly-met-with-obama-at-white-house.html (accessed April 8, 2016).

Sheehan, Rebecca A (2013), "Facebooking the Present: The Biopic and Cultural Instantaneity," in Tom Brown and Belén Vidal (eds), The Biopic in Contemporary Film Culture, 35–51, New York: Routledge.

Sheets, Diana E. (2013), "Obama's 2012 Victory: The Demographic Becomes the

Narrative," *The Huffington Post*, February 20. Available online: http://www. huffingtonpost.com/dr-diana-e-sheets/obamas-2012-victory-the-demographic-becomes-the-narrative_b_2341438.html (accessed September 3, 2015).

Shepherd, Laura J. (2013), *Gender, Violence and Popular Culture*, London: Routledge.

Shippey, Tom (2012), "Historian Fiction and the Post-Imperial Arthur," in Helen Fulton (ed.), *A Companion to Arthurian Literature*, 449–462, Malden: Blackwell.

Sigerson, David (2008), "Oliver Stone," *Interview*, November 25. Available online: http://www.interviewmagazine.com/film/oliver-stone/#_ (accessed August 15, 2015).

Silk, Michael (2012), *The Cultural Politics of Post-9/11 American Sport: Power, Pedagogy and the Popular*, London: Routledge.

Silverstein, Melissa (2015), "Women Are Shut Out of Directing Roles, and It's Hurting Movies," *The Washington Post*, May 12. Available online: https://www. washingtonpost.com/posteverything/wp/2015/05/12/women-are-shut-out-of-directing-roles-and-its-hurting-movies/ (accessed August 6, 2015).

Smith, Kyle (2009), "Thunder Before Victoria's Reign," *New York Post*, December 18. Available online: https://www.google.gr/search?q=the+new+york+post&gws_rd=cr, ssl&ei=v9bIVeuqOIOvswGgjIu4Bg (accessed August 10, 2015).

Smith, Rosslyn (2012), "Media's Obama Narrative Collides with Reality," *American Thinker*, October 11. Available online: http://www.americanthinker.com/ articles/2012/10/medias_obama_narrative_collides_with_reality.html (accessed April 8, 2016).

Sommers, Ryan J. (2007), "Matthew Michael Carnahan Explains Lions For Lambs Agenda," *Rotten Tomatoes*, November 8. Available online: http://editorial. rottentomatoes.com/article/matthew-michael-carnahan-explains-lions-for-lambs-agenda/ (accessed August 16, 2015).

Staiger, Janet. "Hybrid or Inbred: The Purity Hypothesis and Hollywood Genre," in Barry K. Grant (ed.), *Film Genre Reader III*, 185–202, Austin, TX: University of Texas Press.

Sterritt, David (2012), "George Clooney: The Issues Guy," in Murray Pomerance (ed.), *Shining in Shadows: Movie Stars of the 2000s*, 220–37, Brunswick: Rutgers University Press.

Stevens, Dana (2007), "*Elizabeth: The Golden Age*. Just like a 16th-century episode of *The Hills*," *Slate*, October 11. Available online: http://www.slate.com/articles/arts/ movies/2007/10/elizabeth_the_golden_age.html (accessed August 10, 2015).

Storey, John (2015), *Cultural Theory and Popular Culture. An Introduction*, 5th edn, Harlow: Pearson-Longman.

Stubbs, Jonathan (2013), *Historical Film: A Critical Introduction*, New York: Bloomsbury.

Sullivan, Chris (2011), "Getting Political With Film Stars Clooney, Hoffman, and Wood," *Redbull*, October 27. Available online: http://www.redbull.com/cs/Satellite/

en_INT/Article/LFF-2011-Ides-of-March-Interview-with-film-stars-Clooney,-Hoffman-and-Wood-021243110845961 (accessed August 7, 2015).

Tasker, Yvonne (1993), *Spectacular Bodies: Gender, Genre and the Action Cinema*, London: Routledge.

Thanouli, Eleftheria (2013), *Wag the Dog: A Study on Film and Reality in the Digital Age*, New York: Bloomsbury.

The Economist (2013), "Taking on Terror," January 24. Available online: http://www.economist.com/blogs/prospero/2013/01/qa-kathryn-bigelow (accessed August 17, 2015).

Thompson, Lauren (2007), "The Death of Diana," *Express*, February 23. Available online: http://www.express.co.uk/news/uk/275/The-death-of-Diana (accessed August 11, 2015.

Tolson, Jay and Linda Kulman (2006), "The Other Jesus: How a Jewish Reformer Lost His Jewish Identity," in Paula Fredriksen (ed.), *On The Passion of the Christ: Exploring the Issues Raised by the Controversial Movie*, 17–30, Berkeley: University of California Press.

Toner, Robin (1992), "The 1992 Campaign: Primaries; Tsongas Abandons Campaign, Leaving Clinton a Clear Path Toward Showdown with Bush," *New York Times*, March 20. Available online: http://www.nytimes.com/1992/03/20/us/1992-campaign-primaries-tsongas-abandons-campaign-leaving-clinton-clear-path.html (accessed August 18, 2015).

Totman, Sally-Ann (2009), *How Hollywood Projects Foreign Policy*, New York: Palgrave MacMillan.

Towlson, Jon (2014), *Subversive Horror Cinema: Countercultural Messages of Films from Frankenstein to the Present*, Jefferson: McFarland.

Travers, Pete (2010), "*Robin Hood*," *Rolling Stone*, May 13. Available online: http://www.rollingstone.com/movies/reviews/robin-hood-20100513 (accessed August 12, 2015).

Tzioka-Evangelou, Pinelopi (2005), "Introduction," in Pinelopi Tzioka-Evangelou (trans.), *Aristotle. Politics V & VI*, 23–67, Athens: Zitros (in Greek).

Vanairsdale, S. T. (2010), "Exclusive: Doug Liman on *Fair Game*: 'It's a Really Great Movie," *Movieline*, April 28. Available online: http://movieline.com/2010/04/28/exclusive-doug-liman-on-fair-game-its-a-really-great-movie/ (accessed August 17, 2015).

Vanhala, Helena (2011), *The Depiction of Terrorists in Blockbuster Hollywood Films, 1980–2001: An Analytical Study*, Jefferson: McFarland.

Verrier, Richard (2015), "Digital Jobs Help Drive Hollywood Employment to Highest Level in Decade," *Los Angeles Times*, February 10. Available online: http://www.latimes.com/entertainment/envelope/cotown/la-fi-ct-hollywood-jobs-20150210-story.html (accessed August 22, 2015).

Vidal, Belén (2012), *Heritage Film: Nation, Genre and Representation*, New York: Wallflower Press.

Voinova, Natalia (2013), *The Cold War in Science Fiction: Soviet and American Science Fiction Films in the 1950s*, Hamburg: Anchor Academic Publishing.

Walker, Janet (ed.) (2001), *Westerns: Films Through History*, London: Routledge.

Ward, Stephen J. A. (2014), "Radical Media Ethics," *Digital Journalism* 2 (4): 455–471.

Warnicke, Retha M. (2003), *The Rise and Fall of Anne Boleyn: Family Politics at the Court of Henry VIII*, Cambridge: Cambridge University Press.

Watercutter, Angela (2015), "The Political-Comedy-Starring-Sandra-Bullock Trailer: *Our Brand Is Crisis*," *Wired*, September 8. Available online: http://www.wired.com/2015/09/our-brand-is-crisis-trailer/ (accessed October 26, 2015).

Weber, Max (1958), *From Max Weber: Essays in Sociology*, edited by H. H. Gerth, translated by C. Wright Mills, Oxford: Oxford University Press.

Weinard, Will (2012), "'Safe House' Director Daniel Espinosa Talks Character Development, Audience Perspective and the Power of Information," *IFC*, February 14. Available online: http://www.ifc.com/fix/2012/02/safe-house-director-daniel-espinosa-interview (accessed July 17, 2015).

Weiner, Allison Hope (2014), "A Journalist's Plea On 10th Anniversary Of 'The Passion Of The Christ': Hollywood, Take Mel Gibson Off Your Blacklist," *Deadline*, March 11. Available online: http://deadline.com/2014/03/mel-gibson-career-hollywood-deserves-chance-697084/ (accessed July 23, 2015).

Weintraub, Steve 'Frosty' (2007a), "Chris Cooper Interviewed—*Breach*," *Collider*, February 15. Available online: http://collider.com/chris-cooper-interviewed-breach/ (accessed December 14, 2015).

Weintraub, Steve 'Frosty' (2007b), "Paul Greengrass Interview, *Bourne Ultimatum*," *Collider*, July 25. Available online: http://collider.com/paul-greengrass-interview-the-bourne-ultimatum/ (accessed July 17, 2015).

Weintraub, Steve 'Frosty' (2010), "Matt Damon Interview *Green Zone*," *Collider*, March. Available online: http://collider.com/matt-damon-interview-green-zone-read-or-listen-to-an-extended-interview-with-this-great-actor/ (accessed December 14, 2015).

Weir, Alison (2007), *The Six Wives of Henry VIII*, New York: Vintage.

Wheeler, Mark (2006), *Hollywood Politics and Society*, London: BFI.

Wilcox, David (2012), "'Lincoln's' Seward: A Conversation with David Strathairn about Portraying Auburn's Favorite Son," *The Auburn Citizen*, September 2. Available online: http://auburnpub.com/lifestyles/lincoln-s-seward-a-conversation-with-david-strathairn-about-portraying/article_532c9928-2048-5b5d-af83-279b3603ab50.html (accessed December 14, 2015).

Wilson, Joseph C. (2004), *The Politics of Truth: A Diplomat's Memoir: Inside the Lies that Led to War and Betrayed My Wife's CIA Identity*, New York: Public Affairs.

Winter, Jessica (2013), "Kathryn Bigelow: The Art of Darkness," *Time*, February 4.

Available online: http://content.time.com/time/magazine/article/0,9171,2134499-
2,00.html (accessed August 17, 2015).

Wise, Damon (n.d.a), "Damon Wise Talks To Doug Liman," *Empire*. Available online:
http://damonwise.blogspot.gr/2011/03/interview-with-doug-liman-director-of.html
(accessed April 13, 2016).

Wise, Damon (n.d.b), "Naomi Watts On *Fair Game*," *Empire*. Available online: http://
damonwise.blogspot.gr/2011/03/interview-with-naomi-watts-star-of-fair.html
(accessed April 13, 2016).

Wolin, Sheldon S. (2004), *Politics and Vision. Continuity and Innovation in Western
Political Thought*, expanded edn., Princeton: Princeton University Press.

Woods, Sean (2012), "Q&A: Ben Affleck on Directing 'Argo' and Surviving Hollywood,"
Rolling Stone, October 12. Available online: http://www.rollingstone.com/movies/
news/q-a-ben-affleck-on-directing-argo-and-surviving-hollywood-20121012
(accessed August 17, 2015).

Zeitz, Joshua (2012), "Fact-Checking 'Lincoln': Lincoln's Mostly Realistic; His Advisers
Aren't," *The Atlantic*, November 12. Available online: http://www.theatlantic.com/
entertainment/archive/2012/11/fact-checking-lincoln-lincolns-mostly-realistic-his-
advisers-arent/265073/ (accessed July 30, 2015).

Zinoman, Jason (2012), "Late at Night, Comedy Gets Pointed and Political," *New York
Times*, October 3. Available online: http://www.nytimes.com/2012/10/04/arts/
television/comedy-and-politics-uneasy-bedfellows-but-snuggling.html (accessed
October 25, 2015).

Index

3:10 to Yuma, 22
24, 2, 50
42, 163
300, 33, 121, 122, 124, 125, 127, 164, 168
300: Rise of an Empire, 164
2016: Obama's America, 3

Abraham Lincoln: Vampire Hunter, 22
Abu Ghraib, 71
Academy Award, 2, 36, 54, 91, 93, 105,
    106, 130, 131, 132, 150, 173 *see also*
    Oscar
Act of Valor, 168
actant, 18, 38, 39, 44, 46, 68, 86, 98, 127
action thriller, 4, 14, 32, 37, 74, 75, 105,
    168, 169
Adjustment Bureau, 22
Affleck, Ben, 28, 89, 91, 101, 102, 108, 148
Aiken, Frederick, 107, 111, 112, 114
Alexander, 28, 30, 121, 124, 125
Alford, Matthew, 24, 26, 90, 93, 173
All The King's Men, 19, 36
All The President's Men, 108, 146
Allen, Joan, 84
Altman, Rick, 10, 11, 40, 108, 109, 131
Amazing Grace, 121, 130
American exceptionalism, 82, 161, 169
American Gangster, 22
American Sniper, 9, 168
Argo, 1, 2, 10, 29, 32, 67, 89, 91, 95, 97, 99,
    100, 101, 102, 116, 147, 148, 164
Aristotle, 6, 62
Arkin, Alan, 101
Arnold, William, 108, 126
Ashcroft, John, 96, 97
Atonement, 173
Australia, 12
Avengers, The, 36
Aykroyd, Dan, 39

Bad Company, 31
Bale, Christian, 165

Banks, Alicia, 164
Barker, Martin, 9, 92, 93, 173
Barnes, Henry, 118
Barry, Paul, 70
Battleship, 22, 162
Beatty, Ned, 77
Bellucci, Monica, 25
Benedikt, Katrin, 161
Between Two Ferns, 48
Bigelow, Kathryn, 28, 30, 96, 154, 167
Bilmes, Alex, 148
bin Laden, Osama, 89, 98, 101, 103
biopic, 4, 10, 32, 105, 118, 121, 122, 139,
    140, 146, 163
Black Hawk Down, 92
Blanchett, Kate, 130, 136
Blitzer, Wolf, 46
Bloody Sunday, 147
Bloom, Orlando, 124
Blunt, Emily, 136
Boal, Mark, 100, 154
Body of Lies, 28, 29, 69, 70, 72, 75, 76, 79,
    80, 81, 82, 85, 165, 168
Boklund-Lagopoulou, Karin, 16
Booker, Keith M., 12, 13, 26, 105, 171
Booth, John Wilkes, 112
Bordo, Susan, 135
Borgen, 43
Boss, 2
Bourne Identity, The, 28, 29, 30, 67, 69, 71,
    75, 79, 81, 82, 83, 85, 87, 155
Bourne Legacy, The, 67, 69, 70, 85, 139
Bourne Supremacy, The, 28, 29, 67, 69, 75,
    79, 81, 86, 147
Bourne Ultimatum, The, 28, 29, 67, 69, 75,
    79, 81, 83, 85, 86, 88
Bowling for Columbine, 3
Boynton, Rachel, 158
Breach, 29, 32, 89, 91, 95, 96, 97, 98, 99,
    102, 154
Brevet, Brad, 152
Brighi, Elisabetta, 66

Brockes, Emma, 148, 154
Brolin, Josh, 111, 114
Browne, Patrick, 113, 115, 117
Bryant, Nick, 50
Brzezinski, Mika, 46
Buckland, Warren, 95
Bukszpan, Daniel, 122
Bullock, Sandra, 158
Bush, George W., 1, 48, 49, 82, 89, 90, 92,
    93, 96, 99, 102, 117, 118, 146, 171
Butler, Gerard, 124, 127, 161
Butler, The, 163

Caiaphas, 122, 123
Campaign, The, 1, 31, 35, 36, 37, 38, 39,
    40, 41, 42, 44, 45, 46, 47, 49, 57, 58,
    61, 62
Candidate, The, 15, 36, 146
Capra, Frank, 6, 31
Carnahan, Matthew Michael, 28, 108,
    152
Carr, David, 155
Carter, Jimmy, 43, 152
Cavill, Henry, 158
Cetti, Robert, 71, 82, 88
Changeling, 27
Channing, Tatum, 161
Chapman, James, 124
Charlie Wilson's War, 31, 35
Chastain, Jessica, 98, 167
Cheney, Dick, 71, 82, 93, 102, 117, 118
Chernobyl Diaries, 22
China Syndrome, 108
Christensen, Terry, 9, 12, 14, 15, 16, 28,
    49, 51, 89, 92, 100, 101, 116, 137,
    143, 157, 162, 171
Christianity, 93, 122, 123, 126
Citizen Kane, 12
Clear and Present Danger, 150
Clinton, Hillary, 130
Clinton, Bill, 1, 89, 118
Clooney, George, 23, 28, 29, 89, 91, 93, 94,
    105, 118, 144, 147, 148, 158, 173
Clueless, 37
Cohen, Sacha Baron, 37
Colbert Report, The, 47, 48
Colbert, Stephen, 37, 47, 52, 53, 159
Cold Light of Day, The, 68, 76

Cold Mountain, 12
Cold War, 12, 70, 78, 82, 117, 124, 168
Collateral Damage, 92
communism, 65
Company You Keep, The, 145
Condell, Kate, 30
Congress, 38, 40, 59, 62, 115, 116, 130
Conspirator, The, 19, 28, 29, 30, 32, 105,
    106, 107, 109, 112, 113, 115, 117,
    145
Contagion, 162
Coontz, Stephanie, 134
Cooper, Chris, 29, 75, 98, 154
Corporation, The, 3
Costa-Gavras, 150
Costner, Kevin, 36, 38, 54, 55
Courtés, Joseph, 17, 18
Cox, Brian, 124
Coyne, Michael, 13, 15, 62, 171
Crash, 27, 163
Crick, Bernard, 5
Crowe, Cameron, 165
Crowe, Russell, 75, 108, 127
Cruise, Tom, 30, 146, 160, 161
Curic, Katie, 154

Daily Show with Jon Stewart, The, 47, 48
Dahan, Olivier, 116
Damon, Matt, 29, 75, 90, 91, 93, 154
Daniels, Lee, 28
Dargis, Manohla, 43, 50, 136, 138
Davies, Philip John, 12, 171
Day After Tomorrow, The, 161
Debord, Guy, 42
Debt, The, 30, 121
Deep Impact, 50
Déjà vu, 22
Demme, Jonathan, 154
democracy, 25, 26, 38, 48, 54, 65, 71, 77,
    126, 129, 153
Democracy in America, 169
Denby, David, 80
Departed, The, 22
Derry, Charles, 67
Dexter, 173
Diana, 165, 166
DiCaprio, Leonardo, 75
Dictator, The, 31, 35, 37

Distinguished Gentleman, The, 36
Django Unchained, 27, 163
documentary, 3, 9, 10, 20, 23, 92, 94, 95,
    97, 98, 111, 143, 158, 171
Douglas, Michael, 74
Downfall, The, 166
Duplicity, 66
DuVernay, Ava, 163

Easton, David, 5
Eastwood, Clint, 26, 27, 52
Ebert, Roger, 146, 149
Eckhart, Aaron, 161
Elizabeth: The Golden Age, 30, 33, 121,
    130, 132, 133, 134, 135, 136, 138
Elliott, Andrew B. R., 124
Elsaesser, Thomas, 95
Emmerich, Roland, 161
epic, 10, 33, 121, 122, 124, 125, 126, 127,
    128, 129, 167, 168, 169, 170
Espinosa, Daniel, 150, 151
Exodus: Gods and Kings, 164, 165
Experiment, The, 166
Extremely Loud and Incredibly Close, 24

Fahrenheit 9/11, 3, 92, 93
Fair Game, 29, 30, 89, 90, 91, 95, 96, 97,
    98, 99, 102, 103, 153, 154, 168
Farrell, Colin, 66, 125
Ferrell, Will, 36, 38
Finney, Albert, 83
Flags of Our Fathers, 26, 27, 105
Fontanille, Jean, 18, 86
Ford, Elizabeth A., 130, 140
foreign policy, 2, 65, 66, 77, 168, 173
Foster, Jodie, 147
Foxx, Jamie, 161
framing, 47
Franco, James, 158
Franklin, Daniel P., 12, 13, 77
Frears, Stephen, 139, 140, 141
Freedom Writers, The, 27, 163
Freeman, Morgan, 50
Frost/Nixon, 2, 20, 28, 152, 153
Fuchs, Cynthia, 109
Fuller, Jamie, 159
Fun in Acapulco, 108
Fuqua, Antoine, 28, 125, 144, 161

Galifianakis, Zach, 38, 48
Game of Thrones, 173
Gardies, André, 18, 95
Geluardi, John, 114, 115
gender, 12, 27, 30, 130, 136, 140, 160,
    167
Genette, Gérard, 17
genocide, 26
Get Smart, 30, 31, 37
Gianos, Philip L., 12, 22, 110, 111, 129
Gibson, Mel, 122, 123, 150
Giddens, Anthony, 7, 8
Giglio, Ernest, 2, 7, 10, 12, 14, 15, 40, 55,
    89, 91, 143, 144, 147
Gilroy, Tony, 28, 29, 108
Giroux, Jack, 152
Gladiator, 126
Gleeson, Brendan, 124
Gleiberman, Owen, 138
Glitre, Katharine, 11
Goldberg, Evan, 158
Goldblum, Jeff, 53
Gone With the Wind, 15
Good Day to Die Hard, A 160
Good Morning Vietnam, 52
Good Night, and Good Luck, 28, 29, 32,
    105, 109, 113, 114, 115, 117, 119,
    148, 151, 168
Good Shepherd, The, 29, 76
Good Wife, The, 173
Goodman, John, 101
Gordon, Richard, 140
Grace of Monaco, 165, 166
Grammer, Kelsey, 56
Gray, Jonathan, 48
Great Debaters, The, 27, 163
Green Zone, 28, 29, 68, 89, 90, 91, 95, 96,
    99, 100, 102, 103, 153, 154, 168
Greengrass, Paul, 23, 28, 102, 144, 145,
    147, 150, 151
Greimas, Algirdas J., 18, 39, 46
Grey's Anatomy, 173
Guantanamo, 71
Guevara, Ernest "Che", 24
Gulf War, 4, 8, 26
Gyllenhaal, Jake, 26

Haas, Elizabeth, 9, 12, 14, 15, 16, 28, 49,

51, 89, 92, 100, 101, 116, 137, 143, 157, 162, 171

Haas, Peter J., 9, 12, 14, 15, 16, 28, 49, 51, 89, 92, 100, 101, 116, 137, 143, 157, 162, 171

Hanssen, Robert, 89, 97, 98, 99

Hay, Colin, 7, 8, 49, 51, 54, 60, 71, 88, 120, 139, 169

Haysbert, Dennis, 50

Head of State, 31, 35, 36, 37, 38, 39, 40, 41, 42, 43, 44, 45, 46, 49, 50, 51, 52, 53, 56, 58, 139, 168

Helgeland, Brian, 28

Help, The, 27, 163

heritage film, 129, 130, 135

Heslov, Grant, 28, 89, 105, 147, 151, 152, 158

Hirschbiegel, Oliver, 166

Hiscock, John, 145

history film, 9, 30, 109, 113, 115, 116, 119, 120, 124, 126, 129, 163, 164

Hochscherf, Tobias, 114, 115

Hogan, Jackie, 107

Holloway, David, 24, 94, 117

Homeland, 2, 31

Hopper, Dennis, 56

Hornaday, Ann, 117

House of Cards, 2

House of Sand and Fog, The, 27

Human Stain, The, 27

Hunger Games, The, 4, 22

Huston, Danny, 111, 112

Hutcheon, Linda, 29

Hyde Park on Hudson, 28

I Spy, 30, 31

iconography, 40, 44, 79

Ides of March, The, 10, 20, 28, 105, 147, 148, 152

In The Loop, 28

In The Valley of Elah, 68

Independence Day, 15

Inglorious Basterds, 21

Interpreter, The, 29, 30, 32, 67

interventionism, 25, 26, 82, 84, 162, 169

Interview, The, 158

Invictus, 121

Iran, 82, 97

Iraq, 49, 75, 77, 84, 90, 93, 100, 124, 126, 145, 147, 148, 152, 162, 171 *see also* Iraq War

Iraq War, 52, 89, 91, 96, 97, 125

Iron Lady, The, 28

Irvine, Lindesay, 148, 149

Islam, 125, 126

isotopy, 17, 18, 74, 77, 79, 81, 85, 109, 128, 132, 162, 168

Jack Ryan: Shadow Recruit, 160

Jacobson, Harlan, 151

Jarhead, 4, 8, 26

Jefferson, Thomas, 55

JFK, 88

Johansson, Scarlett, 134

Joireman, Sandra Fullerton, 135

Jolie, Angelina, 30, 66, 71, 75, 167

Jones, James Earl, 50

Jones, Jeffrey P., 48

Kaklamanidou, Betty, 6, 11, 29

Kellner, Douglas, 13, 23, 42, 43, 56, 82, 92, 93, 117, 168, 171, 172, 173

KGB, 84, 158

Khomeini, Ayatollah, 97

King Arthur, 28, 121, 124, 125, 126, 161, 167

King, Geoff, 74

Kingdom, The, 28, 29, 68, 126, 127, 152, 168

Kingdom of Heaven, 28, 29, 33, 121, 124, 126, 127, 148, 149, 164

King's Speech, The, 21, 29, 121, 122, 130, 132

Kinnear, Greg, 90

Kline, Kevin, 111, 112, 113

Koslow, Jessica A., 116

Kreitner, Richard, 112

Krieger, Jennifer, 154

Kruger, Diane, 124

Krutnik, Frank, 117, 118

Kuhn, Annette, 36

Kushner, Tony, 28, 116, 149

La Vie en Rose, 166

Lagopoulos, Alexandros Ph., 16

Larson, Kate Clifford, 106

Lasswell, Harold, 5
Last Samurai, The, 12
Laucht, Christoph, 114, 115
Lear, Norman, 148
Legally Blonde 2, 21, 30, 31, 35, 37
Leno, Jay, 47
Lenon, Suzanna, 119
Leonard, Elizabeth D., 112
Leonard, Tom, 54
Letterman, David, 47
Letters of Iwo Jima, 26
Levinson, Barry, 52, 53, 98
Levy, Emanuel, 151
Lewis, Jacob, 127
Life of David Gale, The, 32, 105, 107, 109
Lim, Dennis, 118
Liman, Doug, 28, 82, 144, 153, 155
Lincoln, 2, 4, 10, 21, 27, 28, 29, 32, 105,
    106, 109, 112, 113, 115, 116, 117,
    119, 146, 147, 154, 168
Linney, Laura, 39
Lions for Lambs, 20, 28, 68, 145, 152, 168
Lithgow, John, 39
Live Free or Die Hard, 67
Lord of the Rings, The, 92
Ludlum, Robert, 75, 82

Mac, Bernie, 51
Macdonald, Kevin, 108
Mackaman, Tom, 164
Madam Secretary, 2, 31, 173
Maddow, Rachel, 48
Maher, Bill, 46
Man from U.N.C.L.E., The, 157
Man of the Year, 14, 20, 31, 35, 36, 37,
    38, 39, 40, 41, 42, 44, 45, 46, 47,
    49, 52, 53, 54, 56, 58, 61, 62, 81,
    139, 168
Manchurian Candidate, The, 30, 32, 76,
    86, 154
Marsh, David, 7, 8
Matthews, Chris, 46
Mazelis, Fred, 164
McAvoy, James, 107
McDaniel, Hattie, 93
McFarlane, Brian, 29
McMaken, Ryan, 165
Meacham, John, 123

media spectacle, 40, 41, 42, 56
Meet the Press, 71
Men Who Stare at Goats, The, 29, 31, 35,
    147
Mendez, Antonio J., 89, 101, 169
Metz, Walter, 107
MI6, 66, 84, 161
Milk, 2, 29, 32, 105, 106, 107, 109, 114,
    118, 119, 154, 168
Miller, Claire Caine, 171
Miller, Dennis, 46
Miller, Elizabeth, 166
Mirren, Helen, 130, 131, 139, 140
Missing, The 22
Mission: Impossible III, 67
Mission: Impossible - Ghost Protocol, 67
Mission: Impossible—Rogue Nation, 160
Mist, The, 173
Mitchell, Alison, 171
Mitchell, Deborah C., 130, 140
monarchy film, 33, 121, 122, 129, 130,
    131, 132, 138, 140, 164, 167
Money Monster, 147
Moore, Michael, 3
Morgan, Peter, 28, 131, 152, 153
Morgan, Piers, 44
Morris, Wesley, 136
mortification, 107
Mossadegh, Mohammad, 97
Moulin Rouge, 92
Mr. Smith Goes to Washington, 13, 31, 40
Munich, 28, 29, 121, 149, 150
Murrow, Edward R., 105, 111, 114, 115,
    117, 118, 120

Nader, Ralph, 53
Namesake, The, 27
narrative
    grammar, 18, 18, 23, 70, 166
    program, 21, 27, 38, 39, 46, 68, 75,
        136, 163
Natural Born Killers, 15
Neale, Steve, 19
Nelson, Willie, 56
Neve, Brian, 12, 13
No Way Out, 40
North Country, 27
Northup, Solomon, 163

Nothing But The Truth, 153
Noyce, Philip, 206, 150

O'Sullivan, Michael, 108, 126, 127
Obama, Barack, 1, 2, 42, 43, 48, 49, 50, 54,
    56, 58, 82, 102, 103, 116, 147, 153,
    163, 171
Olechnowicz, Andrzej, 140
Olympus Has Fallen, 161, 162
Omagh, 151
One Flew Over The Cuckoo's Nest, 173
Open Range, 22
Oscar, 2, 91, 93, 101, 106, 119, 131, 147
Other Boleyn Girl, The, 28, 30, 33, 121,
    130, 131, 132, 133, 134, 135, 136,
    138, 139, 152
Our Brand is Crisis, 157, 158
Overpeck, Deron, 160
Owen, Clive, 66, 125, 136

Pacino, Al, 67
Palmer effect, 50
Palmer, William J., 65
Pan's Labyrinth, 28
Parallax View, The, 98, 108, 151
Parker, Alan, 65
Pascal, Amy, 30
Passion of the Christ, The, 21, 33, 92, 93,
    121, 122, 123, 150
Patriot Act, 118
Patriot Games, 150
Patton, Paula, 46
Pearl Harbor, 129
Pelosi, Nancy, 52
Penn, Sean, 119, 154
Perot, Ross, 58
Pianist, The, 28
Piers Morgan Live, 44
Pilate, Pontius, 122, 123
Pitt, Brad, 127
Plame, Valerie, 89, 90
Plummer, Christopher, 125
Portman, Natalie, 135
presentism, 124
Presley, Elvis, 108
Pretty Woman, 15, 59
Primary Colors, 36
Public Enemies, 22

Quaid, Dennis, 71, 74
Queen, The, 28, 29, 30, 33, 121, 130, 131,
    132, 133, 139, 140, 141, 152

race, 27, 51, 125, 165
Rancière, Jacques, 5
Reagan, Ronald, 2, 43, 48, 52, 82, 119, 160
Real Time With Bill Maher, 159
Recruit, The, 66
Redford, Robert, 28, 106, 107, 108, 113,
    117, 144, 145, 146, 152
Reign Over Me, 24
Rendition, 7, 30
Reynolds, Ryan, 71, 75
Richards, Jeffrey, 126, 127, 129
Richardson, Miranda, 137
Richie, Guy, 157
Richman, Jason, 54
Riefenstahl, Leni, 143
Road, The, 162
Roberts, Julia, 59, 66
Robin Hood, 28, 121, 122, 124, 126, 127,
    129, 164, 167
Rock, Chris, 37, 49, 50, 51
Rogen, Seth, 158
Rollins, Peter, 9, 26
Romney, Mitt, 1, 42, 43
Rosenstone, Robert A., 32, 105, 109, 115,
    116, 120
Rosenthal, Joe, 26
Rothenberger, Creighton, 161
Russell, Catherine, 107
Rylance, Mark, 134

Safe House, 67, 69, 70, 71, 73, 75, 76, 81,
    84, 85, 86, 87, 88, 151
Saldana, Zoe, 87
Salt, 14, 28, 30, 67, 69, 70, 71, 72, 73, 75,
    76, 77, 78, 79, 80, 81, 85, 88, 150,
    167
Samuelsohn, Darren, 159
Sant, Gus Van, 119
Scandal, 54
Schaff, Barbara, 109
Scheuneman, Stacy, 117
Schuessler, Jennifer, 164
Schultz, Ed, 46
Schwarzenegger, Arnold, 52, 119, 160

Sciretta, Peter, 146
Scott, A. O., 43, 50
Scott, Ian, 4, 12, 14, 88
Scott, Ridley, 28, 80, 126, 129, 144, 145, 148, 149, 150, 151, 155, 164, 165
Selma, 9, 163, 164, 172
semiotics, 5, 16, 17, 109, 166
Sentinel, The, 32, 74
Shapiro, Michael, 22
Sheehan, Rebecca A., 139
Shepard, Sam, 86
Shooter, 21, 28, 76, 77, 161
Sicko, 3
Silverstein, Melissa, 30
Singin' in the Rain, 108
Skerritt, Tom, 26
slavery, 27, 106, 112, 116, 117, 125, 146
Sloan, Ray, 114, 115
Spartan, 19
Spiderman, 92
Spielberg, Steven, 28, 106, 108, 112, 116, 144, 146, 147, 149, 150, 151
Spy Game, 66, 71
Staiger, Janet, 11, 19, 171, 172
Stallone, Sylvester, 160
State of Play, 28, 29, 32, 105, 108, 109, 152
Sterling, Dan, 158
Stern, Joshua Michael, 54
Stewart, Jon, 37, 47, 52, 53, 159
Stone, Oliver, 23, 24, 28, 30, 102, 125, 144, 145, 146
Storey, John, 6
strategic-relational approach, 7, 8, 49, 60, 120, 139, 169
Strathairn, David, 29, 84, 154
Streep, Meryl, 146, 154
Stubbs, Jonathan, 149
Sullivan, Chris, 148
Sum of All Fears, The, 67, 69, 70, 71, 78, 79
Swing Vote, 7, 20, 31, 35, 36, 37, 38, 40, 41, 42, 44, 45, 46, 54, 55, 56, 57, 60, 61, 62
Swofford, Anthony, 26
Syriana, 20, 29, 32, 68, 89, 90, 91, 93, 94, 95, 99, 100, 102, 103, 148, 168

Tasker, Yvonne, 160
Tears of the Sun, 25, 26

Terrio, Chris, 89
terrorism, 53, 81, 82, 87, 88, 92, 125, 149, 151
Thanouli, Eleftheria, 45, 98, 118
Thomas, Betty, 30
Thompson, Lauren, 140
Three Days of the Condor, 151
Three Kings, 4, 8
Tinker, Tailor, Soldier, Spy, 28
Tocqueville, Alexis de, 169
torture, 71, 82, 88, 94, 96, 97, 101, 154, 164
Tourist, The, 66
Traitor, 32, 68, 168
Travers, Pete, 127
Travis, Pete, 150, 151
Triumph of the Will, 143
Troy, 33, 121, 122, 124, 125, 127, 128, 168
Tudor, Andrew, 19

United 93, 23, 24, 102, 147

V for Vendetta, 22
Valkyrie, 14, 21
Vampire Diaries, 173
Vantage Point, 2, 32, 67, 68, 69, 70, 71, 74, 76, 77, 85, 86, 87, 88, 150, 151
Veep, 2, 31
Verrier, Richard, 155
Vidal, Belén, 129, 130, 138, 139, 140
Vietnam, 12, 13, 52, 148, 163
Vikander, Alicia, 158
Visitor, The, 27

W., 2, 20, 28, 146
Wag the Dog, 45, 52, 98, 118, 119
Walhberg, Mark, 77
Walken, Christopher, 47
War Horse, 27
Warnicke, Retha M., 135
Washington, Denzel, 71, 147, 154
Watercutter, Angela, 158
Watts, Naomi, 96, 154, 166
Wayne, John, 52
Weaver, Sigourney, 87
Weber, Max, 5
Weinard, Will, 151
Weiner, Allison Hope, 150

Weinstein, Harvey, 166
Weintraub, Steve 'Frosty, 147, 154
Weir, Alison, 134
Wells, Paul, 12, 171
West Wing, The, 2, 14
western, 7, 9, 10, 11, 12, 15, 18, 20, 22, 40,
    65, 172
Whitaker, Forest, 163
White House Down, 161, 162
Why We Fight, 143
Wibberley, Marianne, 30
Williams, Robin, 36, 38, 52
Willis, Bruce, 25, 160, 161
Wilson, Joseph C., 89, 90
Windtalkers, 27
Witherspoon, Reese, 37

Wolin, Sheldon S., 3, 6, 123
Woods, Sean, 148
World Trade Center, 23, 24, 102
World War Z, 222
Wright, Jeffrey, 136, 145

xXx: State of the Union, 32, 105, 108, 109

Young Victoria, The, 30, 121, 130, 131,
    133, 136, 138

Zeitz, Joshua, 112, 115, 116
Zero Dark Thirty, 2, 7, 30, 89, 91, 95, 97,
    98, 99, 100, 102, 103, 116, 154, 164,
    167
Zinoman, Jason, 159

Lightning Source UK Ltd.
Milton Keynes UK
UKOW05n1610210417
299645UK00001B/21/P